The person charging
spe...

# LILLIAN HELLMAN

GARLAND REFERENCE LIBRARY
OF THE HUMANITIES
(VOL. 141)

# LILLIAN HELLMAN
## *An Annotated Bibliography*

Steven H. Bills

GARLAND PUBLISHING, INC. • NEW YORK & LONDON
1979

**Library of Congress Cataloging in Publication Data**

Bills, Steven H
   Lillian Hellman, an annotated bibliography.

   (Garland reference library of the humanities ; v. 141)
   Includes index.
   1. Hellman, Lillian, 1905–　—Bibliography.
I. Title.
Z8395.52.B49　[PS3515.E343]　　016.812'5'4　　78-68280
ISBN 0-8240-9803-X

Printed on acid-free, 250-year-life paper
Manufactured in the United States of America

to the memory of
my teacher, counselor, and friend
A. STUART PITT

# CONTENTS

# ACKNOWLEDGMENTS

My thanks are extended to my friends and associates who have been vigilant in watching for Hellman news as it has been published. I am deeply indebted to the librarians at the Library of Congress, at the U.S. Naval Academy, and at the Library for the Performing Arts (New York Public Library), Lincoln Center, New York, for their assistance. Dr. Jackson R. Bryer, of the University of Maryland, has been an inspiration, guide, and prodder in leading me to the numerous bibliographical resources consulted. The patience and support of Martha, my wife, in this three-year effort certainly deserve recognition. To Linda Fauvie, the expert typist who prepared the final manuscript, I extend my sincere thanks.

# INTRODUCTION

Diverse conflict and controversy have always surrounded the life and works of Lillian Hellman. She has been labeled a Communist, her plays have been banned for being "filthy," and to this day her presence evokes intense scorn and contempt from her critics. Simultaneously, however, she has been championed as a political hero, her plays have earned her the title "greatest American woman playwright," and she has been officially honored and praised by presidents, first ladies, and countless others. Since her first play, *The Children's Hour*, was first produced in 1934, Miss Hellman seems to have been involved in continuous public controversy. The numerous lawsuits by and against her, her heated exchanges with actors, directors, censors, and publishers, and her battle with the United States Congress have all been part of her nonstop struggle for justice and survival.

This bibliography documents the wide range of activities in which Hellman has been involved. Hellman's public life is traced bibliographically in entries depicting her political activism, her successes and failures in the theatre, her literary development, and even her interest in Creole cooking. Through the friendships and contacts she has developed during her lengthy career, she has been influential in the lives of many prominent people. For instance, entries are included that trace her relationships with Dorothy Parker, Dashiell Hammett, Tallulah Bankhead, Leonard Bernstein, Jane Fonda, and numerous others. Hellman's academic life is surveyed through entries about her college teaching and her participation in a variety of political and dramatic seminars, conferences, and workshops. The excellence of Hellman's life and works has been recognized for years, as shown by the numerous awards, honorary degrees, and political and personal tributes that are cited in the bibliography.

In addition to the biographical view of Hellman, the bibliography attempts to cover comprehensively the critical reception of her work. Cited are reviews of Broadway openings, major revivals, and various other performances of Hellman's eight original plays and her two adaptations (*The Lark* and *Montserrat*). Also included are reviews of *Candide*, the operetta adapted from Voltaire for which Hellman wrote the libretto. A section of the bibliography is also devoted to reviews of these plays in book form.

Several of Hellman's plays were made into motion pictures. Miss Hellman wrote or collaborated on screenplays for these as well as for other motion pictures. *The Children's Hour* was made into two films, a 1936 version (entitled *These Three*) and the 1962 version. The earlier version was altered to avoid the censorship problems that the play encountered. Reviews of these and other Hellman motion pictures are included in the bibliography.

In 1969, Hellman's first autobiographical work, *An Unfinished Woman*, was published. *Pentimento: A Book of Portraits* (1973) and *Scoundrel Time* (1976) followed. Reviews of these three volumes from newspapers and magazines are cited.

A section of the bibliography is devoted to scholarly works and critical surveys of Hellman's plays and to evaluations of Miss Hellman as a playwright. Over the years there have been surprisingly few scholarly critical works about Miss Hellman. Richard Moody's book *Lillian Hellman, Playwright* (IVG14) is a good bio-bibliographical study that considers the development of Hellman's plays. Jacob H. Adler's pamphlet *Lillian Hellman* (IVG2) is also a good source for blending the biography with her playwriting. Only two other book-length works have been devoted solely to Hellman. Lorena Ross Holmin's *The Dramatic Works of Lillian Hellman* (IVG9) analyzes the eight original plays and is helpful to an understanding of the progress made in moving from realism in *The Children's Hour* to impressionism in *Toys in the Attic*. Manfred Triesch's *The Lillian Hellman Collection at the University of Texas* (IVG24) is a valuable bibliography documenting the manuscripts of plays, letters, and other Hellman contributions to the library.

Few critics have written about Miss Hellman's work without assuming a biographical stance. Serious studies analyzing the technique, thematic development, rhetoric, and political and historical aspects of the Hellman canon need to be undertaken.

The bibliography is organized in eight major sections (I through VIII). Each section is divided alphabetically into subsections; within each subsection the entries are individually numbered. This organization will assist the user to find material quickly on specific areas of interest. Section IA, for example, includes entries about Hellman's political activities, and Section IIIC includes reviews of *The Little Foxes*. (The lower-case "i," instead of "I," is used in subdividing sections II, III, V, and VI to avoid confusion in numbering.) Each entry is annotated, with the exception of articles whose title is self-explanatory. These reviews are short, or their message merely reiterates the title of the article. Other short reviews lacking substantive material are described simply by stating whether the review is positive or negative.

The subdivisions (A through E) in Section I are arranged chronologically. This arrangement allows the user to trace the progress of events in specific areas of interest. For example, in IA, a reader may follow Hellman's early anti-fascist political activities through her confrontation with McCarthyism and her suit against Richard Nixon over the Watergate tapes. Similar patterns are found in IB through IE. In cases where one specific event is covered by numerous news and feature articles, only one entry has been made in the bibliography. If, however, a series of articles published subsequently presents new developments on a topic, the articles are entered separately and appropriate cross-references are provided.

Section II includes interviews, previews, features, and news concerning Hellman's books and plays. The subdivisions (A through O) deal with specific Hellman works and are arranged chronologically by the first appearance of the work. Therefore, *The Children's Hour*, 1934, is IIA and *Scoundrel Time*, 1976, is IIO. Works within these subdivisions are also arranged chronologically.

Reviews of plays, subdivided (A through L) according to their initial production date, are cited in Section III. Alphabetical ar-

rangement is used within the subdivisions; specific productions—for example, the Broadway *Children's Hour* and the London *Children's Hour*—are considered as entities within the sub-
division IIIA. A rubric identifying the location precedes each new
production considered. The critical reception and reputation of
each play become quite clear in this section.

Section IV, ''Scholarly Articles, Books, and Surveys of
Hellman's Works,'' is subdivided into eight sections (A through
H), dividing the plays into logical groupings based on scholarly
material which has appeared in print. Articles comparing and
contrasting *The Lark* as discussed in conjunction with Anouilh's
original *L'Alouette* and Christopher Fry's translation of the original version are listed together. The two plays about the Hubbard
family, *The Little Foxes* and *Another Part of the Forest*, are also
grouped together (IVB). See the table of contents for a complete
breakdown of this section.

Divisions within Section V, ''Reviews of Drama in Book
Form,'' Section VI, ''Reviews of Hellman Screenplays,'' and
Section VII, ''Reviews of Hellman Autobiographies,'' are arranged chronologically, as in Section III. Within each subdivi-
sion, alphabetical arrangement is used. Section VIII lists graduate
work devoted to Hellman's plays and is arranged alphabetically
by author.

Names, places, and events are indexed. The index will be
useful in tracing various personalities as they appeared throughout Hellman's career. Additionally, it will enable the user to follow a particular critic's view of her work over the years. No
attempt has been made to completely index the bibliography by
topic (''well-made play,'' ''evil'' in Hellman's work, female
characters, etc.).

In compiling the bibliography, all major indices were consulted. The *Reader's Guide to Periodical Literature*, the *MLA
International Bibliography*, the New York *Times Index*, and
others were very useful. Numerous Hellman checklists (Moody,
Triesch, and others) also were helpful in finding Hellman articles
for which annotations were supplied. Numerous reviews of the
Hellman autobiographies were obtained by writing to over 300

newspapers nationwide and by scanning microfilm of major newspapers during dates when the reviews would most likely have appeared. (The publisher of the Hellman autobiographies would not allow me to examine the files of reviews that they hold.) A major source of information was the Library for the Performing Arts (New York Public Library), Lincoln Center, New York. The library's collection of clippings about plays and playwrights was very helpful. Many of the clipping folders are deteriorating rapidly, and in fact, some Hellman clippings there are decomposed beyond recognition. Thus, a cataloging of these articles at this time is especially important.

No other comprehensive Hellman bibliography, annotated or otherwise, has been compiled. There are numerous checklists which may be useful for the casual student of Miss Hellman's plays. For those who desire a comprehensive view of this complex woman, it is hoped this volume will serve well.

# ABBREVIATIONS

| | |
|---|---|
| *AG* | *The Autumn Garden* |
| *APF* | *Another Part of the Forest* |
| *CH* | *The Children's Hour* |
| *DC* | *Days to Come* |
| HUAC | U.S. House of Representatives Committee on Un-American Activities |
| *LF* | *The Little Foxes* |
| LH | Lillian Hellman |
| *MMMF&M* | *My Mother, My Father and Me* |
| *ST* | *Scoundrel Time* |
| *SW* | *The Searching Wind* |
| *TIA* | *Toys in the Attic* |
| *UW* | *An Unfinished Woman* |
| *WR* | *Watch on the Rhine* |

# LILLIAN HELLMAN

# I. BIOGRAPHICAL MATERIAL

## IA. Political Activities of Hellman
### (See also Section VIIC, Reviews of *ST*)

IA1. "Columnar Freedom," *Time*, XXXV (Feb. 14, 1938), 28.

Reports that LH's article on the Spanish Civil War
written at Walter Winchell's request was rejected by
Hearst editors because it was "loyalist propaganda."

IA2. "Miss Hellman and Miss Ferber Discuss Jewish Author's
Plight; Bigotry Rising in U.S. as It Is Abroad, Play-
wright Warns Book Luncheon; Novelist Urges Teaching of
Tolerance Through Reading in Schools," New York *Herald
Tribune*, Jan. 10, 1940, p. 19. See also "Lin Yutang
Holds 'Gods' Favor China; Says 3 'Divinities' on Her
Side in War Are 'Arithmetic, Geography, and Philosophy';
2000 at Literary Fete; Edna Ferber, Lillian Hellman,
and Arthur Guiterman Give Talks at Luncheon," New York
*Times*, Jan. 10, 1940, p. 19.

Quotes LH's talk about growing bigotry against Jews.
The speech was given at American Booksellers' Association luncheon at the Astor Hotel, New York.

IA3. Sheaffer, Louis. "Who Fought the Finnish Benefits; and
Why?" New York *World-Telegram*, Apr. 6, 1940, p. 6.

Notes that Sheaffer was attacked by the New York State
Communist Party for organizing theatre benefits for
Finland. He claims that the Party line is similar to
the "isolationist" plea of LH and Shumlin in not wanting
to support the Finnish cause.

IA4. "Governor to Shun Communist Forum; He Rescinds Sponsor-
ship of Dinner for Fascist Victim Calling Committees
Red; Lillian Hellman in Reply; Co-Chairman Voices Regret

But Says She Can Vouch for Distribution of Funds," New
York *Times*, Oct. 4, 1941, p. 34.

Reports that LH, co-chairman with Ernest Hemingway of
the forum and dinner on "Europe Today," says forum will
go on despite Governor Lehman's withdrawal of support.
(See Item IA5.)

IA5.  "Scores Attack on Fund; Lillian Hellman Speaks at Dinner
to Aid Anti-Nazis in France," New York *Times*, Oct. 10,
1941, p. 9.  See also "Dinner-Forum for Exiled Writers
Even Without Lehman," *PM* (New York), Oct. 10, 1941, p.
11.

Includes quotations from LH's speech before an anti-
fascist forum in which she called her critics "cowardly
and malicious."  (See Item IA4.)

IA6.  "U.S. Town Urged to Take Name of Distomo, Destroyed by
the Nazis with 1,100 Residents," New York *Times*, Aug.
31, 1944, p. 19.

Lists LH as a member of the Committee for the Rebirth
of Distomo, an anti-Nazi organization.

IA7.  "Russia Acclaimed by Miss Hellman; Home, She Says Soviet
Will Deal with Fascism--Hopes We Do the Same in U.S.,"
New York *Times*, Mar. 2, 1945, p. 5.

IA8.  "PAC Joins Forces with Two Groups; Campaign Alliance is
Formed with Citizens' PAC and Ickes' Arts-Science Body,"
New York *Times*, May 12, 1946, p. 9.

Reports that the Political Action Committee of the Congress of Industrial Organizations joined forces with the
National Citizen Political Action Committee and the
Citizens' Committee of the Arts, Sciences, and Profes-
sions.  LH was a delegate at the merger meeting.

IA9.  Calta, Louis.  "2 Burns Musicals Likely This Year;
Hellman Returns from Paris," New York *Times*, Aug. 26,
1947, p. 26.

Reports LH's return to New York after attending UNESCO
meetings in Paris.

IA10. Parke, Richard H.  "Our Way Defended to 2,000 Opening
'Culture' Meeting; Americans Against Reds, Not Against
Peace, Says Norman Cousins at Waldorf Session; But
Russia Sets Theme: Atlantic Pact and Atomic Program

Attacked by Fadeyev--Britain Warns of War Apathy," New
York *Times*, Mar. 26, 1949, p. 1.

Deals with the highly controversial meeting of the
Cultural and Scientific Conference for World Peace.
Reports LH's critical remarks about Cousins' speech.

IA11. "The Russians Get a Big Hand from U.S. Friends," *Life*,
XXVI (Apr. 4, 1949), 40-43. See also "Peace, Everybody
Wars Over It," *Newsweek*, XXXIII (Apr. 4, 1949), 20.

Claims the Cultural and Scientific Conference for World
Peace provided "a sounding board for Communist propaganda." LH is reported to be a great aid to the Communists because of her activities.

IA12. "Hundreds Named as Red Appeasers; California's Tenney
Committee Lists Actors, Musicians, and Others as 'Line'
Followers," New York *Times*, June 9, 1949, p. 5.

Reports blacklisting by the California State Senate
Committee on Un-American Activities. Numerous enter-
tainers were accused of being appeasers or supporters
of the Communist Party. Included on the list with LH
were Sinatra, K. Hepburn, G. Kelly, G. Peck, Hammett,
and others.

IA13. Hill, Gladwin. "Writer Names 100 as Film Reds After
Threats Against his Family," New York *Times*, Sept. 20,
1951, p. 25.

Reveals that LH is among the 100 persons named Communist Party members by Martin Berkely.

IA14. Carr, Robert K. *The House Committee on Un-American
Activities, 1945-1950*. Ithaca, N.Y.: Cornell University Press, 1952, pp. 60-61.

Reports that HUAC labeled LH's *North Star* one of four
films which contain "pro-Communist or pro-Soviet scenes
which had been consciously and deliberately inserted by
Communists or their sympathizers."

IA15. "U.S. House of Representatives Hearings Before the
Committee on Un-American Activities--Communist Infil-
tration of Hollywood Motion Picture Industry"--Part 8,
82nd Congress, 2nd Session, 1952, pp. 3345-3546.

Includes transcription of LH's testimony before HUAC.

IA16.  "Lillian Hellman Balks House Unit; Says She is Not Red
       Now, But Won't Disclose if She Was Lest It Hurt
       Others," New York *Times*, May 22, 1952, p. 15.  See
       also "Lillian Hellman, Writer, Refuses Red Testimony,"
       San Diego *Union*, May 22, 1952, Sect. A, p. 4.  "The
       Theatre;  Meeting Goer," *Time*, LIX (June 2, 1952),
       74.

       Depicts LH's appearance before the House Un-American
       Activities Committee in 1952 where she refused to
       testify against others.  Reports her claim that she was
       not a Communist nor had she been one two years before.
       Asked if she had been three years before, she refused
       to answer; the Committee did not cite her for contempt.
       (See Items IA19, IA25-27.)

IA17.  Bracker, Milton.  "Books of 40 Authors Banned by U.S.
       in Overseas Libraries," New York *Times*, June 22, 1953,
       p. 1.

       Reports that State Department directives banned books
       of LH and others because of alleged Communist ties.

IA18.  "McCarthy Calls 23 for Book Inquiry," New York *Times*,
       June 28, 1953, p. 33.

       Announces that LH would be called along with Rockwell
       Kent and Dorothy Parker as witnesses in the hearing on
       overseas library banning of books.

IA19.  Buckley, William F., Jr.  *The Committee and The Cri-
       tics:  A Calm Review of the House Committee on Un-
       American Activities*.  New York: G.P. Putnam's Sons,
       1962, p. 296.

       Notes briefly that the investigation of "Communist in-
       filtration into the Hollywood motion picture industry"
       included testimony from LH "who invoked the Fifth
       Amendment."

IA20.  Grose, Peter.  "Soviet Writers Given Party Line; Con-
       vention Is Told to Fight West's 'Dirt and Filth,'" New
       York *Times*, May 23, 1962, p. 12.

       Reports that LH, C.P. Snow, and others visited the
       opening session of writers congress in the Soviet Union
       which Kosygin and Brezhnev also attended.

IA21.  Arnold, Martin.  "Lillian Hellman Says She Found Fer-
       ment Among Soviet Writers;  Author Reports a Determined

Drive for Greater Freedom of Literary Expression,"
New York *Times*, May 31, 1967, p. 11.

Reveals that while doing research in the Soviet Union
LH attended the National Congress of the Union of Writers. She found a "determined" will to write with
freedom throughout the gathering.

IA22.   Raymont, Henry. "80 World Intellectuals to Hold Seminar on Problems of U.S.," New York *Times*, Oct. 28,
1968, p. 2.

Lists LH as participant.

IA23.   Ezergalis, A. "Kutnetsov's Exile," New York *Times*,
Aug. 30, 1969, p. 20.

Criticizes LH's remarks concerning Kutnetsov's exile
from the USSR. (See also LH. "Topics: The Baggage
of a Political Exile," New York *Times*, Aug. 23, 1969,
p. 26.)

IA24.   Clines, Francis X. "FBI Head Scored by Ramsey Clark,"
New York *Times*, Nov. 18, 1970, p. 48.

Announces the formation of the Committee for Public
Justice, a group to fight political repression. Lists
LH as executive council member.

IA25.   Bentley, Eric, ed. *Thirty Years of Treason: Excerpts
from Hearings Before the House Committee on Un-American Activities, 1938-1968*. New York: Viking Press,
1971, pp. 533-543.

Included are LH's letter to Committee Chairman Wood
and excerpts from her testimony before HUAC.

IA26.   Kraft, Hy. *On My Way to the Theater*. New York:
Macmillan, 1971, pp. 156, 196.

Lists LH as one of the supporters of the 1968 McCarthy-
O'Dwyer campaign in New York. In discussing HUAC,
Kraft reveals that Sidney Cohn wanted to reach agree-
ment with Representative Walter on the presentation of
a case that would logically excuse Communist ties of
Hollywood artists. Kraft was told that Cohn "thought
of presenting the idea to Lillian Hellman. I knew
Lillian Hellman well enough to predict her vigorous
and violent rejection of any proposal that would lend
even a microscopic shred of dignity" to HUAC.

IA27.   Bentley, Eric. *Theatre of War*. New York:  Viking
        Press, 1972, p. 300.

        Discusses briefly LH's appearance before HUAC.

IA28.   Belfrage, Cedric. *The American Inquisition 1945-1960*.
        New York:  Bobbs-Merrill, 1973, p. 98.

        Reports LH's plea for peace at the "Scientific Confer-
        ence for World Peace."

IA29.   Goldstein, Malcolm. *The Political Stage:  American
        Drama and Theater of the Great Depression*. New York:
        Oxford University Press, 1974, passim.

        Documents LH's support of various radical social and
        political campaigns throughout her life.  Notes that
        plays by LH are reflections of the political situations
        during the times in which they were written because of
        the keen social conscience of LH.

IA30.   Ripley, Anthony.  "U.S. Judge Rules Nixon Documents
        Belong to Nation," New York *Times*, Feb. 1, 1975, pp.
        1, 10.  See also Ripley, Anthony. "Appeals Court Will
        Move Quickly on Nixon Records," New York *Times*, Feb.
        2, 1975, Sect. I, p. 44.

        Lists LH as one of four who filed suit to gain access
        to President Nixon's Watergate tapes.

IA31.   Shenker, Israel.  "Rhetoric of Democrats in 1976 Leans
        Heavily on Unity and God," New York *Times*, July 16,
        1976, p. 15.

        Quotes LH on campaign rhetoric:  "Politicians are
        afraid of offending anyone ... so they talk in general-
        ities."

IA32.   "Noting the 'R' in October, Lillian Hellman Hosts a
        Bash at the Oyster Bar," *People*, VIII (Oct. 17, 1977),
        44.

        Features the $100/person reception given by LH in New
        York to benefit her "Committee for Public Justice."
        Attendees included Woody Allen, Leonard Bernstein, and
        Claudette Colbert.

IB.  Awards, Degrees, and Honors

IB1.   "Lillian Hellman Wins Honorary Tufts Degree," New York
       *Journal American*, June 9, 1941, p. 8.

       Reports the awarding of an honorary MA to LH for "con-
       tributions to the theatre."

IB2.   "Academy Elects 116," New York *Times*, May 12, 1960, p.
       22.

       Reports LH's election to the American Academy of Arts
       and Sciences.

IB3.   Calta, Louis.  "Arts Medal Goes to Miss Hellman;  Play-
       wright Named Winner of Brandeis Award--Change in *Romeo
       and Juliet* Cast," New York *Times*, Mar. 11, 1961, p. 15.
       See also "Awards Made for Arts; Brandeis Cities Play-
       wright, Composer, Poet, and Artist," New York *Times*,
       Mar. 30, 1961, p. 21.  "Brandeis U. Honors 9 in Creative
       Arts," New York *Times*, June 11, 1961, p. 63.

       Announces the $1500 prize awarded LH for "a lifetime of
       artistic achievement."

IB4.   "Kennedy Doctor Widens Activity;  She Urges Research
       for Relief of Chronic Pain," New York *Times*, Apr. 20,
       1961, p. 23.

       Reveals that LH and six other women were cited for ex-
       cellence by the Women's Division of the Albert Einstein
       College of Yeshiva University.

IB5.   "Honors," *The New York University Alumni News*, Oct. 1,
       1961, p. 2.

       Reports "Alumna" LH was awarded an honorary degree by
       Wheaton College.

IB6.   "Arts and Letters Institute Names 12," New York *Times*,
       Feb. 13, 1962, p. 40.

       Notes LH's election as a vice-president of the National
       Institute of Arts and Letters.

IB7.   "Rutgers Awards Degrees to 2,730," New York *Times*, June
       6, 1963, p. 24.

       Lists LH as one of eleven to receive honorary doctor-
       ates.

IB8.  Gassner, John. "Too Many Judges?; Procedures in
      Giving Prizes Questioned," New York *Times*, July 21,
      1963, Sect. 2, p. 1.

      Discusses procedures/oversights in choosing prize win-
      ners for drama. Notes that LH has never received a
      Pulitzer Prize despite deserving one.

IB9.  "Miss Hellman and Shumlin Honored," New York *Times*,
      Jan. 28, 1964, p. 28. See also "Gold Medal to Be Given
      to Hellman," San Diego *Tribune*, Jan. 28, 1964, Sect. A,
      p. 13.

      Reports that LH received prize for "achievements in
      drama" from the National Institute for Arts and Letters.

IB10. "Brandeis Commencement," New York *Herald Tribune*, June
      14, 1965, p. 15.

      Notes that LH was among several honored by Brandeis
      during commencement.

IB11. Toohey, John. *A History of the Pulitzer Prize Plays*.
      New York: Citadel Press, 1967, passim.

      Notes LH's plays were contenders for the Pulitzer and
      Drama Critics' Circle Award. The controversy over *CH*'s
      failure to win is discussed. LH's not having won a
      Pulitzer Prize cited as an oversight by the selection
      committee.

IB12. "Miss Hellman Wins Award by College," New York *Times*,
      Apr. 4, 1968, p. 58.

      Reports that Jackson College (Women's Dept., Tufts Uni-
      versity) voted to present an "award of distinction" to
      LH. The prize honors women who are "outstanding in
      their field."

IB13. Handler, M.S. "Lillian Hellman is Among Nine Named to
      City University Chairs," New York *Times*, Sept. 26, 1972,
      p. 38.

      Reports LH's appointment as distinguished professor at
      Hunter College.

IB14. "From Show Biz to Groves of Academe," *Variety*, Oct. 4,
      1972, p. 2.

      Reports that LH was named distinguished professor of
      romance languages at CUNY.

IB15.  "New Jersey Briefs; A.C.L.U. Honors 4 in New Brunswick," New York *Times*, Oct. 29, 1973, p. 79.

Reports that the New Jersey branch of the ACLU presented plaques to LH and 3 others for "outstanding
contributions to civil liberties."

IB16.  "Briefs on the Arts; 15 from Stage in Hall of Fame,"
New York *Times*, Nov. 20, 1973, p. 30.

Reveals that LH and 14 others were named to the
Theatre Hall of Fame.

IB17.  Van Gelder, Lawrence. "Notes on People; Public Photos
of Greece's Gizikis Irk Him," New York *Times*, Dec. 7,
1973, p. 30.

Reports that LH was awarded the first "Woman of the
Year Award" by New York University Alumnae Club for
"outstanding attainments in business and professional
life."

IB18.  "Lillian Hellman, Author and Playwright," *Yale Alumni
Magazine*, XXXVII (June 1974), 20.

Reports honorary doctorate awarded LH.

IB19.  "N.Y.U. Graduates 2,300 in Garden; Commencement Class
Totals 7,500 for University," New York *Times*, June 7,
1974, p. 20.

Notes that LH was awarded an honorary doctorate by
NYU.

IB20.  Bennetts, Leslie. "Lillian Hellman Gives Vivid Reading Here; Literary Giant Takes Post at Bryn Mawr,"
Philadelphia *Bulletin*, Oct. 30, 1974, p. 8.

Reports that LH, Bryn Mawr's Lucy Martin Donnelly
Fellow in Creative Writing, made only one public appearance during her stay, during which she read impressively
from *Pentimento*.

IB21.  Bonin, Jane F. *Major Themes in Prize Winning American
Drama*. Metuchen, N.J.: Scarecrow Press, 1975, pp.
76, 80, 131, 150, 152.

Considers *TIA* as a Circle prize-winning play. Says
that *CH*'s theme of lesbianism kept LH from winning a
Pulitzer Prize, because of "squeamish judges."

IB22.   "8 'Women of the Year' Honored by Magazine," New York
        *Times*, April 20, 1975, p. 16.

        Reports that *Ladies Home Journal* chose LH as one of
        the "Women of the Year."

IB23.   "Suzy Says; A Playwright's Night," New York *Sunday
        News*, Oct. 26, 1975, Sect. 11, p. 12.

        Announces Nov. 9 tribute to LH for her work on the
        Committee for Public Justice.

IB24.   Bachrach, Judith. "A Tribute to the Old Lillian
        Hellman, the Real Lillian Hellman, Lillian Hellman Au
        Gratin," Washington *Post*, Nov. 11, 1975, Sect. B, p.
        7. See also: Bell, Arthur. "Bell Tells," *Village
        Voice*, Nov. 17, 1975, p. 126. Gussow, Mel. "For
        Lillian Hellman, More Honors and a New Book," New
        York *Times*, Nov. 7, 1975, p. 28. "Hellman Tribute
        Benefit Raises War-Chest Fund," San Diego *Union*, Dec.
        8, 1975, Sect. B, p. 4. Nachman, Gerald. "A Tribute
        in Her Own Time," New York *Daily News*, Nov. 11, 1975,
        p. 39. Pinkerton, Ann. "Hellman's Angels," *Women's
        Wear Daily*, Nov. 11, 1975, p. 18. Sullivan, Dan.
        "Celebrity Toast to Lillian Hellman," Los Angeles
        *Times*, Nov. 14, 1975, Sect. 4, p. 1. Vespa, Mary.
        "It's Hellman's Hour, As Scores of Her Pals Salute a
        Distinguished Writer," *People*, IV (Nov. 1975), 18-20.

        Features the benefit celebration held in honor of LH
        at the Circle in the Square, New York. The ceremony
        was to laud LH for her "contributions to literature,
        and to the protection of civil liberties." Proceeds
        from the gathering were donated to LH's Committee for
        Public Justice. A long list of celebrities including
        Jacqueline Onassis, Leonard Bernstein, Mike Nichols,
        Jane Fonda, and others attended. Excerpts from plays
        by LH were read.

IB25.   Cummings, Judith. "Columbia Grants Degrees to 6,700,"
        New York *Times*, May 13, 1976, p. 19.

        Lists LH as recipient of honorary degree.

IB26.   Krebs, Albin. "Notes on People; U.S. Approves Visit
        by Defector to China," New York *Times*, June 30, 1976,
        p. 34.

        Announces that LH is to be awarded "The Edward Mac-
        Dowell Medal for outstanding contributions to litera-
        ture."

IB27.  "Lillian Hellman Gets Lord & Taylor Award," New York
       *Times*, Nov. 10, 1977, Sect. 2, p. 16.

       Reports that LH was given award for bringing "new
       beauty and deeper understanding to our lives."


                IC.  Teaching, Lectures, Speeches


IC1.   "Dramatists Attending Writer's Congress," New York
       *Post*, June 1, 1939, p. 12.

       States that LH will serve as chairman for the drama
       panel sponsored by Third American Writer's Congress.

IC2.   "Drama Still Alive, Stage Experts Say," New York
       *Times*, Dec. 2, 1951, Sect. 1, p. 85.

       Reports that LH took part in a panel discussion spon-
       sored by Harvard Law Forum.  The topic discussed was
       serious drama and its relationship to the musical.
       Richard Rodgers, Marc Connelly, and John Chapman were
       the other panelists.

IC3.   "Lillian Hellman to be Lecturer," New York *Times*, July
       31, 1960, p. 48.

       Announces LH's appointment as guest lecturer at Harvard
       for spring term, 1961.

IC4.   "Lillian Hellman Gives Eulogy at Hammett Funeral," New
       York *Herald Tribune*, Jan. 13, 1961, p. 20.

       Includes excerpts from LH's eulogy.

IC5.   Ross, Don.  "Lillian Hellman Teaches What Can't Be
       Taught," New York *Herald Tribune*, Apr. 23, 1961, Sect.
       4, p. 3.

       Features LH's creative writing course taught at Loeb
       Drama Center in Cambridge.  Notes that the course was
       the idea of McGeorge Bundy, "now special assistant to
       JFK."

IC6.   Hewes, Henry, ed. *The Best Plays of 1963-64*.  New
       York: Dodd, Mead, 1964, p. 363.  (See Item IIA47.)

       Lists LH as narrator for the Marc Blitzstein Memorial
       Concert, Philharmonic Hall, April 19, 1964.

IC7.  Shepard, Richard. "Lillian Hellman Teaching at Yale,"
      New York *Times*, Feb. 1, 1966, p. 28.

      Describes the first class of a freshman seminar taught
      by LH.

IC8.  "Dorothy Parker Recalled as Wit;  Mostel and Lillian
      Hellman Deliver Brief Eulogies," New York *Times*, June
      10, 1967, p. 33.

IC9.  Whitman, Alden. "Lillian Hellman Gives Her Harvard
      Seminar Lesson on Writing for the Screen," New York
      *Times*, May 10, 1968, p. 54.

      Reports LH's guidance on screenplay writing given to
      Harvard students. Emphasizes that screenplay writers
      must have final film product in mind in order to end
      up with a "viable" script. LH read aloud a short
      story by Graham Greene to the students and then specu-
      lated on how to turn it into a good screenplay. The
      key to good screenwriting is "how [well] you develop
      your characters."

IC10. "Seminar Studies U.S. Woes," New York *Times*, Dec. 3,
      1968, p. 49.

      Reveals that Princeton is holding seminars about
      troubles in the U.S. (Vietnam, military industrial
      complex, etc.). Notes that LH participated with other
      intellectuals. (See Item IC11.)

IC11. Shenker, Israel. "A Hit and Myth Gathering of Intel-
      lectuals," New York *Times*, Dec. 9, 1968, Sect. 4, p. 2.

      Indicates that the gathering of "so-called" intellec-
      tuals at Princeton was fruitless. (See Item IC10.)

IC12. Eckman, Fern Marja. "Lillian Hellman--Plenty of
      Class," New York *Post*, Oct. 14, 1972, pp. 3, 12.

      Features literature classes LH taught at Hunter
      College.

IC13. Martin, Judith. "Unsentimental Look at Politics, Life,
      Art," Washington *Post*, Nov. 12, 1974, Sect. B, p. 2.

      Features LH's lecture at the Smithsonian Associates
      series by "distinguished American Women of Letters."
      Notes that LH responded to questions from the audience
      and spoke of her efforts to desegregate Washington,

D.C. theatres.  Includes her criticism of the NAACP
for its handling of the Dorothy Parker estate to which
it was heir.

IC14.  Klion, Stanley R.  "On Damning Business," New York
*Times*, June 21, 1975, p. 26.

Criticizes LH's Barnard College commencement speech
that was published June 4, 1975, in the New York *Times*.

IC15.  Barkin, Don.  "Personalities," Washington *Post*, Aug.
4, 1978, Sect. C, p. 3.

Announces that LH will travel from her Cape Cod home
to speak at Leonard Bernstein's sixtieth birthday
celebration in Washington.

IC16.  McLellan, Joseph, and Lon Tuck.  "Night of Nights for
One of America's Arts Heroes;  Party on the Lawn for
Bernstein's 60th," Washington *Post*, Aug. 26, 1978,
Sect. 6, pp. 1, 4.

Reports LH's remarks at tribute to Leonard Bernstein.
Notes that LH's remarks "interrupted the generally
congratulatory tone of other remarks," by giving a
brief tribute to the late Felicia Bernstein.  Bernstein
gave his approval of her remarks shortly before she
went on stage.


## ID.  Hellman and Hollywood


ID1.  "Screen Notes," New York *Times*, Jan. 18, 1935, p. 27.

Reports that LH was engaged by Herman Shumlin to write
the screenplay for *Dark Angel*.

ID2.  "Lillian Hellman Sees Hollywood as Clique Ridden,"
New York *World Telegram*, June 29, 1935, p. 16.

Reveals in a short interview "what's wrong with Hollywood" according to LH.  "Hollywood groups are tight --
that's why there are so many fights."

ID3.  Creelman, Eileen.  "Picture, Plays, and Players; Lillian
Hellman, Author of *The Children's Hour*, Writes a
Movie," New York *Sun*, July 9, 1935, p. 12.

Notes that LH is in the process of writing the screenplay for *Dark Angel*.

ID4.    "The Films Now Know Miss Hellman," New York *Herald
Tribune*, July 17, 1935, Sect. 5, p. 3.

Reveals information about LH's time in Hollywood following the success of *CH*.  LH explains in the interview that she "had only $55 in the bank" when she
finished the play.  Points out the Shumlin-Hammett
contributions to the play.

ID5.    "Leaves for Hollywood," New York *World Telegram*, Feb.
15, 1937, p. 12.

Announces LH's departure for Hollywood to write the
screenplay for *Dead End*.

ID6.    Morehouse, Ward.  "Broadway After Dark," New York *Sun*,
Mar. 11, 1939, p. 30.

Discusses in an interview LH's plans to alternate working in Hollywood and on Broadway.

ID7.    Creelman, Eileen.  "Picture Plays and Players; Lillian
Hellman Discusses the Filming of her Play, *The Little
Foxes*," New York *Sun*, June 19, 1941, p. 10.

Features interview with LH in which she claims characters in *LF* were based on people she knew in the South.

ID8.    Strauss, Theodore.  "Of Lillian Hellman, a Lady of
Principle," New York *Times*, Aug. 29, 1943, Sect. 2, p.
3.

Discusses LH's screenplay writing.  Notes that she has
been surrounded by controversy in Hollywood because of
her refusal to compromise with producers and directors
on her scripts.

ID9.    _____.  "The Author's Case;  Post-Premiere Cogitations
of Lillian Hellman on *The North Star*," New York *Times*,
Dec. 19, 1943, Sect. 2, p. 5.

Reports LH's complaints about the production of *The
North Star* script which she claims artistically mars
her screenplay.  Maintains that the producer and the
director are at fault.

ID10.  "*Watch on the Rhine* Voted Best Film;  Warner's Movie of Anti-Nazi Play Wins the New York Critics' Award for 1943;  Paul Lukas is Honored;  Chosen as Leading Actor of Year--Ida Lupino, George Stevens Also Cited," New York *Times*, Dec. 29, 1943, p. 19.

ID11.  Pryor, Thomas M.  "By Way of Report," New York *Times*, Aug. 27, 1944, Sect. 2, p. 3.

Reveals that *North Star* film version is playing to capacity crowds in the Soviet Union.

ID12.  Stanley, Fred.  "Escape in Hollywood," New York *Times*, July 1, 1945, Sect. 2, p. 1.

Previews film version of *SW*.  Includes an interview with movie's producer, Hal Wallis.

ID13.  Strauss, Theodore.  "Of Lillian Hellman, a Lady of Principles; The Author of *Watch on the Rhine* and *North Star* Stands by Her Guns," New York *Times*, Aug. 29, 1945, Sect. 2, p. 3.

Features LH's battles with producers/directors over film productions.

ID14.  Pryor, Thomas M.  "At Peace with the World," New York *Times*, July 7, 1946, Sect. 2, p. 3.

Interviews LH concerning the movie version of *SW*.  Reveals an indifferent attitude by LH over the mixed reviews.  Tells of her devotion to work in writing a new play, putting the last one behind her.

ID15.  Green, Abel, and Joe Laurie, Jr.  *Show Biz: From Vaude to Video*.  New York:  Henry Holt, 1951, p. 426.

Points out that LH was making $35 per week as a script writer for Metro when *CH* hit Broadway.  She then demanded $1000 per week before she would go back to work.

ID16.  "Television Play; *Another Part of the Forest*," London *Times*, Jan. 17, 1957, p. 3.

Proclaims in a preview of *APF* that it is "an authentic comment on the virgins of violence."

ID17.  "Broadway Plays to be Filmed," London *Times*, Aug. 2, 1960, p. 11.

Announces Wyler's filming of *TIA*.

ID18.  Schumach, Murray.  "Hollywood Infamous;  Remake of
       *Children's Hour* Comes Closer to Original Play," New
       York *Times*, June 15, 1961, Sect. 2, p. 7.

       Includes an informational preview of new film version
       of *CH*.

ID19.  _____.  "Hollywood Slant;  Transplanted *Toys in the
       Attic* Prompts Some Personal Analysis," New York *Times*,
       Oct. 28, 1962, Sect. 2, p. 7.

       Lists the cast of the film version of *TIA* including
       Dean Martin, Geraldine Page, Wendy Hiller, and others.

ID20.  Bart, Peter.  "On a Grim Chase with 'Sound and Fury,'"
       New York *Times*, June 20, 1965, p. 11.

       Reports that the ongoing shooting of *The Chase* is an
       extremely interesting and hopeful project since the
       talents of LH and Marlon Brando are combined.  This is
       LH's first film script in fifteen years.

ID21.  "Questioning Miss Hellman on Movies," New York *Times*,
       Feb. 27, 1966, Sect. 2, p. 5.

       Discusses her screenplay for *The Chase* and the movies
       of the day.  LH was not pleased with the complete con-
       trol of the director in movie production.

ID22.  Easton, Carol.  "Willy Wyler; The Finishing Touch"
       and "The North Star."  *The Search for Sam Goldwyn*.
       New York:  William Morrow and Co., 1976, pp. 129-139,
       218-222.

       Tells of LH's employment by MGM in 1935.  "The Hellman-
       Goldwyn relationship was a stormy love-hate affair.
       Both were difficult people, forever hurling gauntlets
       at each other....  Hellman made it clear that nobody,
       not even Sam Goldwyn, was going to push her around.
       She was independent and insistent on her terms, take
       it or leave it.  She held out for an exorbitant $2,000
       a week.  Sam took it."  Discusses the production of
       *These Three* and *The North Star*.  LH felt that her
       screenplay for *North Star* was ruined by the producer,
       actors, and director.  She called the picture "a senti-
       mental mess."

ID23.  Shales, Tom.  "The Oscars:  Top Honors to 'Rocky,'
       Finch and Dunaway." Washington *Post*, Mar. 30, 1977,
       Sect. B, p. 13.

Reports that LH received a standing ovation from the Academy prior to her presenting an Oscar to an award winner.

ID24. Arnold, Gary. "The Night of the Star War," Washington *Post*, Apr. 2, 1978, Sect. K, pp. 1, 11.

Recalls that at last year's (1977) Academy Awards when LH presented an award, she was "welcomed like a conquering culture heroine" with a standing ovation.

## IE.  Miscellaneous Biographical Material

IE1. Gassner, John, and Bernard F. Dukore, eds., "Introduction" to *The Little Foxes, A Treasury of the Theatre*, Vol. II.  New York:  Simon and Schuster, 1935, pp. 953-954.

Includes a biographical sketch.

IE2. "Winter's Harvest," *Stage*, XII (Mar. 1935), 9.

Notes new faces to appear on Broadway; LH and others cited.

IE3. Tanner, Juanita.  "They Know Their Heroines," *Independent Woman*, XV (Mar. 1936), 74-75.

Includes portrait of LH with a passing reference to the success of *CH*.

IE4. "Miss Hellman Again," New York *Times*, Dec. 13, 1936, Sect. 11, p. 4.

Includes biographical summary of LH's life.  Notes her successes with *CH* and Hollywood screenplays and thus anxiously awaits her new play, *DC*.  Notes her New Orleans birthplace and also her frequent moves to New York and New Jersey caused by "nomadic elders."  Cites LH's earliest published works in the *Paris Comet* and the *American Spectator*.  Mentions her early collaboration with Hammett.

IE5. "Rialto Gossip;  Merry Christmas, a Play and an Actress from Hollywood--Mr. Woods Files a Report," New York *Times*, Dec. 20, 1936, Sect. 11, p. 1.

Reveals that in the contract between LH and Shumlin, it is stipulated that each time his name appears in an advertisement, hers must also appear. (See Item IE6.)

IE6.    Shumlin, Herman. "On Billing," New York *Times*, Jan. 3, 1937, Sect. 10, p. 3.

Refutes story which reported LH's contract containing a clause requiring a "fifty-fifty" billing. (See Item IE5.)

IE7.    Mantle, Burns. "New Blood; Lillian Hellman." *Contemporary American Playwrights*. New York: Dodd, Mead & Co., 1938, pp. 180-181.

Notes that LH is a dramatist with "potential" after her first two plays. Includes a biographical sketch.

IE8.    "Lillian Hellman," *Wilson Bulletin for Librarians*, XIII (May 1939), 632.

Includes a one-page biographical sketch of LH.

IE9.    "Lillian Hellman Buys Estate of 130 Acres; Playwright Gets Property in Mt. Pleasant, Westchester," New York *Times*, June 7, 1939, p. 43.

IE10.   *Current Biography 1941*. New York: H.W. Wilson Co., 1941, pp. 375-376.

Included is a biographical sketch of LH to 1941. A short checklist of works by LH as well as an account of key events in her life are provided.

IE11.   Hughes, Charlotte. "Women Playmakers," *New York Times Magazine*, May 4, 1941, pp. 10-11.

Surveys careers of several accomplished women playwrights including LH, Rachel Crothers, and others.

IE12.   "Rialto Gossip; News, Comment--A Report or Two--About Various Theatrical Matters," New York *Times*, Oct. 19, 1941, Sect. 9, p. 1.

Announces that LH is at work researching her new play, but is not yet writing it.

IE13.   Harriman, Margaret Case. "Profiles; Miss Lily of New Orleans," *New Yorker*, XVII (Nov. 8, 1941), 22-26. Reprinted in *Take Them Up Tenderly*. New York: Alfred A. Knopf, 1944, pp. 94-109.

Sketches LH's life to age 36 after she had completed *CH*, *DC*, *LF* and *WR*.  Calls LH the "youngest successful woman writing plays in the United States."  Discusses her political stance, her desire to be known as a liberal and not a Communist.  This is an excellent article for viewing LH's youth, family, and growth to maturity.  It is better organized than her own description of her youth in *UW*.

IE14.  Robinson, Clarke.  "Silhouettes of Celebrities," *World Digest*, XV (Jan. 1942), 78-83.

Includes a biographical sketch of LH to 1942.

IE15.  Maney, Richard S.  "From Hellman to Shumlin to Broadway," New York *Times*, Apr. 9, 1944, Sect. 2, p. 1.

Features the extraordinary successes achieved by the LH-Shumlin team in producing Broadway hits.

IE16.  "People are Talking About ..."  *Vogue*, CIII (Apr. 15, 1944), p. 98.

Includes brief biography of LH and photo.

IE17.  Mersand, Joseph.  *The American Drama Since 1930*.  Port Washington, New York:  Kennikat Press, 1949, pp. 47, 139, 147-149, 154.

Makes numerous passing references to LH as a significant woman dramatist.

IE18.  Sherwood, Robert E.  "Footnote to a Preface," *Saturday Review*, XXXII (Aug. 13, 1949), 130, 132-134.

Reminisces about literature and drama of the past and notes that LH was one of the "rising stars" of the twenties.

IE19.  "The Drama Mailbag;  Writers Take Up Issue of Directing Plays," New York *Times*, Oct. 30, 1949, Sect. 2, p. 3.

Includes three letters in response to LH's interview on directing plays.  Proposes that the director's position is superior to the playwright's when a play is to be produced.  (See Item IIG10.)

IE20.  Lumley, Frederick.  *20th Century Drama*.  London:  Rockliff, 1956, pp. 227-228.

Calls LH's work "technically efficient" but "mediocre in content."

IE21.  Rice, Elmer L.  *The Living Theatre*.  New York:  Harper
       and Brothers, 1959, pp. 59, 126, 162, 206, 207.

       Makes numerous passing references to LH and her role in
       the theatre.

IE22.  *Current Biography 1960*.  New York:  H.W. Wilson Co.,
       1960, pp. 186-187.

       Includes a biographical portrait of LH to 1960.  Out-
       lines all of her plays to date and their receptions as
       well as a brief bibliography of works by LH.

IE23.  Brown, Deming.  *Soviet Attitudes Toward American
       Writing*.  Princeton, N.J.:  Princeton University Press,
       1962, p. 189.

       Reports the frequently excellent reception in the USSR
       of LH's plays during WWII.

IE24.  "Miss Hellman Completes Latest Play," San Diego *Union*,
       Nov. 11, 1963, Sect. A, p. 14.

       Announces the completion of LH's play *Emma* based on
       Emma Lazarus.  (Play was not produced or published.)

IE25.  Meehan, Thomas.  "Q:  Miss Hellman, What's Wrong with
       Broadway?  A:  It's a Bore," *Esquire*, LVIII (Dec. 1962),
       140-142.  Reprinted in *The Modern Theatre*.  Edited by
       Robert W. Corrigan.  New York: Macmillan, 1964, pp.
       1108-1112.

       Discusses with LH the "sorry state of the theatre" in
       1962.  LH claims that there is "very little [theatre]
       which is any fun."  She credits the "extraordinary wri-
       ting talents" of the twenties with "breaking new ground";
       therefore there were twice as many play openings
       then as now.  The high price of tickets and the necess-
       ity to buy tickets months in advance have driven LH
       from the theatre.

IE26.  "Curtis Publishing Is Named in a $3 Million Libel Suit,"
       New York *Times*, Feb. 27, 1964, p. 39.

       Reports that LH and Curtis Publishing Company (*Ladies
       Home Journal*) were named in a libel suit over material
       in the article "Sophronia's Grandson Goes to Washing-
       ton," written by LH.  Sheriff Dewey Colvard of Etowah
       County, Alabama, filed the suit.

IE27.  Rabkin, Gerald. *Drama and Commitment: Politics of American Theatre of the Thirties*. Bloomington: Indiana U. Press, 1964, pp. 40-41.

Notes that LH is "the hardiest dramatic survivor of the thirties, perhaps because, unlike Odets, she commanded a technique which could survive abrupt change in the winds of doctrine." Considers briefly *CH*, *DC*, and *LF*.

IE28.  Nolan, Paul T. "Drama in the Lower Mississippi States," *Mississippi Quarterly*, XIX (Winter 1965-66), 20-28.

Makes numerous passing references to LH as a Southern Dramatist. Nothing substantive about her is included.

IE29.  Gould, Jean. "Lillian Hellman." *Modern American Playwrights*. New York: Dodd, Mead, 1966, pp. 168-185.

Includes a biographical sketch of LH. Her birthplace, education, Hollywood and Broadway successes, and other information presented.

IE30.  Styron, William. "Lillian Hellman." *Double Exposure*. Edited by Roddy McDowall. New York: Delacorte Press, 1966, pp. 140-193.

Presents a "fragmented dialogue" by telephone with Styron and LH. They play a word game that ends with high praise for LH as a person who "creates joy" for herself and others amidst "general madness."

IE31.  Drutman, Irving. "Hellman: A Stranger in the Theatre?" New York *Times*, Feb. 27, 1966, Sect. 2, p. 1.

Discusses with LH the widening gap between her and the theatre, her reasons for not producing a new play, and her techniques for teaching writing at Yale.

IE32.  "People and Places; *The Selected Letters of Anton Chekhov*," *Saturday Review*, XLIX (Dec. 17, 1966), 38.

Announces the publication of the LH-edited volume.

IE33.  French, Warren. *The Thirties: Fiction, Poetry, Drama*. Deland, Fla.: Everett Edwards, 1967, pp. 177-178.

Mentions LH as a significant social playwright whose plays will continue to be important contributions to the theatre as time passes.

IE34.   Kaplan, Morris.  "Dorothy Parker's Will Leaves Estate
        of $10,000 to Dr. King," New York *Times*, June 27,
        1967, p. 22.

        Reports that LH was named the executrix for Parker's
        estate.

IE35.   "Lillian Hellman Files Suit over *Little Foxes* Telecast,"
        New York *Times*, Oct. 21, 1967, p. 17.

        Reveals that LH filed $500,000 suit against CBS and
        Samuel Goldwyn Inc. for showing the entire film *LF* when
        the contract said only part could be aired.  (See Item
        IE39.)

IE36.   Cook, Jean.  "Furniture Collection That Charts Lillian
        Hellman's Career," New York *Times*, Nov. 14, 1967, p.
        40.

        Notes that the furniture in her apartment appeared in
        various productions of her plays.

IE37.   Funke, Lewis.  "The Prime of Jay Allen," New York *Times*,
        Mar. 3, 1968, Sect. 2, p. 1.

        Notes that Jay Presson Allen credits LH with encourag-
        ing her in the play adaptation of Muriel Spark's novel
        *The Prime of Miss Jean Brodie*.

IE38.   Haber, Joyce.  "Lillian Hellman; Theatre's Very Bad,"
        New York *Post*, Nov. 1, 1969, p. 46.

        Features a conversation with LH in which she notes that
        Broadway theatre is bad because "it gets a bad audience
        ... and a bad audience gets bad plays."

IE39.   "Miss Hellman Loses *Little Foxes* Plea," New York *Times*,
        Feb. 27, 1970, p. 26.

        Notes that Judge John Scilippi, New York Court of
        Appeals, ruled against LH in her lawsuit against CBS.
        (See Item IE35.)

IE40.   Day, Martin S.  *History of American Literature, 1910 to
        the Present*.  New York:  Doubleday, 1971, pp. 223-225.

        Includes a biographical sketch of LH and notes on her
        first five plays.  Notes the excellent reception of
        *CH* and *LF*.

IE41. Reinhold, Robert. "Academy Split over Plan to Honor Ezra Pound," London *Times*, July 6, 1972, p. 6.

   Notes that LH was on committee to nominate controversial Ezra Pound for the Emerson-Thoreau medal of the American Academy of Arts and Sciences.

IE42. Sokolsky, Bob. "I Just Think That Broadway is Very Dull," Philadelphia *Bulletin*, Nov. 19, 1972, p. 16.

   Interviews LH in Philadelphia where she attended the Y Arts Council Playwright series. "Frankly, I don't like theatre anymore. At least I don't like the Broadway theatre anymore.... I think movies are picking up the slack."

IE43. Wilson, Garff B. *Three Hundred Years of American Drama and Theatre: From "Ye Bare and Ye Cub" to "Hair."* Englewood Cliffs, N.J.: Prentice-Hall, 1973, passim.

   Includes a biographical sketch of LH along with information about the production of *LF* on Broadway. Mentions several of her other plays.

IE44. "Some Notables Name Their Best," New York *Times*, Jan. 6, 1974, Sect. 2, p. 9.

   Features celebrities naming their favorite movies. Includes LH's picks, Marcel Ophuls' *The Sorrow and the Pity* and Ingmar Bergman's *Cries and Whispers*.

IE45. Shenker, Israel. "Perelman Shaken Up by Florida's Charms," New York *Times*, Apr. 27, 1974, p. 25.

   Features a Sarasota, Florida, vacation gathering that included LH, Albert Hackett, Frances Goodrich, and S.J. Perelman.

IE46. Giddins, Susan R. "The Set That Lillian Built," New York *Post*, May 13, 1974, *Magazine*, p. 32.

   Notes that LH's apartment is to be on tour of celebrities of New York.

IE47. Funke, Lewis. *Playwrights Talk About Writing: 12 Interviews with Lewis Funke.* Chicago: Dramatic Publishing Company, 1975, pp. 90-110.

   Includes an excellent interview with LH on playwriting. She notes that she is no longer fond of the theatre. Discusses the extensive writing and re-writing process she used in composing her plays.

IE48.   Day, Martin S.  "The Golden Age of American Drama;
        Playwrights Serious and Comic." *Handbook of American
        Literature*. St. Lucia, Queensland:  U. of Queensland
        Press, 1975, pp. 271-272.

        Labels LH "unquestionably America's greatest woman
        dramatist and perhaps the best playwright of her sex
        in the English language." Considers briefly *CH*, *LF*,
        and *APF*.

IE49.   Reed, Rex.  "Lillian Hellman Remembers ...," New York
        *Sunday News*, Nov. 9, 1975, Sect. 3, p. 5.

        Reveals numerous anecdotes in an interview with LH.
        Her "humility, courage and truthfulness" are proclaimed
        by Reed.

IE50.   "Remarkable American Women," *Life* (Special Report 1776-
        1976), 52.

        Categorizes LH as "a tough uncompromising speaker of
        truths" in a brief biographical sketch.

IE51.   Balfour, Katherine.  "Talking to Lillian Hellman,"
        *Family Circle*, LXXXVIII (Apr. 1976), 24-27.

        Includes an interview with LH which is primarily bio-
        graphical in which she claims  "the priorities of the
        women's movement have to be reordered.  Let's tackle
        the real issues first--the economic ones."

IE52.   Gold, Arthur, and Robert Fizdale.  "Lillian Hellman's
        Creole Cooking," *Vogue*, CLXIII (June 1976), 98-99.

        Includes LH's recipes for "Rich Man's Gumbo," Stuffed
        Eggplant, Baked Fish Creole, and others.

IE53.   Pincus, Ann.  "My Favorite Women," *Good Housekeeping*,
        CLXXXIII (Nov. 1976), 188.

        Features Dustin Hoffman's pick of LH as his favorite
        woman.  "If I spent the rest of my life· in a room with
        this woman she would never bore me."

IE54.   Roeder, Bill.  "Newsmakers," *Newsweek*, LXXXVIII (Nov.
        1, 1976), 61.

        Reveals LH wearing a mink coat in an advertisement.
        The $7,000 coat was her payment.

IE55.  Doudna, Christine. "A Still Unfinished Woman; A
       Conversation with Lillian Hellman," *Rolling Stone*,
       No. 233 (Feb. 24, 1977), 52-57.

       Features an interview with LH which was conducted
       during the July 4th weekend in 1976. Includes LH's
       comments on her autobiographical work, her plays, her
       life, and current events. "Nobody can argue any longer
       about the rights of women. It's like arguing about
       earthquakes." Presents excellent photographs of LH
       taken throughout her life.

IE56.  Cohen, Richard. "Bogie's Widow Famous for Being
       Famous," Washington *Post*, Jan. 25, 1979, Sect. C, pp.
       1, 7.

       Notes in an article on Lauren Bacall that LH is a
       similar personality. Cites the LH-Hammett relationship
       as parallel to Bogart-Bacall. LH "has become a legend
       in her own time and one reason is she lived long enough
       to write it herself."

## II. INTERVIEWS, PREVIEWS, FEATURES, AND NEWS CONCERNING HELLMAN'S PLAYS AND BOOKS

### IIA. Interviews, Previews, Features, and News -- *The Children's Hour*

IIA1. Roughead, William. "Closed Doors; or The Great Drumsheugh Case." *Bad Companions*. New York: Duffield and Green, 1931, pp. 109-146.

Recounts the case from which LH supposedly obtained her material for *CH*.

IIA2. "Reverses Mss. Legend," New York *World-Telegram*, Nov. 17, 1934, p. 10.

Discusses LH–Shumlin collaboration on *CH*. Notes the development of the play from the conceptual stage to production.

IIA3. "New Plays of the Week," New York *Herald Tribune*, Nov. 18, 1934, Sect. 5, p. 1.

Announces *CH* opening and includes drawing of a scene.

IIA4. Mok, Michel. "*The Children's Hour* Had to Be Written; 18th Century Gave Idea for Modern Play; Miss Lillian Hellman Inspired by Scotch Law Case," New York *Post*, Nov. 23, 1934, p. 5.

Includes brief background information on *CH* and biographical material on LH.

IIA5. Morehouse, Ward. "Broadway After Dark; Rediscovering Thirty-Ninth Street and Maxine Elliot Theatre--Standee Trade at *Children's Hour* Brings Memories of 'Romance' and 'Rain' and 'Coquette,'" New York *Sun*, Dec. 15, 1934, p. 6.

Speculates that *CH* will have a long run.

IIA6.  "Summer's Children; A History of Mr. Shumlin's Bracken
Search for Actresses," New York *Times*, Jan. 20, 1935,
Sect. 10, p. 2.

Reviews the acting experience of actresses playing
leading roles in *CH*. Considers the casting of Misses
McGee, Revere, and Emery. The article is sarcastically
critical of Shumlin for his selection.

IIA7.  Brown, John Mason. "Two on the Aisle; The Similarities
Between *The Children's Hour* and *The Great Drumsheugh
Case*, as noted by Edmund Pearson," New York *Post*, Jan.
24, 1935, p. 17.

Quotes Edmund Pearson who claims that a summary of the
plot of *The Great Drumsheugh Case* is the source LH used
in developing *CH* plot. There was some controversy over
the play's origin because of a statement made by LH
claiming originality.

IIA8.  "American Play Banned; English Censor Forbids Presentation of *The Children's Hour*," New York *Times*, Mar.
12, 1935, p. 24.

Reports that the Lord Chamberlain, Earl Cromer, censor
of the English stage, has banned the production of *CH*
"because of its theme."

IIA9.  "London Success Seen for *Children's Hour*; Producer
Regrets Action of Lord Chamberlain Barring Play and
Considers Appealing," New York *Times*, Mar. 15, 1935,
p. 24.

IIA10. Walbridge, Earl. "Closed Doors," *Saturday Review of
Literature*, XI (Mar. 16, 1935), 548.

Includes a letter to the editor claiming LH did not
acknowledge William Roughead's earlier version of *CH*
plot.

IIA11. Reed, Edward. "New Faces; 1935; Lillian Hellman,"
*Theatre Arts*, XIX (Apr. 1935), 270.

Surveys briefly the plot of *CH* and the controversy re-
sulting from the play. Biographical sketch of LH at
age 29 includes information about her birthplace, education at NYU and Columbia, her marriage to Kober, her
work at Metro-Goldwyn-Mayer, and her writing of *My
Dear Queen* in collaboration with Louis Kronenberger.

IIA12.   Shumlin, Herman.  "Seeks to Remove Taboo on 'The
         Children's Hour,'" New York *World-Telegram*, Apr. 13,
         1935, p. 20.

         Protests the London ban on *CH* calling it "highly
         moral."

IIA13.   Vernon, Grenville.  "The Play;  The Pulitzer Award,"
         *Commonweal*, XXII (May 1935), 134.

         Discusses the Pulitzer Prize play, *The Old Maid*, and
         concludes that four other plays of the year, includ-
         ing *CH*, were more deserving of the prize.

IIA14.   "News and Gossip of the Broadway Area," New York *Times*,
         May 5, 1935, Sect. 9, p. 1.

         Includes LH's telegram about another play following
         *CH*.  "I know what the play will be but I have not
         started writing.  Have no title but wish I did.  The
         play will concern a couple of people who are destroyed
         by the time in which they love [live]."

IIA15.   "Broadway at Odds on Pulitzer Award," New York *Times*,
         May 7, 1935, p. 21.

         Expresses discontent over *The Old Maid* selection for
         Pulitzer.  Speculates that *CH* may have been eliminated
         because of subject.

IIA16.   Krutch, Joseph Wood.  "Drama:  'Best Play,'" *The
         Nation*, CXL (May 22, 1935), 610.

         Criticizes the Pulitzer Prize Committee's oversight
         in not recognizing LH's *CH* or Odets' *Awake and Sing* as
         the year's best play.

IIA17.   Maney, Richard.  "Even the Keyhole Was Absent in the
         Real '*CH*,'" New York *Herald Tribune*, Aug. 4, 1935,
         Sect. 5, p. 1.

         Summarizes the plot in *The Great Drumsheugh Case* on
         which *CH* was based.  Notes differences between the two.

IIA18.   ———.  "Miss Hellman's Play Prepares for a Birthday;
         *The Children's Hour* Soon Will Be a Year Old and Still
         Has Original Cast," New York *Herald Tribune*, Nov. 17,
         1935, Sect. 5, p. 4.

         Reports that "more than 300,000 persons" have viewed
         the *CH* production.

IIA19.   "Continuing the Full Saga of Drama's Enterprise; 8,752
         *Children's Hours*;  Miss Hellman's Play Passes Its
         First or Most Difficult Year," New York *Times*, Nov. 17,
         1935, Sect. 10, p. 3.

         Considers the play's success after one year.  Includes
         box office statistics, profit, and changes to the
         script.

IIA20.   "*Children's Hour* Banned In Boston;  Mayor Acts After
         Report by City Censor Who Saw Play Here;  Private
         Showing Banned;  Mansfield Rejects Manager's Offer--
         Drama Was Backed by Guild Affiliate," New York *Times*,
         Dec. 15, 1935, p. 42.

         Reports that *CH* was labeled "indecent" by Boston cen-
         sor and thus was banned from production.  Various
         facets of the Boston ban on *CH* discussed in IIA21-26,
         IIA28-31.

IIA21.   "*Children's Hour* Banned by Mayor, May Be Produced in
         Nearby City," Boston *Herald*, Dec. 15, 1935, p. 1.

IIA22.   "Fight Boston Play Ban;  Author of *The Children's Hour*
         Calls Mayor Arbitrary," New York *Times*, Dec. 16, 1935,
         p. 22.

         Reveals LH's announcement that Shumlin will take "every
         step legally possible" to fight the play's ban by
         Mayor Mansfield.

IIA23.   "*Children's Hour* Ban Extended," New York *Times*, Dec.
         18, 1935, p. 33.

         Proclaims that Mayor James A. Torrey of Beverly,
         Massachusetts, has banned *CH* from his city.

IIA24.   Bullard, F. Lauriston.  "Censor Still Rules Boston
         Theatres;  *The Children's Hour* is Latest Play to Meet
         Ban as City's Old Code Persists," New York *Times*,
         Dec. 22, 1935, Sect. 4, p. 11.

         Criticizes Boston's censoring practices and the banning
         of *CH*.

IIA25.   "Boston Sued on Play Ban;  $250,000 Damages are Sought
         over *The Children's Hour*," New York *Times*, Dec. 27,
         1935, p. 15.

IIA26.   "Two Suits Filed in Boston Play Fight," New York *Times*,
         Dec. 28, 1935, p. 10.

IIA27. "'The Children's Hour' is Weighed in Chicago," New York *Times*, Jan. 10, 1936, p. 17.

Notes that *CH* has been banned by Corporation Counsel of Chicago.

IIA28. "'Children's Hour' Loses Plea," New York *Times*, Jan. 14, 1936, p. 24. (See Item IIA29.)

Reports U.S. court upheld lower court ruling which ruled in favor of governmental ban of *CH* in Boston.

IIA29. "'Children's Hour' Hearing Jan. 29," New York *Times*, Jan. 15, 1936, p. 15. (See Item IIA28.)

Corrects previous day's report on federal ruling stating that the case is still pending. Only the motion for a temporary injunction to stop the play's ban was denied.

IIA30. "Whisper Opposed in Play," New York *Times*, Jan. 30, 1936, p. 14.

Cites in a cursory fashion the objections to *CH* by Boston's mayor and censor.

IIA31. "Disapproved of 'Hour' Before He Read or Saw It, Hub Mayor Admits," *Variety*, Feb. 5, 1936, p. 5.

Reports testimony of Boston's mayor that revealed that banning was based on plot summary given by the city censor.

IIA32. Sobol, Louis. "The Voice of Broadway," New York *Evening Journal*, Oct. 7, 1936, p. 27.

Reveals that LH was scoffed at by friends in her attempt to write, but that because of *CH* she is the "most sought-after playwright in America."

IIA33. "*The Children's Hour* is Hailed in London," New York *Times*, Nov. 13, 1936, p. 27.

IIA34. Gassner, John, ed. *Twenty Best Plays of the Modern American Theatre: 1930-1939*. New York: Crown, 1939, pp. xix, xxii.

Mentions *CH*, *DC*, *LF*. Notes that LH has the ability to manipulate social themes and still maintain realistic characters. *CH* anthologized.

IIA35.   Norton, Elliot.   "Women Writers Hit with a Real Punch;
         Second Thoughts of a First Nighter," Boston *Sunday
         Post*, Mar. 3, 1940, p. 11.

         Features Clare Boothe [Luce] and LH and their theatre
         accomplishments.   Praises *CH*.

IIA36.   Davis, Owen.   *My First Fifty Years in the Theatre*.
         Boston:  Walter H. Baker, 1950, pp. 125-126.

         Considers *CH* very briefly noting that the confronta-
         tion between Mrs. Tillford and the two accused school
         teachers in the play is the "best scene in modern
         drama."

IIA37.   Sheaffer, Louis.   "She Held *Children's Hour* Revision
         to a Minimum," Brooklyn *Daily Eagle*, Dec. 11, 1952,
         p. 8.

         Previews the revival of *CH* at the Coronet, directed
         by LH.   Notes LH's superstitious hindsight pointing
         out that she felt that O'Neill's *Days Without End*, a
         "flop," should have served as an omen for her own *DC*.

IIA38.   Drutman, Irving.   "'The CH' is Here Again," New York
         *Herald Tribune*, Dec. 14, 1952, Sect. 4, p. 1.

         Previews *CH* revival.   Recalls that LH was very sur-
         prised at the play's 1934 success.

IIA39.   Gilroy, Harry.   "The Bigger the Lie," New York *Times*,
         Dec. 14, 1952, Sect. 2, pp. 3-4.

         Reports that LH lost her voice during rehearsals for
         *CH* revival which she directed.   Notes that in original
         *CH* production, none of Broadway's "leading ladies"
         would take parts because of lesbianism suggested in
         the play.   Includes biographical material on LH at the
         time of *CH*'s first production.   LH has made only minor
         changes in original script for revival.

IIA40.   "*Children's Hour* Revived Tonight," New York *Daily News*,
         Dec. 18, 1952, p. 85.

IIA41.   Bloomgarden, Kermit.   "The Pause in the Day's Occupa-
         tion," *Theatre Arts*, XXXVII (May 1953), 32.

         Briefly reviews the original *CH*'s controversial history.
         Notes that many actresses turned down the teachers'
         roles in the play.   The censorship bans and the dis-
         pute over the Pulitzer Prize are noted.   Text of play
         included.

IIA42.   "'Children's Hour' to Tour," *Variety*, Sept. 3, 1953,
         p. 60.

IIA43.   "Lie Believers Guilty, States Lillian Hellman," San
         Diego *Union*, Nov. 13, 1953, Sect. A, p. 17.

         Features LH in Chicago prior to the opening of *CH*.
         Reports LH's contention that there has been a "break-
         down of Christian morality" in the country and the *CH*
         opening is timed well to show us how destructive lies
         can be.

IIA44.   "Chicago Sees *Children's Hour*," New York *Times*, Nov.
         10, 1953, p. 39.

         Reports that *CH*, banned in Chicago in 1936, opened
         there at the Harris Theatre without police interfer-
         ence.

IIA45.   Gassner, John. *The Theatre in Our Times*. New York:
         Crown Publishers, 1954, passim.

         Makes passing reference to many of LH's plays. Dis-
         cusses *CH*: "We may view with some perturbation the
         fact that the plays written in recent years have so
         rarely possessed the power that belongs to *The
         Children's Hour*."

IIA46.   Gaver, Jack, ed. *Critic's Choice: New York Drama
         Critics' Circle Prize Plays 1935-1955*. New York:
         Hawthorn Books, 1955, passim.

         Reports that the failure of the Pulitzer Prize Commit-
         tee to award *CH* its prize angered New York drama
         critics. The play was instrumental in the critics
         establishing their own prize, the Circle Award. Notes
         other LH plays that were Circle Prize contenders/win-
         ners.

IIA47.   Mantle, Burns, ed. *The Best Plays of 1934-35*. New
         York: Dodd, Mead, 1966, pp. 33-66, 345-412.

         The *Best Plays* series was originated by Burns Mantle
         and was continued by John Chapman, Louis Kronenberger,
         Otis L. Guernsey, and Henry Hewes. In the year of a
         play's opening a summary, cast listing, and often some
         excerpts were included in the volume. As well as con-
         sidering the new plays, the yearbooks also list prize
         winners, productions of plays in other cities, and
         other drama information. From the 1934-35 volume on,

news of LH is included in some form in many of the
volumes.  Included here are the history of *CH*, an excerpt from the play, a list of the original cast, and
a biographical sketch of LH.  (See Items IIB7, IIC26,
IIC30, IIE11, IIF6, IIG13, IIG14, IIH9, IIi10, IIJ4,
IIK4, IIL1.)

IIA48.    Bentley, Eric.  *The Theatre of Commitment*.  New York:
          Atheneum Publishers, 1967, pp. 39-40.

          Appraises critically the 1952-53 revival of *CH*.  The
          lie which leads to tragedy in the play is ironically
          similar to the tactics used by McCarthyism that were
          so destructive to LH.

IIA49.    Houghton, Norris.  *The Exploding Stage: An Introduc-
          tion to Twentieth Century Drama*.  New York:  Weybright
          and Talley, 1971, pp. 54, 82, 241, 243.

          Describes the costs of producing a play:  *CH* cost
          $6,000 in 1938, $60,000 in the mid-50's.  Several
          other passing references to *CH*.


          IIB.   Interviews, Previews, Features, and News
                        -- *Days to Come*


IIB1.     Beebe, Lucius.  "An Adult's Hour is Miss Hellman's
          Next Effort," New York *Herald Tribune*, Dec. 13, 1936,
          Sect. 7, p. 2.

          Reveals in an interview the uneasiness LH felt about
          *DC*.  She claimed to have had difficulty making the
          social statements about the labor movement she desired
          to make.  Maintaining an "editorial point of view"
          was difficult for her.  Describes the plot of *DC*
          noting that the urge to write the play began "five or
          six years ago."  LH claims that she now divides her
          time between Broadway and Hollywood.

IIB2.     "The Rise of Lillian Hellman," Brooklyn *Daily Eagle*,
          Dec. 13, 1936, Sect. C, p. 4.

          Anticipates the opening of *DC* with much hope because
          of LH's past success.

IIB3.   "News of the Stage; Miss Hellman's Play Tonight,"
        New York *Times*, Dec. 15, 1936, p. 31.

        Reports *DC* opening.

IIB4.   "News of the Stage; 'Days to Come' Expected to Close
        Next Tuesday," New York *Times*, Dec. 17, 1936, p. 34.

IIB5.   "Closing Tonight," New York *Post*, Dec. 19, 1936, p. 8.

        Announces *DC* closing.

IIB6.   Nichols, Lewis.  "The Nights Before Christmas, Through
        All the Houses," New York *Times*, Dec. 20, 1936, Sect.
        11, p. 5.

        Provides short reviews of all Broadway plays to be on
        stage Christmas Eve.  Announces the closing of *DC* on
        Dec. 22.

IIB7.   Mantle, Burns.  *The Best Plays of 1936-37*.  New York:
        Dodd, Mead, 1966, p. 441.

        Lists the original cast of *DC*.  (See Item IIA47.)


        IIC.  Interviews, Previews, Features, and News
                -- *The Little Foxes*


IIC1.   O'Hara, Frank.  "Comedies Without a Laugh."  *Today in
        American Drama*.  Chicago:  U. of Chicago Press, 1939,
        pp. 83-100.

        Considers comic aspects of *LF*.  Includes summary, not
        critical material.

IIC2.   Mok, Michel.  "Tallulah Bankhead's Birthday Present:
        A Role with a Real Southern Accent!"  New York *Post*,
        Jan. 31, 1939, p. 9.

        Reveals Bankhead's delight with her *LF* role.

IIC3.   "New Plays of the Week," New York *Herald Tribune*, Feb.
        12, 1939, Sect. 6, p. 1.

        Announces opening of *LF* with an artist's portrait of
        Bankhead, cast as Regina.

IIC4.  Ormsbee, Helen.  "A First Night is the Last Mile Until
       She Hears Her Own Voice," New York *Herald Tribune*, Feb.
       12, 1939, Sect. 6, p. 2.

       Notes Bankhead's nervousness prior to *LF* Baltimore
       opening.

IIC5.  Tighe, Dixie.  "Going Places," New York *Post*, Feb. 16,
       1939, p. 11.

       Reports in a gossip column that LH did not appear at
       *LF* opening despite cries for the author by the audience
       during the curtain call.

IIC6.  "Writing a Play Isn't Half of It for This Author;  Six
       Months of Research and Much Thought Take Place Before
       She Begins," New York *Herald Tribune*, Feb. 19, 1939,
       Sect. 6, p. 2.

       Notes in a preview of *LF* that in eight years of writing
       LH has produced four plays.  She has taken two years to
       complete each effort.  The actual writing of *LF* took
       six months.  Includes some biographical information.

IIC7.  Mok, Michel.  "The Man Who Found a Hit for Tallulah
       Just Made Her Forget She Was a Star," New York *Post*,
       Feb. 28, 1939, p. 9.

       Reports that Shumlin credits LH and Bankhead for *LF*
       success.

IIC8.  "Theater;  *The Little Foxes*;  Tallulah Bankhead Has Her
       First US Hit," *Life*, VI (Mar. 6, 1939), 70-73.

       Includes a pictorial feature on *LF*.  Bankhead appears
       on the issue's cover.

IIC9.  Beebe, Lucius.  "Stage Asides," New York *Herald Tribune*,
       Mar. 12, 1939, Sect. 6, pp. 1, 3.

       Explains in an interview what she has attempted to do
       in *LF*.  LH claims that she has tried to teach a moral-
       ity lesson in the play by depicting the evil Hubbard
       family's materialism.  Some of the play was inspired
       by people LH encountered in the South.  Reveals her
       next play may be an adaptation of Zola's *Germinal*.

IIC10. "His Big Trouble was Avoiding a Stuffy Boarding House
       Look," New York *Herald Tribune*, Mar. 19, 1939, Sect. 6,
       p. 4.

       Describes Howard Bay's set design for *LF*.

IIC11.    Atkinson, Brooks. "Critics Lay an Egg," New York *Times*, Apr. 23, 1939, Sect. 10, p. 1.

       Proclaims that *Abe Lincoln in Illinois*, Sherwood's play, should have won Drama Critics' Circle Award. The votes were split between it and *LF* and thus no award was given.

IIC12.    "Footnote on Headliners," New York *Times*, Apr. 23, 1939, Sect. 4, p. 2.

       Reports that New York theatre critics met to select the year's best American play (Critics' Circle Award). Although no play had sufficient votes to win, LH's *LF* came closest.

IIC13.    "*The Little Foxes* Title a S-Parker [sic]," New York *World-Telegram*, June 24, 1939, p. 8.

       Reveals that Dorothy Parker provided the name for LH play from "Song of Solomon."

IIC14.    Wyatt, Euphemia van Rensselaer. "The Drama," *Catholic World*, CXLIX (July 1939), 470.

       Reviews the 1938–39 theatre season noting that *LF* was one of the best plays produced.

IIC15.    Maney, Richard. "Of Time and Tallulah," New York *Times*, Aug. 27, 1939, Sect. 9, p. 2.

       Bankhead praises LH for creating the role of Regina in *LF*.

IIC16.    "Pretty Soft; Southern Speech Absorbed as One Learns Lines," New York *Herald Tribune*, Nov. 26, 1939, Sect. 6, p. 4.

       Comments on the development of Southern dialects in *LF*. Miss Bankhead "needed no coaching" because of her Southern origin.

IIC17.    "Benefits for Finns Stir Theatre Row," New York *Times*, Jan. 19, 1940, p. 21.

       Reports Bankhead's desire to do a benefit performance of *LF* for Finnish relief; Shumlin and LH would not allow it. (See Items IIC18, IIC19.)

IIC18.    "Actors Widen Split on Finn Benefits; Special Meeting Expected in Controversy Over Presenting Performances

for Fund;  Dullzell Criticizes Idea," New York *Times*,
Jan. 20, 1940, p. 17.

Discusses the controversy over whether Broadway theatres
would do benefit performances for Finnish relief.
Quotes Bankhead who questioned "the sincerity of
Shumlin ahd Hellman for not wanting to participate with
*The Little Foxes*." (See Items IIC17, IIC19.)

IIC19.  "Sees Finnish Aid Imperiling Peace;  Lillian Hellman,
Author, Says Benefit Performances Tend to Fan War
Flames;  Reply to Miss Bankhead, Broadway Producers
Go Ahead with Plans for Shows as Actors Mark Time,"
New York *Times*, Jan. 21, 1940, p. 27.

Reports LH's contention that a benefit performance of
*LF* "would give a dangerous impetus to war spirit in
this country." Her statement was in reply to Bankhead's
assertion that LH and Shumlin showed "pro soviet bias."
(See Items IIC17, IIC18.)

IIC20.  Bentley, Eric. *The Playwright as Thinker: A Study of
Drama in Modern Times*. New York:  Reynal and Hitch-
cock, 1946, p. 345.

Considers *LF* briefly, noting that the play is "comedie
rossé--a type of acrid, raw, naturalistic comedy."

IIC21.  Zolotow, Maurice.  "Tallulah Bankhead." *No People
Like Show People*. New York:  Random House, 1947, pp.
21, 63-65, 72-74.

Notes the controversial confrontation between Bankhead
and LH over a benefit performance of *LF* to aid Finland.
(See Items IIC17-19.)

IIC22.  Bankhead, Tallulah.  *Tallulah*. New York:  Harper &
Brothers, 1952, pp. 237-238, 241-244, 304-305.

Discusses Bankhead's relationship with LH in *LF* production.  "Great as is my admiration for Lillian
Hellman as a playwright, I could never again rejoice
in her company."

IIC23.  Hewitt, Barnard.  "Two New Playwrights." *Theatre
U.S.A. 1668-1957*. New York:  McGraw-Hill, 1959, pp.
415-417.

Comments on *LF* with portions of Richard Watts, Jr.'s
*Herald Tribune* review of Feb. 16, 1939, reprinted.
Lists LH's plays following *LF*. (See Item IIIC29.)

IIC24.  Miller, Jordan Y. *American Dramatic Literature*. New York: McGraw-Hill, 1961, pp. 87-90.

Anthologizes *LF* and includes a short critical comment as well as biographical information. *LF* is "one of the finest examples of the craft of playmaking combined with the qualities of excellent realistic drama."

IIC25.  Lenoir, Jean Pierre. "Miss Signoret Seen in Play She Adapted," New York *Times*, Dec. 6, 1962, p. 56.

Reports that Simone Signoret adapted and starred in French version of *LF*. It was not well received by audiences and critics.

IIC26.  Guernsey, Otis L., Jr., ed. *The Best Plays of 1967-68*. New York: Dodd, Mead, 1964, passim.

Includes very brief comment on *LF*. (See Item IIA47.)

IIC27.  Gottfried, Martin. "Theatre," *Women's Wear Daily*, Oct. 22, 1965, p. 81. Reprinted in "The Repertory Theatre of Lincoln Center--Danton's Death (Oct. 22, 1965)." *Opening Nights: Theatre Criticism of the Sixties*. New York: G.P. Putnam's Sons, 1969, pp. 190-197.

Announces the Lincoln Center Repertory schedule and notes that the *LF* revival is being done by an outside company.

IIC28.  Clurman, Harold. *The Naked Image: Observations on the Modern Theatre*. New York: Macmillan, 1966, pp. 202, 209.

Mentions the Paris production of *LF*. LH is called "indomitable" at the 1963 Drama Conference in Edinburgh.

IIC29.  Guernsey, Otis L., Jr., ed. *The Best Plays of 1966-67*. New York: Dodd, Mead, 1967, passim.

Lists Memphis production of *LF*. (See Item IIA47.)

IIC30.  Funke, Lewis. "Nichols to Direct at Lincoln Center, Troupe Turns to Broadway for *Little Foxes* Revival," New York *Times*, Jan. 25, 1967, p. 36.

IIC31.  ———. "'Little Foxes' for Lincoln Center," New York *Times*, Jan. 29, 1967, Sect. 2, pp. 1, 4.

Maintains that *LF* is "an American Classic" and thus merits revival.

IIC32.   Shepard, Richard.  "'Little Foxes' Gets a Start in
         Low Key," New York *Times*, Sept. 20, 1967, p. 40.

         Describes the first rehearsal of Lincoln Center *LF*
         production.

IIC33.   Bankhead, Tallulah.  "Miss Bankhead Objects," New
         York *Times*, Oct. 29, 1967, Sect. 2, p. 5.

         Disagrees with LH claims made in a New York *Times*
         essay, Oct. 22, 1967.  Maintains that *LF* was a plea-
         sant experience for her, despite LH's contention that
         it was not.  It was LH who stopped coming backstage
         for visits after their argument over benefit perform-
         ances of the play.  Bankhead wishes *LF* revival "great
         success."

IIC34.   Zolotow, Sam.  "Changes Coming in 'The Little Foxes,'"
         New York *Times*, Nov. 2, 1967, p. 61.

         Reports that major cast changes in *LF* will be made when
         it moves from Lincoln Center to Broadway.  Mike Nichol
         lavishly praises the play.

IIC35.   "Lincoln Center Rep Swinging as 'Foxes' Clicks,"
         *Variety*, Nov. 8, 1967, p. 63.

         Reports that *LF* is almost sold out for its run.

IIC36.   O'Connor, John J.  "On the Off-Off Circuit," *Wall
         Street Journal*, Nov. 21, 1967, p. 20.

         Announces Lincoln Center *LF* production.

IIC37.   Freedman, Morris.  *The Moral Impulse:  Modern Drama
         from Ibsen to the Present*.  Carbondale and Edwardsvill
         Southern Illinois U. Press, 1968, pp. 101-105.

         Briefly discusses LH as caricaturist in *LF* and compare
         her to Brecht.

IIC38.   "'Foxes' Decision Goes to Subber," *Variety*, Aug. 21,
         1968, p. 56.

         Reports the numerous problems encountered in producing
         *LF* at Lincoln Center.  Criticizes the practice of im-
         porting a play from outside the Repertory Company.

IIC39.   "Best Bets;  On Stage," Seattle *Post Intelligencer*,
         Feb. 20, 1970, Tabloid, p. 2.

         Announces *LF* at Seattle Repertory Theatre.  (See Items
         IIIC58, IIIC59.)

IIC40.  Gill, Brendan W.  *Tallulah*.  New York:  Holt, Rine-
        hart & Winston, 1972, pp. 10, 63, 175, 177.

        Considers Tallulah Bankhead's association with LH in
        the *LF* production and subsequent controversies between
        them.

IIC41.  Israel, Lee.  "*The Little Foxes*."  *Miss Tallulah
        Bankhead*.  New York:  G.P. Putnam's Sons, 1972, pp.
        186-200.

        Tells of Bankhead's starring role in LH's *LF* and the
        bitterness that eventually arose from the association.
        Notes that Bankhead was "a fierce anti-Communist" and
        "it was assumed by many that she simply didn't under-
        stand the play's political ramifications."  Discusses
        the LH-Bankhead-Hammett relationship.

IIC42.  Smiley, Sam.  *The Drama of Attack:  Didactic Plays of
        the American Depression*.  Columbia:  U. of Missouri
        Press, 1972, passim.

        Briefly considers *LF* as a didactic play since the
        villain wins.  *CH* and *DC* receive passing notice.

IIC43.  Aaron, Jules.  "Theatre in Review; *The Little Foxes*,"
        *Educational Theatre Journal*, XXVII (Dec. 1975), 553-
        554.

        Features U. of California production of *LF* in which
        actress Barbara Rush joined a student cast in the play.
        *LF* is called a "marvelous theatrical vehicle ... em-
        bodying Hellman's didactic examination of good and
        evil."


        IID.  Interviews, Previews, Features, and News
                 -- *Watch on the Rhine*


IID1.   Mantle, Burns, ed.  *The Best Plays of 1940-41*.  New
        York:  Dodd, Mead, 1941, passim.

        Lists cast of *WR* and gives plot summary.  Calls *WR* a
        "soberly reasoned and ... convincingly written play."
        (See Item IIA47.)

IID2.   "Opera and Drama Given in Baltimore," New York *Times*,
        Mar. 25, 1941, p. 26.

Announces opening of *WR* at Ford's Theatre, Baltimore, prior to Broadway run.

IID3.     Rice, Robert.  "'Watch on the Rhine,'" *PM*, Mar. 30, 1941, pp. 42, 43.

Previews *WR*, predicting great success.  Includes pictures of cast during rehearsal and lines from the play

IID4.     Morehouse, Ward.  "Broadway After Dark;  Prize, Plays, Critics and Such," New York *Sun*, Apr. 3, 1941, p. 31.

Maintains that if the "Critics' Circle were to meet today *Watch on the Rhine* would undoubtedly win" its award.  "It is my prediction that Miss Hellman will take the honors."

IID5.     "What Is Life Worth," New York *Times*, Apr. 6, 1941, Sect. 4, p. 8.

Mentions briefly the war theme in *WR*.

IID6.     Mantle, Burns.  "The Gestapo Tangles with the Drama; Lillian Hellman's *Watch on the Rhine* Enters Season's Best Play Contest," New York *Sunday News*, Apr. 13, 1941, p. 70.

Comments on upcoming Critics' Circle Awards.  It notes that *Native Son* and *WR* run "neck and neck."

IID7.     "Lukas Gets Holiday from Hisses," New York *Sun*, Apr. 15, 1941, p. 15.

Features Paul Lukas noting that his role as hero in *WR* is the first U.S. role in which he has not played a "rogue" hissed by audiences.

IID8.     Van Gelder, Robert.  "Of Lillian Hellman;  Being a Conversation with the Author of *Watch on the Rhine*," New York *Times*, Apr. 20, 1941, Sect. 9, pp. 1, 3.

Features LH prior to opening of *WR*.  Reveals the difficulty she encountered in choosing a title and notes that Shumlin threatened to stop rehearsals of the play unless she chose one.  LH tells of her attempt to write in longhand, as Mark Twain wrote, but notes that she feels better using a typewriter.  Includes some biographical information.

IID9.     Roosevelt, Eleanor. "My Day," New York *World-Tele-gram*, Apr. 21, 1941, p. 15.

Notes that she enjoyed *WR* production.

IID10.    Anderson, John. "'Watch on the Rhine' Wins Critics' Award," New York *Journal American*, Apr. 23, 1941, p. 10. See also "Critics Prize Goes to *Watch on the Rhine*; Lillian Hellman's Play Wins Annual American Award--Saroyan is Second; *Corn Is Green* Honored; Emlyn Williams' Production Named Best Importation--Seven Ballots Cast," New York *Times*, Apr. 23, 1941, p. 24. "Lillian Hellman's Play is Critics' Choice for 1941," New York *Herald Tribune*, Apr. 23, 1941, p. 18. Mantle, Burns. "*Watch on the Rhine* Wins Critics' Award; *Beautiful People* 2nd," New York *Daily News*, Apr. 23, 1941, p. 55. Whipple, Sidney B. "Critics' Circle Votes for 'Watch on Rhine,'" New York *World-Telegram*, Apr. 23, 1941, p. 23. (See Items IID11-13, IID19.)

IID11.    Atkinson, Brooks. "News of the Broadway Theatre as April Turns to May; Critics' Prize Plays," New York *Times*, Apr. 27, 1941, Sect. 9, p. 1.

Describes the relative merits of *WR*, and *The Beautiful People* (Saroyan), and the voting of the New York drama critics in distinguishing the better of the two for their Critics' Circle Award.

IID12.    Watts, Richard, Jr. "The Theatre," New York *Herald Tribune*, Apr. 27, 1941, Sect. 6, pp. 1, 2.

Justifies his vote for *WR* in Critics' Circle Award.

IID13.    Sylvester, Robert. "Lillian Hellman Talks of Plays," New York *Daily News*, Apr. 28, 1941, p. 35.

Comments on *WR*'s winning Critics' Circle Award. She claims that *WR* and *DC* could be improved by eliminating one character from each.

IID14.    Beebe, Lucius. "Stage Asides; Miss Hellman Speaks Up," New York *Herald Tribune*, May 18, 1941, Sect. 6, p. 1.

LH claims that she does not begin to write plays with a moral or political message. Claims that she took theme for *WR* from Henry James' *European*. Notes the connection between politics and the theatre.

IID15.  Atkinson, Brooks. "Late August News of Broadway Plays
        and Theatres; *Watch on the Rhine*; After Five Months
        the Actors Are Giving a Notable Performance," New York
        *Times*, Aug. 24, 1941, Sect. 9, p. 1.

        Comments on the play's success after a five-month run.
        Notes that the play will be significant "when people
        return to the era to uncover the people [who lived]
        during the rise of Nazism."

IID16.  "Hellman Play in London; One Critic Sees *Watch on the
        Rhine* Best There in Years," New York *Times*, Apr. 24,
        1942, p. 20.

        Reports that *WR* London opening received excellent re-
        views.

IID17.  "'Command' Performance of 'Watch on the Rhine,'" New
        York *Times*, Jan. 6, 1942, p. 26. See also "New Honors
        for Hellman," New York *Herald Tribune*, Jan. 25, 1942,
        Sect. 6, p. 4. (See Item IID18.)

        Reports *WR* was selected as part of FDR's birthday
        celebration.

IID18.  "To Show Hellman Manuscript," New York *Times*, Jan.
        25, 1942, Sect. 1, p. 37.

        Announces Library of Congress display of LH's original
        manuscript of *WR* in connection with the command per-
        formance of the play as part of the Diamond Jubilee
        Birthday Celebration for President Roosevelt.

IID19.  "Drama Award Presented," New York *Times*, Jan. 28,
        1942, p. 10.

        Reports Critics' Circle Award presentation to LH.
        *WR* scenes were performed at ceremony.

IID20.  "Lillian Hellman to be Feted," New York *Times*, Feb.
        19, 1942, p. 22.

        Reveals that proceeds from a party given at the close
        of *WR* went to the Anti-Fascist Refugee Fund.

IID21.  "Special Edition of Hellman Play for Benefit of
        Refugees," *Publishers Weekly*, CXLII (July 1942), 170.

        Reveals that proceeds of a special publication of *WR*
        by Random House will go to the Joint Arts Fascist
        Refugee Committee for general relief of victims in
        French concentration camps.

IID22.   Painter-Downes, Mollie.  "Letter from London," *New Yorker*, XIX (July 17, 1943), 61-63.

Mentions that on the night of the first landings on Sicily, Churchill took his family to see *WR*.

IID23.   "Hellman Play Opens in Moscow," New York *Times*, Feb. 26, 1945, p. 10.

Notes *WR* opening in Moscow, under the title *Trouble in the Parolly Family*.

IID24.   Atkinson, Brooks, and Albert Hirschfeld.  *"Watch on the Rhine." The Lively Years, 1920-1973.*  New York: Association Press, 1973, pp. 163-166.

Includes plot summary of *WR* and calls it one of the great plays of the era.  Notes the contribution to the war effort it made by rallying the audience against the Nazis.


       IIE.   Interviews, Previews, Features, and News
              -- *The Searching Wind*


IIE1.    "How Lillian Hellman Writes a Play," *PM*, Mar. 12, 1944, Magazine, pp. 11-12.

Notes LH's claims that it is very difficult for her to write a play because of her need to revise and rewrite. Discusses her writing of *SW*.

IIE2.    Ormsbee, Helen.  "Miss Hellman All But Dares Her Next Play to Succeed," New York *Herald Tribune*, Apr. 9, 1944, Sect. 4, p. 1.

Previews *SW* in an interview with LH over lunch between rehearsals.

IIE3.    Rascoe, Burton.  "Has Miss Hellman Disappointed 'The Party'?"  New York *World-Telegram*, Apr. 22, 1944, p. 6.

Features a report on LH-Communist ties stating that she is out of favor with the Communists because her new play, *SW*, is not dosed up with the current Party Line propaganda.

IIE4.   "How War Came," *New York Times Magazine*, Apr. 23, 1944,
        p. 19.

        Pictorially features *SW*.

IIE5.   "Drama Critics Fail to Pick a Best Play," New York
        *Post*, Apr. 26, 1944, p. 31.

        Reports LH's *SW* received seven votes, the most for any
        play in Circle competition;  however, eight were
        necessary to win.

IIE6.   Drutman, Irving.  "Herman Shumlin's Favorite Dramatist,"
        New York *Herald Tribune*, May 7, 1944, Sect. 4, p. 1.

        Reveals in an interview that LH is Shumlin's favorite
        dramatist.  The *SW* Broadway opening marked the tenth
        anniversary of their association.  Shumlin claims that
        their relationship has not been "peaceful and calm,"
        but has been intense.  Notes a conflict between the
        two over a scene in *SW*.

IIE7.   "Good Deed," *New Yorker*, XX (May 13, 1944), 22.

        Reveals in a short anecdote how LH arranged for two men
        in the Air Force to see *SW*.

IIE8.   Mower, Margaret.  "Dissent in the Drama Mailbag," New
        York *Times*, July 16, 1944, Sect. 2, p. 1.

        Claims critics missed the point of the love triangle in
        *SW*.  The triangle in the play represents not merely a
        political struggle, but also represents a personal
        struggle.

IIE9.   Randolf, Alan F.  "Dissent in the Drama Mailbag," New
        York *Times*, July 16, 1944, Sect. 2, p. 1.

        Disagrees with critics who favorably reviewed *SW*.

IIE10.  Fleischman, Earl E.  "*The Searching Wind* in the Making,"
        *Quarterly Journal of Speech*, XXXI (Feb. 1945), 22-23.

        Reveals, in an article by an actor in the play, how *SW*
        production took shape over months of performance.  Dis-
        cusses the relationship of actors, director, and author.

IIE11.  Mantle, Burns, ed.  *The Best Plays of 1943-44*.  New
        York: Dodd, Mead, 1965, passim.

        Includes a short positive comment on *SW*, an edited re-
        print, and a list of the original cast.  (See Item IIA47.

IIF.   Interviews, Features, Previews, and News
       -- *Another Part of the Forest*

IIF1.  Funke, Lewis B. "News and Gossip of the Rialto," New
       York *Times*, Mar. 10, 1946, Sect. 11, p. 1.

       Reports LH's return from New Orleans to begin writing
       the second part of the "Hubbard Family trilogy." Notes
       that plans for a Bloomgarden production of *LF* are
       running into difficulties. (The third play in the
       "Hubbard Family trilogy" was never written.)

IIF2.  McLaughlin, Russell. "New Hellman Play Monday Night,"
       Detroit *News*, Nov. 10, 1946, Sect. 2, p. 8.

       Briefly previews *APF* opening in Detroit.

IIF3.  Bald, Wambly. "It's Just Like Having Another Baby,"
       New York *Post*, Nov. 12, 1946, Magazine, p. 17.

       Previews *APF* New York opening. LH compares writing a
       play to "having a baby," considering the intensive
       care which must be provided.

IIF4.  "The Little Foxes as Cubs," *New York Times Magazine*,
       Nov. 17, 1946, pp. 68-69.

       Presents a pictorial display of Broadway's *APF* produc-
       tion.

IIF5.  Wilson, John S. "No First Night Jitters for Playwright
       Lillian Hellman," *PM*, Nov. 17, 1946, pp. 16-17.

       Previews *APF* revealing that LH hopes the play will be
       a success. "But it's not the proper worry of the play-
       wright to think about success. You do the best you can
       and if the people like it--fine."

IIF6.  Mantle, Burns, ed. *The Best Plays of 1946-47*. New
       York: Dodd, Mead, 1947, passim.

       Lists cast of *APF* and includes plot summary. Labels
       it one of the "best plays in years." (See Item IIA47.)

IIF7.    "Moscow Likes Hellman Play," New York *Times*, Oct. 17,
         1949, p. 19.   See also "Moscow Acclaims a Hellman
         Play;   Capacity House Sees *Another Part of the Forest*;
         First U.S. Drama of New Season," New York *Times*, Oct.
         18, 1949, p. 34.

         Reveals that the Russian version of *APF* "was applauded
         at the first performance."

IIF8.    "Soviet Paper Finds Hellman Play Fails," New York
         *Times*, Nov. 13, 1949, p. 83.

         Reveals that *Soviet Art*, a Russian newspaper, criti-
         cized LH's *APF* as being "a merciless and scornful
         exposé of the artful capitalist reality."

IIF9.    Bentley, Eric. *In Search of Theatre*. New York:
         Alfred A. Knopf, 1953, p. 9.

         Proclaims that "if Maxwell Anderson is the King of
         Broadway intelligentsia, the queen is Miss Lillian
         Hellman, whose plays can succeed without the help of
         stars."  Notes that *APF* is a play that is neither
         original in form nor profound in thought;  it is, how-
         ever, a "well-made" play.  The major problem is that
         the center of the play is "hollow," failing to capture
         the audience's attention.

IIF10.   "An Overture to *The Little Foxes*;  Miss Hellman's Play
         at Liverpool," London *Times*, Aug. 31, 1953, p. 3.

         Announces briefly the coming of *APF* to Liverpool
         Theatre.

IIF11.   Watson, E. Bradlee, and Benefield Pressey, eds.  *Con-
         temporary Drama: 11 Plays*. New York:  Charles Scrib-
         ner's Sons, 1956, pp. 204-206.

         Includes anthologized *APF* preceded by two pages of
         positive criticism.

IIG.   Interviews, Features, Previews, and News
       -- *Montserrat*

IIG1.   Morehouse, Ward.  "Broadway After Dark;  Visit with
        Miss Hellman," New York *Sun*, Dec. 16, 1948, p. 18.

        Concerns *Montserrat* and Blitzstein's *Regina*, the
        musical based on *LF*. Quotes LH:  "I think *Montserrat*
        is a good play and can't agree with those who don't."

IIG2.   McCord, Bert.  "News of the Theatre;  Lillian Hellman
        Returns," New York *Herald Tribune*, Feb. 28, 1949, p.
        10.

        Reports LH's return from Hollywood and her casting of
        the anticipated opening of *Montserrat* in New York.

IIG3.   ————.  "News of the Theatre;  *Montserrat* to Prince-
        ton," New York *Herald Tribune*, Aug. 24, 1949, p. 14.

        Reveals that *Montserrat* is to be performed first,
        Oct. 8, 1949, in Princeton prior to a two-week run in
        Philadelphia.

IIG4.   "Hellman Getting 7½% of 'Montserrat' Profits," *Variety*,
        Sept. 28, 1949, p. 65.

IIG5.   "The New Season 1949-50, Lillian Hellman," *Theatre
        Arts*, XXXIII (Oct. 1949), 14.

        Includes a portrait and short announcement of the
        soon-to-open *Montserrat*.

IIG6.   "Hellman Week on Broadway," *Cue*, XXIX (Oct. 1, 1949),
        14-15.

        Proclaims that Broadway will become "Lillian Hellman
        Lane" when two productions, *Montserrat* and *Regina*,
        open.  Reveals that Norman Mailer recommended *Montserrat*
        to LH as a play she should adapt.  The play's production
        was delayed so that Emlyn Williams could play the lead.
        *Regina* is Marc Blitzstein's musical based on *LF*.  In-
        cludes excellent photographs of LH at work.

IIG7.    Harris, Harry. "*Montserrat* and *Goodbye, My Fancy* Open
         Here This Week; Lillian Hellman Says Never Again After
         Adapting New Play from French; 'Too Hard,' She Ex-
         plains," Philadelphia *Bulletin*, Oct. 9, 1949, Sect.
         MI, p. 10.

         Previews *Montserrat* in its pre-Broadway run in Phila-
         delphia. Notes in an interview with LH that the
         adaptation was a very difficult task.

IIG8.    Drutman, Irving. "Lillian Hellman Describes 'First
         and Last Adaptation,'" New York *Herald Tribune*, Oct.
         23, 1949, Sect. 5, p. 1.

         Reports in an interview-preview on *Montserrat* that
         LH will not do another adaptation because she wants to
         devote her time to original writing.

IIG9.    "'Montserrat,'" *New York Times Magazine*, Oct. 23,
         1949, pp. 52, 53.

         Presents photographs of *Montserrat* production.

IIG10.   Schumach, Murray. "Miss Hellman Discusses Direction,"
         New York *Times*, Oct. 23, 1949, Sect. 2, pp. 1, 3.

         Reveals LH's views about directing while she was in
         the process of directing *Montserrat*. Only a few direc-
         tors are able to go beyond the point of "camouflaging
         ignorance with technical jargon." Elia Kazan, Jed
         Harris, Herman Shumlin, and possibly two others now
         make "creative contributions" to the stage. Discusses
         techniques pointing out that "there shouldn't be any
         ruler in the theatre." Claims she learned a great
         deal from Shumlin. (See Item IE19.)

IIG11.   "Venezuelan Venture," *Theatre Arts*, XXXIII (Nov.
         1949), 44.

         Concerns Irene Sharaff, costume designer for *Montserrat*,
         and others. Discusses the play's costumes with LH.

IIG12.   Morehouse, Ward. "Visit with Miss Hellman," New York
         *Sun*, Dec. 16, 1949, p. 18.

         LH discusses *Montserrat* in an interview. Argues that
         it is not a great play but is "simple and honest."
         She disagrees with those who did not have positive
         reactions.

IIG13.  Chapman, John, ed.  *The Best Plays of 1949-50*.  New
        York:  Dodd, Mead, 1950, passim.

        Comments briefly on *Montserrat* and lists the original
        cast.  *Montserrat* was "an extraordinarily grim melo-
        drama....  a failure."  (See Item IIA47.)

IIG14.  Kronenberger, Louis, ed.  *The Best Plays of 1960-61*.
        New York:  Dodd, Mead, 1961, passim.

        Comments briefly on the New York *Montserrat* revival.
        (See Item IIA47.)

IIG15.  "*George Dillon* May End Run," New York *Times*, Feb. 14,
        1961, p. 46.

        Announces closing of *Montserrat* Feb. 21 at Gate Theatre.


        IIH.  Interviews, Features, Previews, and News
              -- *The Autumn Garden*


IIH1.   McCord, Bert.  "News of the Theatre;  Hellman Hard at
        Work," New York *Herald Tribune*, May 30, 1950, p. 7.

        Reports that LH is hard at work on a play "with its
        setting in the South."

IIH2.   ———.  "News of the Theatre;  Hellman Almost Fin-
        ished," New York *Herald Tribune*, Nov. 16, 1950, p. 23.

        Reports LH's claim that she has three to four weeks
        more work on her play, which, if she completes it, will
        be presented at Kermit Bloomgarden Theatre.

IIH3.   ———.  "News of the Theatre;  Clurman to Direct,"
        New York *Herald Tribune*, Dec. 18, 1950, p. 16.

        Notes that LH has decided against directing her own
        play, *AG*, at Kermit Bloomgarden Theatre as Harold
        Clurman will do the job.

IIH4.   Gilroy, Harry.  "Lillian Hellman Drama Foregoes a
        Villain," New York *Times*, Feb. 25, 1951, Sect. 2, p.
        1.

        Comments on the absence of villains in *AG* in a preview-
        interview.  LH's plays are usually filled with evil
        characters, yet *AG* has none.  It has no heroes either.

IIH5.   Morehouse, Ward.  "'Garden' Pleases Miss Hellman,"
        New York *World-Telegram and Sun*, Mar. 3, 1951, p. 7.

        Notes in an interview with LH that *AG* is "her most
        satisfying play."  The play took LH "nine or ten
        months" to write.  "Perhaps in the play, I've wanted
        to say that if you've had something to stand on in-
        wardly when you reach the middle years you have a
        chance of being all right;  if you haven't, you just
        live out your life."  Proclaims her respect for
        Tennessee Williams and Arthur Miller and she argues
        that "now Mr. [George Bernard] Shaw is dead, nobody
        is next to Mr. [Sean] O'Casey for my money."

IIH6.   Clurman, Harold.  "Miss Hellman's New Play;  No
        Message but a Meaning," New York *Herald Tribune*, Mar.
        4, 1951, Sect. 4, pp. 1, 2.

        Maintains in a preview-interview with Clurman, *AG*'s
        director, that LH's new play "has 'no message' that
        can be reduced to a formula."  The play's structure
        is "made up of a garland of plots, each of them twin-
        ing about and merging with the others."  The play "fits
        no convenient designation" and is "unsentimental."

IIH7.   Rice, Vernon.  "Curtain Cues;  Lillian Hellman;
        Frankfurter Expert," New York *Post*, Mar. 6, 1951, p.
        38.

        Previews *AG* New York opening in an interview with LH
        as she ate hot dogs during a break in the play's re-
        hearsals.  LH explains the title by noting that "an
        autumn garden is one which by winter time will fade
        and not be a garden any more.  It's a chrysanthemum
        garden.  The people of the play are coming into the
        winter of life."

IIH8.   Drutman, Irving.  "Author's Problems—What To Do After
        Play Opens?  Lillian Hellman Feeling Completely Lost
        Now That *The Autumn Garden* Is On," New York *Herald
        Tribune*, Mar. 18, 1951, Sect. 4, p. 2.

        Notes that after a play opens, LH is very bored.  The
        intense work in preparation for opening night contrasts
        sharply with the copious amounts of free time after
        opening.

IIH9.   Chapman, John, ed.  *The Best Plays of 1950-51.*  New
        York:  Dodd, Mead, 1951, passim.

Notes that *AG* is a "Chekhovian comedy." Lists original cast and other *AG* box-office statistics. (See
Item IIA47.)

IIH10.  Howard, Lewis. "The Drama Mailbag," New York *Times*,
May 13, 1951, Sect. 2, p. 3.

Argues in a letter that *AG* is flawed because it has
no redeeming character to contrast with the hopeless
characters in the play.

IIH11.  Schutte, Louis H. "The Drama Mailbag," New York *Times*,
May 13, 1951, Sect. 2, p. 3.

Maintains that reviewers failed to convey *AG*'s power
and stature.

IIH12.  "'Garden' Loss $75,000 Tour Deficit $25,000," *Variety*,
Mar. 19, 1952, p. 55.

Reports that *AG* lost all of its original investment.

IIH13.  Bowers, Faubion. *Broadway, USSR*. New York: Thomas
Nelson and Sons, 1959, pp. 61, 75, 89-91.

Discusses the production of *AG* in the Soviet Union at
the Moscow Art Theatre. The play "presents an exqui-
sitely drawn portrait of a number of people in the
autumnal clarity and helplessness of age."


IIi.  Interviews, Features, Previews, and News
-- *The Lark*


IIi1.  McCord, Bert. "Theater News," New York *Herald Tribune*,
Mar. 16, 1954, p. 20.

Reports that LH will adapt *The Lark*. William Wyler
will direct.

IIi2.  Chapman, John. "'Lark' Could Break a Jinx," New York
*Sunday News*, Aug. 21, 1955, Sect. 2, p. 3.

Anticipates success in LH's adaptation of *The Lark*.
Notes that Anouilh has had a long string of Broadway
failures and this could change his fortunes.

IIi3.  Schumach, Murray. "Shaping a New Joan," New York
*Times*, Nov. 13, 1955, Sect. 2, pp. 1, 3.

Notes in an interview prior to *The Lark*'s Broadway
opening the problem LH encountered adapting the play.
LH sees Joan of Arc as "gayer and more fragile" than
Shaw's Joan.  Shaw's *St. Joan* was more political and
*The Lark* is more of "a conflict of individual wills."
LH states that she will never do another adaptation
because of the difficulties she encountered.

IIi4.    "Amusements; *The Lark* Opens at Longacre Tonight,"
         *Women's Wear Daily*, Nov. 17, 1955, p. 43.

IIi5.    Calta, Louis.  "All Critics Unite in Lauding *Lark*;
         Seven Drama Reviews Here Hail Joan of Arc Drama--
         Patrons Form Early Lines," New York *Times*, Nov. 19,
         1955, p. 23.

         Reports *The Lark*'s critical/popular/financial successes
         after the play's opening.

IIi6.    "A Fiery Particle," *Time*, LXVI (Nov. 28, 1955), 76-78.

         Proclaims Julie Harris' performance in *The Lark* as
         magnificent in the issue's cover story.

IIi7.    Peck, Seymour.  "The Maid in Many Guises," *New York
         Times Magazine*, Dec. 4, 1955, pp. 28, 29.

         Surveys the numerous plays dramatizing St. Joan.
         Shaw's portrayal and LH's adaptation of *The Lark* are
         discussed briefly.  Photos of Julie Harris as Joan are
         included.

IIi8.    Guernsey, Otis L., ed.  *The Best Plays of 1969-70*.
         New York:  Dodd, Mead, 1970, passim.

         Lists *The Lark* production at Sarasota, Florida.  (See
         Item IIA47.)


    IIJ.  Interviews, Features, Previews, and News -- *Candide*


IIJ1.    "Broadway Goes Song and Dance," New York *Times*, Nov.
         4, 1956, Sect. 6, p. 28.

         Reviews pictorially musicals on Broadway including
         *Candide*.

IIJ2.    Bernstein, Leonard.  "Colloquy in Boston," New York
         *Times*, Nov. 18, 1956, Sect. 2, p. 1.

Previews *Candide* prior to Boston opening. Proclaims
that LH is a "thoroughly American playwright," who
has done more than just adapt Voltaire's *Candide*. "She
has added, deleted, rewritten, replotted, composed
brand new sequences, provided a real ending, and, I
feel, made it infinitely more significant for our
country and our time. *Candide* will be American because Miss Hellman is American."

IIJ3.   Ross, Don. "Voltaire's *Candide* is Set to Music,"
New York *Herald Tribune*, Nov. 25, 1956, Sect. 4, pp.
1, 2.

Previews the *Candide* production in New York by interviewing LH and Bernstein. LH claims that she feels
she has been working on *Candide* all her life. Notes
LH's admiration for Voltaire despite her changing the
ending of the play to make it happy.

IIJ4.   Kronenberger, Louis, ed. *The Best Plays of 1956-57.*
New York: Dodd, Mead, 1957, passim.

Includes *Candide* summary and cast list. Notes that
the book fails to capture the flavor of Voltaire.
(See Item IIA47.)

IIJ5.   Ewen, David. "Leonard Bernstein." *American Musical
Theatre.* New York: Henry Holt, 1958, pp. 36-37, 42.

Summarizes several reviews of *Candide* in an article
on Bernstein.

IIJ6.   Guthrie, Tyrone. *A Life in the Theatre.* New York:
McGraw-Hill, 1959, pp. 241-242, 244.

Divulges Guthrie's view of *Candide* in New York: "Miss
Hellman's stooped fatally to conquer. None of her
good qualities, even great qualities, as a writer
showed to advantage. This was no medium for hard
hitting argument, shrewd humourous characterization,
the slow revelation of true values and the exposure
of false ones."

IIJ7.   "*Candide* in London; Audience, Critics Divided--Bern-
stein's Music Liked," New York *Times*, May 1, 1959,
p. 35.

Reports that mixed reviews were received in London
production.

IIJ8.   Briggs, John. *Leonard Bernstein. The Man, His Work
and His World.* Cleveland: World Pub. Co., 1961, pp.
195-201.

Briefly discusses the Bernstein-LH collaboration on
*Candide*.


IIK.   Interviews, Features, Previews, and News
      -- *Toys in the Attic*


IIK1.   Gelb, Arthur.  "Lillian Hellman Has Play Ready;
        Dramatist Plans Only Minor Revisions--She Opposes
        'Deep Collaboration,'" New York *Times*, Nov. 9, 1959,
        p. 35.

        Reveals that LH's play, which has been rewritten four
        times over a two-year period, is ready.  LH will ask
        Dorothy Parker to provide a title.

IIK2.   Little, Susan W.  "Lillian Hellman Names New Play
        *Toys in the Attic*," New York *Herald Tribune*, Dec. 17,
        1959, p. 18.

        Reveals LH's difficulty deciding on the title, *TIA*.
        She made her decision with only two and one-half months
        remaining before the play's opening.

IIK3.   Chapman, John, ed.  *Broadway's Best: 1960: The
        Complete Record of the Theatrical Year*.  Garden City,
        N.Y.:  Doubleday, 1960, pp. 19, 62-72, 152-153, 239.

        Includes extensive plot summary and excerpts from *TIA*.
        The Broadway cast listed and production matters con-
        sidered.

IIK4.   Kronenberger, Louis, ed.  *The Best Plays of 1959-1960*.
        New York:  Dodd, Mead, 1960, passim.

        Includes *TIA* summary and cast list.  Remarks that LH's
        characterizations are "probing and wide-ranging."
        (See Item IIA47.)

IIK5.   Little, Stuart W.  "Reading of Her New Play Heard by
        Lillian Hellman," New York *Herald Tribune*, Jan. 13,
        1960, p. 23.

        Features LH listening to actors read *TIA* prior to
        beginning of rehearsals.

IIK6.    Peck, Seymour. "Lillian Hellman Talks of Love and 'Toys,'" New York *Times*, Feb. 21, 1960, Sect. 2, p. 3.

Reports in an LH interview "twenty-five years and three months after the opening of *CH*" that she feels society is not the proper subject for plays, people are. She was surprised when critics saw *LF* as social drama. Explores the theme of love in *TIA* noting that she rewrote the play four times.

IIK7.    Ross, Don. "Lillian Hellman's First New Play in 8 Years," New York *Herald Tribune*, Feb. 21, 1960, Sect. 4, p. 1.

Includes a brief preview of *TIA* prior to its opening.

IIK8.    Marja, Fern. "A Clearing in the Forest," New York *Post*, Mar. 6, 1960, Magazine, p. 2.

Previews *TIA* in an LH interview. Biographical anecdotes about her marriage to Kober and her relationship with Hammett are included.

IIK9.    Zolotow, Sam. *"Toys in the Attic, Fiorello* Cited; *5 Finger Exercise* Also Named by Critics' Circle," New York *Times*, Apr. 20, 1960, p. 44.

Reveals that *TIA* was voted best American play of the 1959-60 season by New York critics.

IIK10.   Gelb, Arthur. "Notes and Gossip Gathered on the Rialto," New York *Times*, Aug. 21, 1960, Sect. 2, p. 1.

Describes Jason Robards' makeup for the final scene of *TIA*; reveals that it was so shocking that the house physician had to treat members of the audience for shock and hysteria.

IIK11.   "Broadway Success for London," London *Times*, Sept. 16, 1960, p. 16.

Reports the production of *TIA* in London.

IIK12.   "'Toys' Net is $100,241 to Date," *Variety*, Sept. 21, 1960, p. 69.

Reports *TIA* profits.

IIK13.  "The Unpredictable Miss Hellman;  No Doctrinaire in
        Playmaking," London *Times*, Nov. 9, 1960, p. 8.

        Previews London opening of *TIA*.  States that the sub-
        jects of LH's plays are difficult to predict because
        she has chosen so many different topics.  LH assisted
        with direction of production.  Argues that tight
        craftsmanship of the well-made play is the style LH
        likes best.  The "diffuse nature" of modern plays such
        as *Waiting for Godot* is presently popular and accepted
        by critics;  LH prefers more disciplined writing.  LH
        confesses that she "crumbled" under the pressures of
        the *Candide* production.

IIK14.  Downer, Alan S. *Recent American Drama*.  Minneapolis:
        U. of Minnesota Press, p. 41.

        Briefly considers *TIA*.  "There is nothing decadent in
        the style or structure of the play, and the audience
        is not asked to pity the characters, the act is spare,
        the judgement unsparing."

IIK15.  Stapleton, Maureen.  "Maureen Stapleton." *Actors Talk
        About Acting:  Fourteen Interviews with the Stars of
        the Theatre*.  Edited by Lewis Funke and John E. Booth.
        New York:  Random House, 1961, pp. 159-195.

        Uses her role in *TIA* as an example in her discussion
        of method acting.

IIK16.  "Connie Bennett Pans 'Toys' in Chi. TV Spiel,"
        *Variety*, Jan. 17, 1962, p. 69.  Reprinted in *Variety*,
        Jan. 31, 1962, p. 62.

        The actress playing Albertine Price criticized *TIA*
        during a TV interview, calling it a "sick and heavy
        play."  (See Item IIK17.)

IIK17.  Bloomgarden, Kermit.  "Maybe Daring--Hardly Amusing,"
        *Variety*, Jan. 31, 1962, p. 62.

        Attacks Bennett's criticism of *TIA* in a letter to the
        editor.  (Bloomgarden directed the Broadway production.)
        (See Item IIK16.)

IIL.   Interviews, Features, Previews, and News
       -- *My Mother, My Father and Me*


IIL1.  "Hellman Comedy to Open in March," New York *Times*, Nov.
       19, 1962, p. 39.

       Reports opening of *MMMF&M*.  LH notes that it will be
       substantially different from the novel by Blechman from
       which it was adapted.

IIL2.  "Lillian Hellman Adapting Book," San Diego *Tribune*,
       Jan. 4, 1963, Sect. C, p. 11.

       Announces LH's adaptation of *MMMF&M*.

IIL3.  Stern, Harold.  "Gordon to 'Mother,'" New York *Standard*,
       Jan. 22, 1963, p. 24.

       Reports beginning of *MMMF&M* rehearsals.

IIL4.  Goldman, William.  *The Season:  A Candid Look at
       Broadway*.  New York:  Harcourt, Brace, and World, 1969,
       pp. 264-265, 272, 413.

       Reveals that Gower Champion was director of *MMMF&M*'s
       seventeen performances.  The play lost $175,000.

IIL5.  Hewes, Henry, ed.  *The Best Plays of 1962-63*.  New
       York: Dodd, Mead, 1969, pp. 6-7, 303-304, 373.

       Reports *MMMF&M*'s Broadway failure.  Includes a carica-
       ture of LH and a list of the original cast of the play.
       (See Item IIA47.)



IIM.   Interviews, Features, Previews, and News
       -- *An Unfinished Woman*


IIM1.  Dudar, Helen.  "Woman in the News; Lillian Hellman;
       A Long Look Backward at the Comedy," New York *Post*,
       June 3, 1967, Magazine, p. 1.

       Interviews LH concerning the untitled book (*UW*) she is
       writing.  Reports that she traveled to the USSR in pre-
       paration for writing.  LH claims that the Russian in-
       telligentsia is knowledgeable about American literature.
       She notes their familiarity with Roth, Malamud, Bellow,

Styron, Updike, and Cheever.  Briefly mentions items
she intends to include in her book.  Some brief anecdotes about Hammett and a comment about the publication
of his book *The Big Knockover*, edited by LH, are included.

IIM2.  "A New Lillian Hellman Looks at Yesterday and Today,"
       New York *Times*, July 1, 1969, p. 33.

       Reports various biographical anecdotes in an interview
       with LH.  LH's friendship with Dorothy Parker, the
       death of Dashiell Hammett, her teaching activities at
       Harvard and MIT, and her life in New York are noted.
       Previews the publication of *UW*.

IIM3.  Seligson, Marcia.  "Book Buzz; Parties," *Book World*
       (Washington *Post*, Chicago *Tribune*), Aug. 31, 1969, p.
       2.

       Reports that Little, Brown, hosted two parties in cel-
       ebration of *UW* publication.

IIM4.  Eichelbaum, Stanley.  "A Playwright's Distaste for
       Theatre," San Francisco *Examiner*, Oct. 6, 1969, *Books*,
       p. 31.

       Interviews LH while on tour promoting *UW*.  Presents
       brief biographical information.

IIM5.  Raymont, Henry.  "Winners of 1969 Book Awards Named,"
       New York *Times*, Mar. 3, 1970, p. 34.

       Reveals that LH won the National Book Award for *UW*.

IIM6.  Beam, Alvin.  "The Glamourous Lillian Hellman," Cleve-
       land *Plain Dealer*, Mar. 10, 1970, Sect. A, p. 11.

       Notes that LH's speech after receiving the National
       Book Award for *UW* "was a grand performance.  The
       applause was long and loud."

IIM7.  Martin, Judith, and Aaron Latham.  "Lillian Hellman
       Keeps Her Secrets," Louisville *Courier Journal*, May
       17, 1970, Sect. E, p. 7.

       Discusses in this syndicated article LH's writing of
       *UW* and her handling of Dorothy Parker's estate.

IIM8.  *Best Sellers*, XXIV (Dec. 15, 1974), 429.

       Announces briefly Bantam paperback publication of *UW*.

IIM9.   Edmiston, Susan, and Linda D. Cirino. *Literary New
        York; a History and Guide.* Boston:  Houghton Mifflin,
        1976, pp. 210-211, 232, 238, 244, 253.

        Quotes *UW* and includes a great deal of biographical
        material about LH in New York:  her houses, addresses,
        neighbors, etc.


        IIN.   Interviews, Features, Previews, and News
                        -- *Pentimento*


IINI.   Horwitz, Carey.  "For the Future LJ Takes Notice of:
        *Pentimento:  A Book of Portraits*," *Library Journal,*
        XCVIII (July 1973), 2157.

        Previews briefly LH's forthcoming autobiography.

IIN2.   Emerson, Gloria.  "Lillian Hellman; At 66, She's Still
        Restless," New York *Times,* Sept. 7, 1973, p. 24.

        Features LH at Martha's Vineyard having just completed
        *Pentimento.*  Discusses her career, life, and political
        views.

IIN3.   Ephron, Nora.  "Lillian Hellman Walking, Cooking, Wri-
        ting, Talking," *New York Times Book Review,* Sept. 23,
        1973, pp. 2, 51.

        Reports in an interview at age 67 that she is not
        equipped to grow old.  She says she doesn't like any
        of the warm places her doctors have recommended and
        also claims that she will not stop smoking.  Notes that
        the diaries she used in writing *Pentimento* were scat-
        tered and thus she had a difficult time with the book.
        She no longer reads new novels, but prefers poetry,
        biography, and letters.  When asked if she worries
        about what will happen to her work when she dies, LH
        states that she does.  She proclaims success in stopping
        biographies of Hammett from being published, but was
        unsuccessful in stopping one on Dorothy Parker.  "It's
        a silly point because what do you give a damn when
        you're dead.  Any life can be made to look a mess of.
        Mine certainly can."

IIN4.   Caen, Herb.  "La Vie Litteraire," San Francisco
        *Chronicle,* Nov. 1, 1973, p. 81.

Previews LH's *Pentimento* while she was on tour in San Francisco promoting the book. Some biographical material is included.

IIN5.  Beam, Alvin. "The Best to You from the Reviewers; Books for Christmas," Cleveland *Plain Dealer*, Dec. 2, 1973, Sect. G, p. 2.

Recommends *Pentimento* as a choice for Christmas giving.

IIN6.  "Best and Brightest," *Book World* (Washington *Post*, Chicago *Tribune*), Dec. 9, 1973, p. 2.

Lists *Pentimento* among the best books of the year.

IIN7.  Levine, JoAnn. "Author Lillian Hellman -- A Portrait in Words," *Christian Science Monitor*, Dec. 21, 1973, Sect. 2, p. 2.

Features briefly a biographical view of LH looking at *UW* and *Pentimento*.

IIN8.  Vetter, Craig. "Book," *Playboy*, XXI (Apr. 1974), 26.

Includes an LH interview while she was on tour in California promoting *Pentimento*. Provides some brief anecdotes about LH and Hammett.

IIN9.  "Lillian Hellman's 'Julia' Chapter into Film," *Variety*, July 10, 1974, p. 7.

Notes Columbia Pictures' plan to film *Julia* based on a chapter from *Pentimento*.

IIN10. "Hellman Memoir Yields 'Willie' for a Film and Separate from 'Julia,'" *Variety*, July 31, 1974, p. 6.

Announces Paramount's plans to produce movie *Willie*, based on a chapter from *Pentimento* about "a young girl's idolatry of her uncle...."

IIN11. McLellan, Joseph. "Paperbacks," *Book World* (Washington *Post*, Chicago *Tribune*), Oct. 20, 1974, p. 4.

Announces *Pentimento* as Signet paperback publication.

IIN12. Brady, Kathleen. "Lillian Hellman's Hour," *Village Voice*, Jan. 13, 1975, pp. 35-36.

Presents a feature article on LH and her activities promoting *UW* and *Pentimento*.

IIN13.   Thomas, Bob.  "Fonda Filming Hellman Story," Jackson
         (Miss.) *Clarion-Ledger*, Nov. 24, 1976, p. 3.

         Features in this syndicated article the movie starring
         Jane Fonda based on "Julia," a chapter from *Pentimento*.
         Notes that Fred Zinnemann is the producer.

IIN14.   Ferris, Susan.  "The Making of Julia," *Horizon*, XX
         (Oct. 1977), 86-94.

         Discusses Fred Zinnemann's desire to film *Julia* based
         on *Pentimento* chapter.  Jane Fonda's casting as LH
         was labeled a "natural."  Cast also includes Vanessa
         Redgrave, Jason Robards, and Maximilian Schell.  LH
         and Zinnemann collaborated on casting.  States that it
         is difficult to portray writers on film but that *Julia*
         "softens the Hellman personality."  Excellent LH photos
         included.

IIN15.   "Show Business;  Growing Fonda of Jane;  The Rebel Has
         Mellowed," *Time*, CX (Oct. 3, 1977), 90-91.

         Features Jane Fonda playing the role of LH in *Julia*.
         Includes Fonda's impressions of LH.  Fonda speaks with
         fond admiration for LH, her courage, her political
         stance, and her femininity.



            IIO.  Interviews, Features, Previews, and News
                      -- *Scoundrel Time*


IIO1.    de Pue, Stephanie.  "Lillian Hellman;  She Never Turns
         Down an Adventure," Cleveland *Plain Dealer*, Dec. 28,
         1975, Sect. 5, p. 2.

         Features interview with LH promoting her new book, *ST*.
         LH offers a brief summary of the book and her memories
         of the McCarthy era.

IIO2.    Fremont-Smith, Eliot.  "Making Books," *Village Voice*,
         Feb. 16, 1976, p. 52.

         Announces the publication of "the book Hellman said
         she couldn't write," *ST*.

IIO3.    Baker, John F.  "PW Interviews;  Lillian Hellman,"
         *Publishers Weekly*, CCIX (Apr. 26, 1976), 6-7.

Reveals in an interview promoting *ST* that she is working on a fourth book of memories, but has not worked
on it recently.

II04.   Leonard, John.  "Critic's Notebook;  An Evening with
        Two Walking Anachronisms," New York *Times*, May 26,
        1976, p. 24.

        Features publisher's dinner party honoring LH for *ST*.

II05.   "Lillian Hellman at Mount Holyoke," *Mount Holyoke
        Alumnae Quarterly*, LX (Summer, 1976), 16–17.

        Features LH at Mount Holyoke addressing seniors and
        publicizing *ST*.  "Conveying a message close to that in
        her new book *ST*, she told the seniors that they were
        too passive for her taste.  Contrasting them with the
        rebellious students of the sixties, she said that we
        have gone backwards in a frightening fashion."

II06.   Alexander, Roy.  "Letters from Readers;  The 50's and
        Beyond," *Commentary*, LXII (Sept. 1976), 6.

        Supports Glazer's article (Item VIIC18) by pointing to
        historical evils of Communists and LH's ties to them.

II07.   Brier, Peter A.  "Letters from Readers;  The 50's and
        Beyond," *Commentary*, LXII (Sept. 1976), 4.

        Includes a letter critical of Nathan Glazer's review of
        *ST* (Item VIIC18).  Declares that Glazer "exaggerates the
        menace [of] Communist conspiracies" of the fifties and
        ignores the fact that LH's stand before HUAC was the
        "beginning of the end of the 'witch hunt.'"

II08.   Glazer, Nathan.  "Letters from Readers;  The 50's and
        Beyond," *Commentary*, LXII (Sept. 1976), 6.

        Answers critics of his *ST* review (Item VIIC18).

II09.   Kroll, Betty.  "Letters from Readers;  The 50's and
        Beyond," *Commentary*, LXII (Sept. 1976), 4.

        Criticizes Glazer's review of *ST* (Item VIIC18).  Kroll
        poses questions as to the ultimate legality of the
        suppression McCarthyism created.

II010.  Wessel, Andrew E.  "Letters from Readers; The 50's and
        Beyond," *Commentary*, LXII (Sept. 1976), 4.

        Harshly criticizes Glazer's *ST* review (Item VIIC18).

II011.  McFadden, Robert D. "Diana Trilling Book is Cancelled, Reply to Lillian Hellman is Cited," New York *Times*, Sept. 28, 1976, p. 1. See also Kernan, Michael. "Friends Amid 'Scoundrels': Publishing Fray Centered on the '50's," Washington *Post*, Sept. 29, 1976, Sect. B, p. 1. "Mrs. Trilling's Book Killed," San Francisco *Chronicle*, Sept. 29, 1976, p. 4. Parker, Jerry. "Data/II: A Literary Dispute," *Newsday*, Sept. 29, 1976, Sect. A, p. 7. Carmody, Deirdre. "Trilling Causes Publisher Loyalty Debate," New York *Times*, Sept. 30, 1976, p. 34.

Reports that publication of Diana Trilling's book was cancelled because she refused to delete material critical of LH's negative comments about Lionel Trilling in *ST*. (See Items II012, II013, II017, II020.)

II012.  Bachrach, Judith. "Lillian Hellman on the Trilling Controversy," Washington *Post*, Sept. 30, 1976, Sect. B, p. 4. See also Klemsrud, Judy. "Lillian Hellman Denies Having Played a Role in Little, Brown's Rejection of Trilling Book," New York *Times*, Sept. 29, 1976, p. 28.

Reports LH's claim that she had no knowledge of Diana Trilling's book criticizing her until Little, Brown had already cancelled it. (See Items II011, II013, II017, II020.)

II013.  Smith, Liz. "Gossip by Liz Smith," Annapolis *Evening Capital*, Oct. 26, 1976, p. 7.

Features in a syndicated article the LH-Diana Trilling controversy. Notes the New York *Times*'s commissioning and then rejecting of an LH article interviewing Rosalynn Carter. Smith speculates that the interview will appear in the November *Rolling Stone Magazine*. (The article did appear in the Nov. 1976 *Rolling Stone*.) (See Items II011, II012, II017, II020.)

II014.  Maclean, A.D. "To the Editor; 'Scoundrel Time,'" *Times Literary Supplement*, Dec. 3, 1976, p. 1516.

Comments on Mayne's use of the word "revisionism" in his review of *ST* (Item VIIC43).

II015.  Trilling, Diana. "To the Editor; 'Scoundrel Time'" *Times Literary Supplement*, Dec. 3, 1976, p. 1516.

Lashes out at Mayne for his review of *ST* (Item VIIC43),
and reveals that Little, Brown refused to publish her
new book because she would not delete four sentences
critical of LH.

II016.   Mayne, Richard.   "To the Editor;   'Scoundrel Time,'"
*Times Literary Supplement*, Dec. 10, 1976, p. 1560.

Includes Mayne's proclamation that he "stands by his
review of *ST*." Notes that since he is being criti-
cized by both sides of the controversy, he claims his
impartiality is proven.   (See Items II014, VIIC43.)

II017.   Trilling, Diana.   *We Must March My Darlings*.   New
York:   Harcourt, Brace, 1977, pp. 42-45, 46n, 47n,
48n, 49-50n.

Takes exception to *ST* by parenthetically inserting
comments about LH's book.   The work was originally a
contribution of Trilling's to an anti-Communist sympo-
sium.   Little, Brown refused to publish the new version
because of her criticism of LH.   Disputes *ST* as an
accurate account of the McCarthy era.   Defends her
own and her husband's political stance during the era.
(See Items II011-13, II020.)

II018.   Abrahams, William.   "To the Editor;   'Scoundrel Time,'"
*Times Literary Supplement*, Jan. 7, 1977, p. 13.

Defends LH and attacks those who defended Diana
Trilling for her stand against LH.   (See Item II015.)

II019.   Buckley, William F.   "On the Right;   Night of the
Cuckoo," *National Review*, XXIX (Apr. 29, 1977), 513.

Cites Sidney Hook's "devastating essay" against *ST*.
Notes with displeasure that LH received a standing
ovation at the Academy Awards ceremony.   Criticizes
her for her Communist ties for which she was "morally
guilty."   (See Item VIIC27.)

II020.   Kazin, Alfred.   "The Legend of Lillian Hellman,"
*Esquire*, LXXXVIII (Aug. 1977), 28, 30, 34.

Reveals the details of the conflict that occurred
when Little, Brown refused to publish Trilling's *We
Must March My Darlings* because she refused to remove
"critical references" to LH and Dashiell Hammett.
When LH was told what Trilling's book said about her,
she replied, "I don't give a damn, .... My goodness

what difference would that make." *ST*, though extremely popular "among the young" and the liberals, is
"inattentive to historical facts," and is called
"sentimental," "inaccurate," and "evasive."  The
copious use of dialogue in the volume is noted.  Considers Trilling's book "heavy" and "totally humorless."

III.  REVIEWS OF HELLMAN'S PLAYS


IIIA.  Reviews of *The Children's Hour*


*Broadway Opening*
*Maxine Elliott Theatre*
*Nov. 20, 1934*
*247 Performances*

IIIA1.  Anderson, John.  "How Child's Lie Brought Ruin to 2 Teachers' Lives Told in Play," New York *Evening Journal*, Nov. 21, 1934, p. 20.

Reports that *CH* is a "morbid tragedy" that is "adult, literate, and interesting."

IIIA2.  Atkinson, Brooks.  "The Play--*The Children's Hour*, Being a Tragedy of Life in a Girls' Boarding House," New York *Times*, Nov. 21, 1934, p. 23.

Proclaims LH "has written and Mr. Shumlin has pro-duced a pitiless tragedy and both of them have daubed it with grease paint in the last quarter of an hour...."  By altering the last act they could turn the play "into vivid drama."

IIIA3.  ————.  "The Drama Rests in Its Headlong Winter Flight; *Children's Hour*; Circumstantial Tragedy Set in a Girls' Boarding School--The Disputed Ending to a Swiftly Written Play," New York *Times*, Dec. 2, 1934, Sect. 10, p. 1.

Criticizes drawn-out nature of Act Three.  The theme is completed before the third act.  "It is as though Miss Hellman did not realize what a fine and sentient tragedy she has written."

IIIA4.   Brown, John Mason.  "The Play;  Katherine Emery and
         Anne Revere Excellent in an Interesting Play Called
         *The Children's Hour*," New York *Post*, Nov. 21, 1934,
         p. 13.

IIIA5.   ————.  "Two on the Aisle;  'The Children's Hour'
         and 'The Great Drumsheugh Case'--Mr. Walbridge Points
         Out Some Similarities," New York *Post*, Nov. 26, 1934,
         p. 15.

         Claims that LH has handled the lesbian subject matter
         in *CH* expertly.  The play "offers theatre goers one of
         the most absorbing evenings."

IIIA6.   Gabriel, Gilbert W.  "'The Children's Hour'--An Excel-
         lent Play Most Excellently Acted with Neither Fear
         Nor Folderol," New York *Journal American*, Nov. 21,
         1934, p. 13.

         Proclaims that *CH* "is a genuine contribution to the
         American Theatre.  It is that wise, that interesting,
         that significant.  It is that all-fired good."

IIIA7.   Garland, Robert.  "*Children's Hour* a Moving Tragedy;
         Play at Maxine Elliott's Theatre a Study of Wrecked
         Lives."  New York *World-Telegram*, Nov. 21, 1934, p.
         16.

IIIA8.   Gruber, Ide.  "The Playbill," *Golden Book*, XXI (Feb.
         1935), 28A.

         Reports that *CH* is "powerful and gripping; it is well-
         written and well-acted."

IIIA9.   Hammond, Percy.  "The Theatres -- 'The Children's
         Hour,' a Good Play About a Verboten Subject," New
         York *Herald Tribune*, Nov. 21, 1934, p. 16.

         Contends that *CH* "will make your eyes start from their
         sockets.  Well acted, well directed, and well written
         scenes that come so fast they almost tread upon one
         another's heels."

IIIA10.  ————.  "The Theatres," New York *Herald Tribune*, Dec.
         9, 1934, Sect. 5, p. 1.

         Maintains that the final scene of *CH* does not drag as
         others have suggested.  Disagrees with Atkinson's
         harsh review of the play.  (See Item IIIA2.)

IIIA11.  Isaacs, Edith J.R.  "Without Benefit of Ingenue,
         Broadway in Review; *The Children's Hour*," *Theatre
         Arts*, XIX (Jan. 1935), 13-14.

         Claims that *CH* is an excellent "realistic play" which
         has "clear, real, and potent" characters.  Labels it
         a "drama of doom."

IIIA12.  Kauf.  "Plays on Broadway; *The Children's Hour*,"
         *Variety*, Nov. 27, 1934, p. 52.

         Maintains that *CH* is "a finely conceived and tightly
         constructed drama" that is "sensitively and beauti-
         fully presented."  It will be a strong Pulitzer candi-
         date.

IIIA13.  Krutch, Joseph Wood.  "Drama; The Heart of a Child,"
         *The Nation*, CXXXIX (Dec. 5, 1934), 656-657.

         Argues that the first two acts are "tense" and "grip-
         ping," but Act Three is "so strained, so impossible,
         and so thoroughly boring that the effect is almost
         completely destroyed, and one is left to wonder that
         anything so inept was ever allowed to reach produc-
         tion."

IIIA14.  Lockridge, Richard.  "The New Play -- 'The Children's
         Hour,' Interesting Tragedy, Opens at Maxine Elliott's,"
         New York *Sun*, Nov. 21, 1934, p. 17.

         Calls *CH* a "sensitively written tragedy" containing
         "biting irony."

IIIA15.  ————.  "The Stage in Review;  Recapitulation," New
         York *Sun*, Dec. 1, 1934, p. 8.

         Calls *CH* "a thoughtful and absorbing drama ... admir-
         ably acted and in a mood of quiet sincerity.  For
         adults only, but for them [it is] virtually compul-
         sory."

IIIA16.  Mantle, Burns.  "'Children's Hour' Smashing Tragedy;
         Adult and Frankly Psychopathic Drama Holds Audience
         Fascinated," New York *Daily News*, Nov. 22, 1934, p.
         59.

IIIA17.  ————.  "An Exciting Drama Stirs the Town; 'The
         Children's Hour' Pregnant with Debatable Subjects,
         Wildly Welcomed," New York *Daily News*, Nov. 25, 1934,
         p. 74.

IIIA18.  ————.  "Paging Miss Taylor, Revealing Miss Lillian,"
New York *Daily News*, Dec. 2, 1934, p. 84.

Reveals that the title for *CH* was chosen by LH over
objections by Shumlin, her director. Shumlin is
lauded for his direction and for letting the author
have the last word in the title choice.

IIIA19.  Nathan, George Jean. "The Theatre," *Vanity Fair*,
XLIII (Feb. 1935), 37.

Argues that the last act of *CH* is realistic and belongs in the play. "Although the final scene is ex-
trinsic in performance, it is essential to the manuscript."

IIIA20.  Pollock, Arthur. "The Theatre--Bold and Honest Drama
is Presented at Maxine Elliott's Theatre Under the
Disarming Title, 'The Children's Hour,'" Brooklyn
*Daily Eagle*, Nov. 21, 1934, p. 19.

IIIA21.  Ruhl, Arthur. "Second Nights; A 'Children's Hour'
Bearing No Resemblance to Longfellow's," New York
*Herald Tribune*, Nov. 25, 1934, Sect. 5, p. 2.

Claims *CH* is a performance for adults only. It rep-
resents "a real contribution to the adult theatre."

IIIA22.  *Stage*, XII (Jan. 1935), 3.

Reports that "there is superb acting in this haunting,
gnawing play; and power and punch in its writing.
One of Broadway's most literate and exciting evenings.

IIIA23.  "*The Children's Hour*," *Stage*, XII (Jan. 1935), 28-29.

Includes an unidentified high school student's review
of the play. "I enjoyed it tremendously and found it
an honest and convincing discussion of subjects which
are a part of every girl's life."

IIIA24.  "The Theatre," *Time*, XXIV (Dec. 3, 1934), 24.

Praises LH for knowing "how to put a play together."
Concentrates primarily on cast.

IIIA25.  "The Thunderbolt of Broadway," *Literary Digest*,
CXVIII (Dec. 1, 1934), 20.

Argues that *CH* will "wring the heart and fire respect
an adult, steadfast play as conspicuously fine, and

intelligent that, beside it, much of the theatre's
present crop becomes shoddy and futile.  This is the
first play of this erratic season in which power,
intellect, and a glowing sense of theatre combine for
a terrifying and ennobling experience.  By the force
of its own stature, it has become the most important
play in New York."

IIIA26.   Winchell, Walter.  "Tense Drama at Elliott a New
          Hit," New York *Daily Mirror*, Nov. 21, 1934, p. 10.

          Maintains that lesbian theme is handled with excep-
          tionally good taste by LH.  Predicts a long run.

IIIA27.   Wyatt, Euphemia van Rensselaer.  "The Drama; *The
          Children's Hour*," *Catholic World*, CXL (Jan. 1935),
          466-467.

          Notes that *CH* "touches upon a subject which we have
          always felt should be taboo but it tiptoes across
          unholy ground with such unrelenting loathing of the
          slime and is so saturated with truth that it seems
          at times not to be the theatre at all...."

IIIA28.   Young, Stark.  "Two New Plays," *New Republic*, LXXXI
          (Dec. 19, 1934), 169.

          Points out that "there is no play in town whose first
          two acts hold the audience to so strict attention as
          *The Children's Hour*.  As for the last act, nobody
          could play it.  It constantly drops into the sort of
          adolescent banality that we sometimes got years ago
          at the Provincetown Playhouse....  Such drama is
          explicit rather than creative, sepulchral rather than
          intense."

*London Production*
*Gate Theatre*
*1936*

IIIA29.   Morgan, Charles.  "American Week in London," New
          York *Times*, Nov. 29, 1936, Sect. 12, p. 2.

          Criticizes the play for not fully developing the
          "lesbian theme."  Predicts that "wide popularity is
          doubtful because of the gloom of the third act."

IIIA30.   "Plays and Pictures; *The Children's Hour*, at the Gate
          Theatre," *New Statesman and Nation*, XII (Nov. 21,
          1936), 810.

Argues that *CH* "lacks all literary or permanent values, [but] is a vehicle for really magnificent acting." The first two acts are "entirely, hideously, convincing."

IIIA31.    "Theatre Notes; *The Children's Hour*; Gate Theatre," *Saturday Review* (London), CLXII (Nov. 21, 1936), 671.

Labels *CH* a "sincerely written" play.

*New York Library Production*
*1936*

IIIA32.    Coleman, Robert. "*The Children's Hour*," New York *Daily Mirror*, Dec. 16, 1936, p. 26.

Claims that *CH* has such "jumbled" and "tangled" themes that they ultimately become unclear.

*Brooklyn Production*
*1938*

IIIA33.    Pollock, Arthur. "Local Premiere," Brooklyn *Daily Eagle*, Mar. 29, 1938, p. 9.

Calls the revival a "thoroughly competent" production

*Brooklyn Schubert Theatre Production*
*1938*

IIIA34.    "Lillian Hellman Comes to Brooklyn Schubert," Brooklyn *Daily Eagle*, Nov. 9, 1938, p. 19.

Notes that *CH* "stands up sturdily and keeps the audience on the edge of their seats."

*New York Public Library Production*
*1945*

IIIA35.    Freedley, George. "The Stage Today; *Children's Hour*, *Gentlemen* Are Worthwhile Off Broadway Shows," New York *Morning Telegraph*, May 29, 1945, p. 2.

Claims *CH* "is enormously effective in the theatre."

IIIA36.  Garland, Robert. "*Children's Hour* at Library," New York *Journal American*, May 23, 1945, p. 8.

Proclaims that *CH* production is still an effective drama.

*London Production*
*New Bolton's Theatre*
*1950*

IIIA37.  "Entertainment; New Bolton's Theatre; *The Children's Hour* by Lillian Hellman," London *Times*, Nov. 22, 1950, p. 10.

Argues that "with a shade more technical cunning the piece would rise above the level of melodrama, but as it is its development has at some points the air of contrivance, as though the author were intent on forcing a misery in excess of the probabilities...."

*Broadway Revival*
*Coronet Theatre*
*Dec. 18, 1952*
*189 Performances*

IIIA38.  Atkinson, Brooks. "At the Theatre," New York *Times*, Dec. 19, 1952, p. 35.

Reports that *CH* "is still powerful and lacerating...."

IIIA39.  ————. "*Children's Hour*; Lillian Hellman's First Drama Has Lost None of Its Power or Pertinence," New York *Times*, Dec. 29, 1952, Sect. 2, p. 1.

IIIA40.  Beaufort, John. "Tragic 'Children's Hour,'" *Christian Science Monitor*, Dec. 27, 1952, p. 4.

Maintains that *CH* "has lost none of its power to astound and appall in the 18 years since it was first presented...."

IIIA41.  Bentley, Eric. "Hellman's Indignation," *New Republic*, CXXVII (Jan. 5, 1953), 30-31. Reprinted in *The Dramatic Event*. New York: Horizon, 1954, pp. 74-77.

Criticizes LH for her direction of *CH*. Claims that "everything on the stage seems unreal, inorganic, unrelated.... there is an absence of genuine passion."

IIIA42.  Beyer, William H.  "Reports;  The State of the
         Theatre;  First Nights," *School and Society*, LXXVII
         (Feb. 21, 1953), 117-118.

         "Miss Hellman directed the current revival and it is
         inevitable that she should have accentuated the neg-
         ative--propelled the melodramatic rather than evoked
         the psychologically characterful...."

IIIA43.  Bloomgarden, Kermit.  "The Pause in the Day's Occupa-
         tion," *Theatre Arts*, XXXVII (May 1953), 33.

         Reviews plot/production history of *CH*; no critical
         material is included.

IIIA44.  Bolton, Whitney.  "'Children's Hour' Still Taut
         Powerful Drama," New York *Morning Telegraph*, Dec. 20,
         1952, p. 4.

         Notes that LH's "aging play" is still "crisp and
         tragic, tight at every seam."

IIIA45.  Chapman, John.  "Revival of *The Children's Hour*
         Strong in Plot, Weak in Acting," New York *Daily News*,
         Dec. 20, 1952, p. 17.

IIIA46.  Dash, Thomas R.  "*The Children's Hour*, Coronet
         Theatre," *Women's Wear Daily*, Dec. 19, 1952, p. 32.

         Argues that the *CH* revival "demonstrates that it is
         impervious to the ravages of time.  Superbly acted...."

IIIA47.  Field, Rowland.  "*The Children's Hour*;  Lillian
         Hellman's Impelling Psychological Study Returns to
         Broadway with Good Cast," Newark *Evening News*, Dec.
         19, 1952, p. 48.

         Notes that *CH* is "as splendid as the original."

IIIA48.  Freedley, George.  "Off Stage -- And On," New York
         *Morning Telegraph*, Dec. 26, 1952, p. 3.

         Calls *CH* "a sturdy play which stands up well in re-
         vival."

IIIA49.  Gibbs, Wolcott.  "The Theatre;  No Pause," *New Yorker*,
         XXVIII (Jan. 3, 1953), 30.

         Claims LH has "written one of the most honest, per-
         ceptive, and distinguished plays of our time and I
         doubt whether she can be given too much credit."

IIIA50. Hawkins, William. "'Children's Hour' at 18, Still
Shocks," New York *World-Telegram and Sun*, Dec. 19,
1952, p. 19.

Claims that *CH* is "just as shattering as it was in
the first place."

IIIA51. Hayes, Richard. "The Stage; *The Children's Hour*,"
*Commonweal*, LVII (Jan. 1953), 377.

Discusses the "theatricality of the work--the sheer,
exhilarating sense it conveys of a positive dramatic
talent, of a playwright who is not afraid to calcu-
late her exits and entrances, to drop her curtain at
a provocative moment, or to expose her characters to
passion and violence. It is this imaginative bold-
ness which has carried Miss Hellman past the failures
of realism to a secure and irreproachable ground."

IIIA52. Hewes, Henry. "Between the Dark, and the Dark, Dark
Darkness," *Saturday Review*, XXXVI (Jan. 10, 1953),
30.

Exclaims that *CH* "for all its expertly drawn suspense,
is filled with puppet characters who in the throes of
dramatic climaxes come out with such uninspired utter-
ances as 'damn you'...."

IIIA53. Hobe. "Plays on Broadway; *The Children's Hour*,"
*Variety*, Dec. 24, 1952, p. 50.

Suggests that *CH* "remains not only taut and exciting
theatre, but has acquired a stimulating new quality
of contemporary significance."

IIIA54. Kerr, Walter F. "*The Children's Hour*," New York
*Herald Tribune*, Dec. 19, 1952, p. 18.

Labels *CH* "a remarkably shrewd and incisive melodrama,
but one which has lost a good deal of its vitality
through unsuitable, unshaded playing."

IIIA55. McClain, John. "'The Children's Hour' -- a Welcome,
Though Gruesome, Addition," New York *Journal American*, Dec. 19, 1952, p. 18.

Notes that *CH* "still stacks up as a compelling evening in the theatre."

IIIA56. Marshall, Margaret. "Drama," *The Nation*, CLXXVI (Jan.
3, 1953, 18-19.

Notes that *CH* is the "imaginary, clinically perfect case history which a specialist in the motives and behavior of children might draw up for the instruction of parents or students. As a play it is well written and very well put together, but it is neither genuinely convincing nor genuinely moving...."

IIIA57.   "'Mary, What Are You Saying?'" *Life*, XXXIV (Jan. 19, 1953), 51–54.

Reviews the revival of *CH* claiming that though the lesbian suggestion may not today be so shocking, the "evils of character assassination" make the play "remarkably timeless and valid."

IIIA58.   Nathan, George Jean. "Gossip Column," New York *Journal American*, Jan. 11, 1953, p. 20. Reprinted in *The Theatre in the Fifties*. New York: Alfred A. Knopf, 1953, pp. 49–52.

Recommends *CH* for "dramatically starved" audiences.

IIIA59.   "Old Play in Manhattan; *The Children's Hour*," *Time*, LX (Dec. 29, 1952), 55.

Calls *CH* "still vivid and powerful."

IIIA60.   "*The Children's Hour*," *Newsweek*, XL (Dec. 29, 1952), 40.

Argues that *CH* "is far and away the finest drama to be offered on Broadway this season." It has not lost its power to "shock an audience."

IIIA61.   Watts, Richard, Jr. "Two on the Aisle; 'The Children's Hour' Scores Again," New York *Post*, Dec. 19, 1952, p. 45.

Suggests that *CH* "is a sort of terror melodrama of enormous fascination."

IIIA62.   Winchell, Walter. "*Children's Hour* Revival Spellbinde as in '34," New York *Daily Mirror*, Dec. 19, 1952, p. 42.

IIIA63.   Wyatt, Euphemia van Rensselaer. "Theatre; *The Children's Hour*," *Catholic World*, CLXXVI (Feb. 1953), 388.

Argues that *CH* "just misses being great tragedy because there is a lack of any spiritual development in Karen. All she can say when Mrs. Tilford humbles

herself in contrition is 'Get out of here.'  The
final curtain has the darkness of frustration and
futility."

*London Production*
*1956*

IIIA64.   "Arts Theatre;  *The Children's Hour*, by Lillian
          Hellman," London *Times*, Sept. 20, 1956, p. 5.

          Evaluates *CH* as "naturally slow, and ... made to
          seem almost preternaturally slow by acting which is
          woefully deficient in the power of attack."

IIIA65.   Clem.  "'The Children's Hour,'" *Variety*, Oct. 3,
          1956, p. 82.

          Reports that censor's ban of the play has not
          been lifted in London.  It is "not shocking" to the
          modern audience.  The production is "pallid."

IIIB.   Review of *Days to Come*

*Broadway Opening*
*Vanderbilt Theatre*
*Dec. 15, 1936*
*7 Performances*

IIIB1.    Anderson, John.  "John Anderson Reviews;  Labor and
          Family Crisis Give Theme to New Play by Lillian
          Hellman," New York *Evening Journal*, Dec. 16, 1936,
          p. 24.

          Proclaims that *DC* is "pretentious and tiresome ...
          a plot that breaks out on the play like an epidemic."

IIIB2.    Atkinson, Brooks.  "The Play; 'Days to Come' on
          Ethics of Strikebreaking is Lillian Hellman's New
          Drama," New York *Times*, Dec. 16, 1936, p. 35.

          Argues that *DC* is an attempt to make "a spiritual
          tragedy out of a labor impasse."  The attempt is a
          "tortured" one.

IIIB3.    Brown, John Mason.  *"Days to Come* Produced at
          Vanderbilt Theatre," New York *Post*, Dec. 16, 1936,
          p. 17.

          Criticizes *DC* for being a "dull incredibly muddled
          drama" that is also "unpleasant."

IIIB4.    Coleman, Robert.  "The Theatre," New York *Daily
          Mirror*, Dec. 16, 1936, p. 25.

          Labels *DC* a "wooden drama" with dialogue and charac-
          ters that are "poorly conceived."  The direction
          "seems to emphasize the weaknesses."

IIIB5.    Dexter, Charles E.  "Strikes and Strikebreakers
          Viewed by Lillian Hellman; *Days to Come* by the
          Author of *The Children's Hour* Opens at Vanderbilt
          Theatre," *Daily Worker* (New York), Dec. 18, 1936, p.
          7.

          Praises LH for her ability to write "incisive dia-
          logue" and create "forceful action."  Her inability
          "to get under the skin of the characters" mars *DC*.

IIIB6.    Gabriel, Gilbert W.  *"Days to Come*; Florence Eldudy
          in Lillian Hellman's New Play," New York *American*,
          Dec. 16, 1936, p. 15.

          Views *DC* with disapproval for being "down in the
          mouth" and a "rather dullish fabrication."

IIIB7.    Gilbert, Douglas.  "'Days to Come' Opens at Vander-
          bilt Theatre," New York *World-Telegram*, Dec. 16,
          1936, p. 32.

          Disapproves of *DC* noting that it has "some of the
          most preposterous and brutal lines uttered this
          season ... not a good play."

IIIB8.    Ibee.  "'Days to Come,'" *Variety*, Dec. 23, 1936, p.
          59.

          Reacts with disappointment to *DC* after the skill and
          promise *CH* demonstrated.  *DC* has "little appeal."

IIIB9.    Krutch, Joseph Wood.  "Drama;  Plays, Pleasant and
          Unpleasant," *The Nation*, CXLII (Dec. 26, 1936), 769-
          770.

          Notes that *DC*, like *CH*, is likeable but it "produces
          and sustains an agonizing tension.  It also leaves
          the nerves sore."

IIIB10.  Lockridge, Richard.  "The New Play;  Lillian Hellman's
         *Days to Come* Opens at Vanderbilt Theatre," New York
         *Sun*, Dec. 16, 1936, p. 42.

         Criticizes *DC* noting that LH's "art deserts her with
         a yelp of protest."

IIIB11.  Mantle, Burns.  "*Days to Come* a Tragic Drama;  Story
         of a Strike That Shook a Town and Shattered a Few
         Souls," New York *Daily News*, Dec. 16, 1936, p. 61.

         Notes that "honesty has gone into the writing" of
         *DC*.  Reports that audience reaction was unenthusias-
         tic.

IIIB12.  Pollock, Arthur.  "The Theatre;  A New Play by Lillian
         Hellman, 'Days to Come' Arrives at Vanderbilt Theatre,"
         Brooklyn *Daily Eagle*, Dec. 16, 1936, p. 20.

         Calls *DC* "a ponderous drama hardly worth its weight
         in ideas."

IIIB13.  "Strike Breakers;  New Theme Utilized in *Days to
         Come* by Lillian Hellman," *Literary Digest*, CXXII
         (Dec. 26, 1936), 22-23.

         Recalls the poor audience response and blunt critical
         reaction to *DC*.  LH, "apparently unable to decide
         whether to throw her sympathies toward Rodman or his
         workmen, belabors instead the thug theme, uses the
         Rodman family misfortunes as a springboard for some
         mild interfamily criticism."

IIIB14.  Taylor, Alexander.  "Sights and Sounds," *New Masses*,
         XXII (Dec. 26, 1936), 27.

         Claims that *DC* "was a rather absorbing play."  LH is
         "a person who knows a lot about how the world wags...."
         Predicts that interesting things can be expected from
         LH.

IIIB15.  Vernon, Grenville.  "The Play and Screen;  *Days to
         Come*," *Commonweal*, XXV (Jan. 1, 1937), 276.

         Criticizes LH for failing to be content with making
         *DC* "a melodrama with a purpose."  If she had, it
         might have turned out to be a "workmanlike job."

IIIB16.  Watts, Richard, Jr.  "The Theatre," New York *Herald
         Tribune*, Dec. 16, 1936, p. 22.

Asserts that *DC* displays "sincerity and frequent
skill" but is ultimately "a grave disappointment."

IIIB17.    Young, Stark.  "Social Drama," *New Republic*, LXXXIX
(Dec. 30, 1936), 273-274.

Claims that *DC* demonstrates an "intuition of sub-
stance" in LH.  "For the material ... we must say
bravo."


IIIC.    Reviews of *The Little Foxes*


*Baltimore Production*
*Ford's Theatre*
*Feb. 2, 1939*

IIIC1.    Burm.  "'The Little Foxes,'" *Variety*, Feb. 8, 1939,
p. 50.

Reports that the play has "dynamic writing, acting,
and directing," but still needs to be improved before
it opens on Broadway.  Suggests that the theme needs
clarification.

IIIC2.    Kirkley, Donald.  "'Little Foxes,'" Baltimore *Sun*,
Feb. 3, 1939, p. 10.

Calls the play "bitter and cheerless."  There is a
great deal of power and tension;  however, the third
act needs cutting to keep it from dragging.


*Pittsburgh Production*
*Nixon Theatre*
*Feb. 15, 1939*

IIIC3.    Monahan, Kaspar.  "Tallulah at Nixon," Pittsburgh
*Press*, Feb. 7, 1939, p. 12.

Praises Bankhead for her portrayal of Regina.  Calls
the part ideal for her talents.

*Broadway Opening*
*National Theatre*
*Feb. 15, 1939*
*143 Performances*

IIIC4.   Anderson, John.   "'Little Foxes' Opens at National
         Theatre," New York *Journal American*, Feb. 16, 1939,
         p. 16.

         Praises *LF* as "a deeply absorbing drama, both thought-
         ful and exciting, better than her first [*CH*]."

IIIC5.   ———.   "The Season's Theatre," *Saturday Review*,
         XIX (Apr. 19, 1939), 14-15.

         Argues that if *LF* "seems slightly overplotted and
         occasionally melodramatic, it has the advantages of
         sharp observation, and incisive character drawing.
         The exposition of the plot is superbly managed, and
         the action stems directly from the characters as they
         reveal themselves...."

IIIC6.   Atkinson, Brooks.   "The Play; Tallulah Bankhead
         Appearing in Lillian Hellman's Drama of the South,
         *The Little Foxes*," New York *Times*, Feb. 16, 1939, p.
         16.   Reprinted in "*The Little Foxes*." *Broadway Scrap-
         book*.   New York:   Theatre Arts, Inc., 1947, pp. 107-
         110.

         Points out that compared to *CH*, *LF* "will have to take
         a second rank.   For it is a deliberate exercise in
         malice--melodramatic rather than tragic."   It is,
         however, a "vibrant play."

IIIC7.   ———.   "Miss Bankhead Has a Play; Lillian Hellman's
         Stinging Drama About Rugged Individualism Provides a
         Number of Good Acting Parts," New York *Times*, Feb.
         26, 1939, Sect. 9, p. 1.

         Praises *LF* for being "worth acting and worth serious
         discussion...an excoriating drama of greed."

IIIC8.   Brown, John Mason.   "Two on the Aisle; Tallulah
         Bankhead and *The Little Foxes*; Miss Hellman's Engross-
         ing Play is Compared to Miss Du Maurier's *Rebecca*,"
         New York *Post*, Mar. 11, 1939, p. 8.   Reprinted in
         *Broadway in Review*.   New York:   W.W. Norton, 1940,
         pp. 116-121.

         Notes that the play is "an evening of extraordinary
         interest and almost anguishing tension."

IIIC9.     Cambridge, John.  "*The Little Foxes* a Story of
           Southern Aristocrats," *Daily Worker* (New York), Feb.
           17, 1939, p. 7.

           Calls *LF* LH's best drama and maintains that it is
           "the most consistently tense play of the season."

IIIC10.    ————.  "The Stage," *Sunday Worker* (New York), Feb.
           19, 1939, p. 7.

           Maintains that *LF* is LH's "best drama."  Elements of
           melodrama appear in the play, but they are carefully
           structured and controlled.

IIIC11.    Coleman, Robert.  "In 'The Little Foxes' Is Good
           Acting of Grim Play," New York *Daily Mirror*, Feb.
           16, 1939, p. 26.

           Speculates that LH "started out to pen a play of
           special significance, to belabor the Southern aristo-
           crats...."  She unfortunately has written a "flam-
           boyant melodrama."

IIIC12.    Ferguson, Otis.  "A Play, a Picture," *New Republic*,
           XCVIII (Apr. 12, 1939), 279.

           Proclaims that *LF* "makes a sure-fire play ... [pro-
           viding] a satisfying evening" for audiences.  "In
           its story the bad characters of a Southern family work
           out their dog-eat-dog plans of aggrandizement for all
           to see...."

IIIC13.    Gassner, John.  "The Theatre," *One Act Play Magazine*,
           II (Feb. 1939), 746-749.

           Calls *LF* "provocative," yet "flawed."

IIIC14.    Gilder, Rosamond.  "Sweet Creatures of Bombast;
           Broadway in Review; *The Little Foxes*," *Theatre Arts*,
           XXIII (Apr. 1939), 244-248.

           Labels *LF* an "incisive drama ... built about machina-
           tions of a greedy Southern family of a generation
           ago...."

IIIC15.    Ibee.  "Plays on Broadway -- 'The Little Foxes,'"
           *Variety*, Feb. 22, 1939, p. 50.

           A mixed review.

IIIC16.  Kronenberger, Louis.  "Greed," *Stage*, XVI (Apr. 1,
         1939), 36-37, 55.

         Argues that greed of the Hubbards in *LF* completely
         dehumanizes them.  Their immoral and evil actions do
         not degrade them as much as the greed which motivates
         those actions.

IIIC17.  Krutch, Joseph Wood.  "Drama; Unpleasant Play," *The
         Nation*, CXLVIII (Feb. 25, 1939), 244-245.

         Argues that "shrewd, tart, and biting" dialogue is
         expected from LH.  One also expects the "situation,
         the characters, and the catastrophe" to be "thoroughly
         unpleasant."  Suggests that LH "indubitably possesses
         the Ancient Mariner's gift--one stays in one's seat
         because one cannot choose but hear."

IIIC18.  Lockridge, Richard.  "The New Play; Lillian Hellman's
         *The Little Foxes* Opens at the National Theatre," New
         York *Sun*, Feb. 16, 1939, p. 12.

         Claims that *LF* is "a play which is steadily interest-
         ing and almost, but never quite, more."

IIIC19.  ————.  "The Stage in Review; Universality in the
         Drama, with a Note on Its Absence in *The Little
         Foxes*," New York *Sun*, Feb. 19, 1939, p. 26.

         Maintains that by omitting the quality of universal-
         ity LH has "disappointed many of us" with *LF*.  With
         this exception the play is "admirable."

IIIC20.  McKenney, Ruth.  "Sights and Sounds," *New Masses*,
         XXX (Feb. 28, 1939), 29-30.

         Claims that *LF* makes a brutal attack on the rich.
         The play is "theatre at its ... best."

IIIC21.  Mantle, Burns.  "'The Little Foxes' -- Tart Drama of
         a Ruthless Southern Family," New York *Daily News*,
         Feb. 16, 1939, p. 45.

         Predicts that "you might not like *The Little Foxes*,
         but I'll guarantee that you'll be at least a little
         fascinated."

IIIC22.  ————.  "Mean Minded Humans Make Good Drama: 'The
         Little Foxes' a Credit to Honesty of Lillian Hellman
         and Herman Shumlin," New York *Daily News*, Feb. 26,
         1939, p. 77.

Maintains that in *LF* "there is never a moment when
interest is not keen, but also very few moments
when the emotions are not stirred with sympathy or
compassion."

IIIC23.    Nathan, George Jean.   "Dour Octopus," *Newsweek*, XIII
           (Feb. 27, 1939), 26.   Reprinted in *The Encyclopedia
           of Theatre*.   Rutherford, N.J.:   Fairleigh Dickinson
           U. Press, 1970, pp. 170-171.

           Argues that *LF* "provides fresh evidence of its author'
           high position among American women writers for the
           stage ... she indicates a dramatic mind, an eye to
           character, a fundamental strength, and a complete
           unremitting integrity that are rare among her native
           playwriting sex."

IIIC24.    "New Play in Manhattan;   *The Little Foxes*," *Time*,
           XXXIII (Feb. 27, 1939), 38-40.

           Reports that LH "capitalizes on melodrama" to increase
           the "emotional intensity of a higher power" in her
           play.

IIIC25.    Pollock, Arthur.   "Lillian Hellman's 'The Little
           Foxes' Opens at the National Theatre with Tallulah
           Bankhead and Excellent Cast," Brooklyn *Daily Eagle*,
           Feb. 16, 1939, p. 11.

           Maintains that LH "can put a play together more
           skillfully than any other dramatist ... in the Amer-
           ican theater...."  *LF* "keeps you squirming with
           tension in your seat."

IIIC26.    Ross, George.   "Decay of the South Hellman Play
           Theme;   Tallulah Bankhead Gives Superb Performance
           in Leading Role of Fine Drama, *The Little Foxes*,"
           New York *World-Telegram*, Feb. 16, 1939, p. 24.

           Claims that *LF* is a "play of dramatic voltage ... and
           electricity."

IIIC27.    Vernon, Grenville.   "The Stage and Screen;   *The Little
           Foxes*," *Commonweal*, XXIX (Mar. 3, 1939), 525.

           Argues that LH "has a tender spot in her heart for the
           South of the aristocrats, but for the South of the
           mill owners she has contempt and hatred.  But what-
           ever her social beliefs Miss Hellman is an artist and
           does not load the dice unduly.  Her Hubbards are a

base lot indeed, but they are believable, and at
least the courage of the sister and elder brother
are admirable."

IIIC28. Waldorf, Wilella. "'The Little Foxes' Opens at the
National Theatre," New York *Post*, Feb. 16, 1939, p.
12.

Evaluates LH's "latest opus ... as a 'period piece.'"

IIIC29. Watts, Richard, Jr. "Theaters; Dixie," New York
*Herald Tribune*, Feb. 16, 1939, p. 14.

Reports that *LF* is a "merciless study; a drama more
honest, more pointed and more brilliant than even
her triumphant previous work."

IIIC30. ————. "The Theater; Miss Hellman's Play," New
York *Herald Tribune*, Feb. 26, 1939, Sect. 6, pp. 1, 2.

Concludes that *LF* is a "finer play" than *CH*. "Perhaps it is not always as shrewd in its theatrical
effectiveness, but it is a deeper, sharper and more
direct work than its brilliant predecessor."

IIIC31. Wyatt, Euphemia van Rensselaer. "The Drama; *The
Little Foxes*," *Catholic World*, CXLIX (Apr. 1939),
87–88.

Argues that "gone with the wind may be the ugly era
of reconstruction and the Northern carpetbaggers but
the exploitation of the South is not ended" for LH
has shown that "the South can now exploit itself.
It is not written for any particular locality, but as
a general exposure to those foxes who run amuck
through our social order careless of the vines they
may destroy to reach the grapes they desire."

*London Production*
*Picadilly Theatre*
*1942*

IIIC32. Darlington, W.A. "American in London," New York
*Times*, Nov. 1, 1942, Sect. 8, p. 2.

Notes that the "subtle essence" that made *LF* great in
the U.S. has "been allowed to evaporate" in the
London version.

IIIC33.  Redfern, James.  "The Theatre;  'The Little Foxes,'"
         *The Spectator*, CLXIX (Oct. 30, 1942), 407.

         Proclaims that *LF* is a "sordid, realistic account of
         moral downfall."

IIIC34.  Whitebate, William.  "Plays and Pictures;  *The Little
         Foxes* at the Picadilly," *New Statesman and Nation*,
         XXIV (Nov. 7, 1942), 304.

         Argues that "those who saw the picture will be dis-
         appointed" in the Picadilly production.  It is "slow,
         uncertain, [and] crude rather than emphatic in its
         effects."

*New York Revival*
*Lincoln Center*
*1967*

IIIC35.  Barnes, Clive.  "Theatre;  Return of 'The Little
         Foxes,'" New York *Times*, Oct. 27, 1967, p. 53.

         Praises the George C. Scott, Anne Bancroft, E.G.
         Marshall revival as "magnificent."

IIIC36.  ————.  "Theatre;  'The Little Foxes' Revisited,"
         New York *Times*, Jan. 6, 1968, p. 24.

         Claims that "something of the original gusto of the
         Lincoln Center performance has evaporated" since
         move to Broadway.  It is a play which should only be
         seen "once in a lifetime."

IIIC37.  Bolton, Whitney.  "Revival;  Lillian Hellman's 'The
         Little Foxes,'" New York *Morning Telegraph*, Oct. 28,
         1967, p. 3.

         Notes that "time has not weakened it or wrinkled" *LF*.

IIIC38.  Bunce, Alan U.  "*Little Foxes* Powerfully Revived,"
         *Christian Science Monitor*, Nov. 3, 1967, p. 4.

IIIC39.  Chapman, John.  "Lincoln Center Rep Revival of 'The
         Little Foxes' a Humdinger," New York *Daily News*,
         Oct. 27, 1967, p. 70.

IIIC40.  ————.  "Pleasant Musical, Strong Drama," New York
         *Daily News*, Nov. 5, 1967, Sect. 2, p. 3.

Notes that LH's "drama of greed, suspicion and venom
is just as solid and strong as when it was produced
in 1939...."

IIIC41.  Cooke, Richard P.  "The Theatre;  A Well-Acted
Revival," *Wall Street Journal*, Oct. 30, 1967, p. 18.

Notes that *LF* is a play "whose parts are considerably
better than the whole."  LH's "knowledge of character
is sure, and her play is fortunate in its casting."

IIIC42.  Gottfried, Martin.  "Theatre;  'The Little Foxes,'"
*Women's Wear Daily*, Oct. 27, 1967, p. 84.

Maintains that *LF* is an "absurdly naturalistic and
heavily built play about opportunistic materialism in
the Old South."  Considers the play to be of little
value.

IIIC43.  "Greedy Lot," *Time*, XC (Nov. 3, 1967), 64.

Argues that *LF*'s power is "unsopped" after twenty-
eight years.  The "craftsmanship remains tight in the
play."

IIIC44.  Hardwick, Elizabeth.  "*The Little Foxes* Revived,"
*New York Review of Books*, IX (Dec. 21, 1967), 4-5.

Summarizes the plot.  Provides no critical comment.

IIIC45.  Hewes, Henry.  "The Crass Menagerie," *Saturday Review*,
L (Nov. 11, 1967), 26.

Proclaims that *LF* "concentrates on showing us the
graceless behavior of a society in which the more
ambitious become scoundrels and the more decent stand
by and let them get away with exploiting the poor."

IIIC46.  Hipp, Edward Sothern.  "New York Stage -- 'Little
Foxes' at Beaumont," Newark *Evening News*, Oct. 27,
1967, p. 28.

Suggests that *LF* "plays well despite spouts of purple
prose and a few plot twists which may seem overdrawn
after 28 years."

IIIC47.  Hobe.  "Show on Broadway;  *The Little Foxes*,"
*Variety*, Nov. 1, 1967, p. 58.

Reports that *LF* "holds up well after 28 years ... a
fine start to the Lincoln Center season."

IIIC48.    Kemper, Robert Graham.  "Evil Revisited," *Christian
           Century*, LXXXV (Mar. 13, 1968), 332.

           Notes that modern audiences are divided from *LF*.
           "When it is over we know what we have seen:  evil--
           gross corruption and malevolence.  Such evil invites
           us to be Pharisees, thankful that we are not as de-
           based as the Hubbards.  We have come together not to
           ponder the nature of the personal and social evils
           that infect our being, but to observe what evil has
           done to them--and they are distant from us."

IIIC49.    Kerr, Walter.  "We Could Have Five *Little Foxes*,"
           New York *Times*, Nov. 5, 1967, Sect. 2, p. 1.
           Reprinted in *Thirty Plays Hath November*.  New York:
           Simon and Schuster, 1969, pp. 129-132.

           Proclaims that *LF* "literally makes you hold your
           breath."

IIIC50.    Kroll, Jack.  "Chasing the Fox," *Newsweek*, LXX (Nov.
           6, 1967), 86.

           Argues that *LF* "was an appropriate play to end the
           1930's in America.  From the perspective of 28 years
           later, it seems to sum up the liberalism, the social
           concern, which was the major force of the American
           stage throughout that decade."

IIIC51.    Lewis, Theophilus.  "Theatre;  *The Little Foxes*,"
           *America*, CXVII (Dec. 9, 1967), 723.

           Praises *LF* noting that it "rates a place in world
           drama beside works by Ibsen and Strindberg.  It is as
           distinctively American as the hot dog and as univer-
           sal in impact as *Tartuffe*.  The vitality of the play
           is in the strength of Miss Hellman's writing."

IIIC52.    McCarten, John.  "The Theatre;  Low Jinks," *New
           Yorker*, XLIII (Nov. 4, 1967), 162.

           Calls *LF* an "account of the vulgar machinations of an
           avaricious Southern tribe, socially on a par with
           Faulkner's 'Snopeses,' [it] is a mechanical melodrama,
           and I don't think that Mr. Nichols' direction has
           supplied enough lubrication to still the clanking of
           the plot."

IIIC53. O'Connor, John S. "On the Off-Off Circuit," *Wall Street Journal*, Nov. 21, 1967, p. 20.

A favorable review.

IIIC54. Simon, John. "The Stage; Tally Ho!," *Commonweal*, LXXXVII (Dec. 1, 1967), 305-306.

Asserts that LH "enjoys the reputation of a major American playwright" and *LF* "should make everyone wonder why. It is easy enough to find a place in the short and simple annals of the poor American stage, but is that any reason for an author who is so clearly a melodramatist rather than a dramatist to usurp a position of prominence?"

IIIC55. "The Theatre," *Time*, XC (Nov. 3, 1967), 64, 69.

Proclaims that after twenty-eight years *LF* is still a "significant" play that has been splendidly cast.

IIIC56. Watts, Richard, Jr. "Two on the Aisle -- Ruthlessness of the Hubbards," New York *Post*, Dec. 27, 1967, p. 45.

Declares *LF* to be "still a fine powerful play." It is "as absorbing as it had seemed originally."

IIIC57. Weales, Gerald. "What Kind of Fool Am I?" *The Reporter*, XXXVIII (Jan. 11, 1968), 36.

Vehemently attacks *LF* revival for being "sloppily performed and ineptly directed." The play has been "ridiculously overpraised."

*Seattle Production*
*Seattle Repertory Theatre*
*1970*

IIIC58. Johnson, Wayne. "'Little Foxes' Superb at Rep," Seattle *Times*, Feb. 23, 1970, Sect. A, p. 15.

Reports that LH's play "is excellent." It is a "consistently engrossing, [and] entertaining piece of theater."

IIIC59. Stromberg, Rolf. "Acting Saves Hokey 'Foxes,'" Seattle *Post Intelligencer*, Feb. 23, 1970, p. 5.

*American College Theatre Festival*
*(North Carolina School of Arts)*
*Washington, D.C.*
*1972*

IIIC60.   Coe, Richard L. "Dated *Little Foxes* at ACTF,"
          Washington *Post*, Apr. 22, 1972, Sect. B, p. 5.

          Claims that *LF* is now a "period piece."


IIID.   Reviews of *Watch on the Rhine*


*Baltimore Opening*
*Ford's Theatre*
*Mar. 24, 1941*

IIID1.   Barn. "'Watch on the Rhine,'" *Variety*, Mar. 26, 1941,
         p. 52.

         Maintains *WR* has skillfully shaped dialogue avoiding
         the propaganda found in other plays with war themes.
         One of LH's best.

IIID2.   Kirkley, Donald. "Premiere of Lillian Hellman's
         Anti-Nazi Drama," Baltimore *Sun*, Mar. 25, 1941, p. 8.

         Predicts that *WR* will win the Pulitzer Prize. Balti-
         more audiences have witnessed "the birth of a great
         drama."


*Broadway Opening*
*Martin Beck Theatre*
*Apr. 1, 1941*
*87 Performances*

IIID3.   Abel. "Plays on Broadway; *Watch on the Rhine*,"
         *Variety*, Apr. 9, 1941, p. 42.

         Calls *WR* "one of the more worthwhile plays of the
         current Broadway season, highly meriting strong
         public support...."

IIID4.   Allen, Kelcey. "Amusements; *Watch on the Rhine*,"
         *Women's Wear Daily*, Apr. 2, 1941, p. 27.

Contends that *WR* is filled with "suspense and force."
The dialogue is vigorous, "ranking with the best
drama seen on our stage."

IIID5.  Anderson, John.  "*Watch on the Rhine* at the Martin
        Beck;  Lillian Hellman's New Play Concerns Conflict
        in U.S. Over Fascism;  Paul Lukas' Acting Brilliant,"
        New York *Journal American*, Apr. 2, 1941, p. 12.

        Emphasizes that *WR* is "passionately anti-Fascist and
        often deeply moving, yet ... falters badly in its
        craftsmanship and loses its most vivid and vigorous
        points in overwriting."

IIID6.  ————.  "Plays and Players;  Author Tests Skill on
        Anti-Nazi Drama," New York *Journal American*, Apr. 6,
        1941, Sect. 5, p. 11.

        Suggests *WR* represents "a powerful step upward, clums-
        ily trying to adjust her playmaking apparatus to the
        larger scale and higher level of her subject matter."

IIID7.  Atkinson, Brooks.  "The Play;  Lillian Hellman's
        'Watch on the Rhine' Acted with Paul Lukas in the
        Leading Part," New York *Times*, Apr. 2, 1941, p. 26.

        Demonstrates "how deeply fascism penetrates into the
        hearts and minds of human beings ... a compassionate
        drama."

IIID8.  ————.  "Hellman's *Watch on the Rhine*;  Author of
        *The Children's Hour* and *The Little Foxes* Writes of an
        American Family Drawn into the Nazi Orbit," New York
        *Times*, Apr. 13, 1941, Sect. 9, p. 1.

        Notes that LH's writing is full and spontaneous.  Her
        writing is like that "of a person who has mastered
        the craft, and is now released, perhaps by the nobil-
        ity of the subject, from the bondage of making things
        fit and working according to pattern."

IIID9.  Beaufort, John.  "*Watch on the Rhine*;  Voices Struggle
        Against Nazism," *Christian Science Monitor*, Apr. 2,
        1941, p. 10.

        Claims that *WR* "emerges through despair, bitterness,
        fear, and anger, into nobility, hope, courage and
        poignancy.  The plot is distinctly ... melodramatic
        ...."

IIID10.   Bessie, Alvah. "Sights and Sounds," *New Masses*,
          XXXIX (Apr. 15, 1941), 26-28.

          Argues that the anti-fascist message LH is attempting
          to portray needs to be clarified. The definition of
          anti-fascism needs to be "redefined in socialist
          terms."

IIID11.   Brown, John Mason. "Lillian Hellman's *Watch on the
          Rhine* Presented," New York *Post*, Apr. 2, 1941, p. 16.

          Points out that *WR* "is not as overpowering as one had
          hoped. It nonetheless comes as an addition to the
          season."

IIID12.   ————. "'Watch on the Rhine,' Seen a Second Time,"
          New York *Post*, Apr. 17, 1941, p. 10.

          Reaffirms his opening-night review noting that the
          play has fine things, but fails to arouse emotions in
          the audience. Claims that he will not vote for it
          for the Critics' Circle Award because of its flaws.

IIID13.   Claxton, Oliver. "A Great Anti-Nazi Play," *Cue*,
          XXI (Apr. 5, 1941), 30. Reprinted in *Cue*, XXI (Apr.
          12, 1941), 30-31.

          Includes positive review.

IIID14.   Field, Rowland. "Broadway; Hellman Play Stirring
          Rebuke to Nazism," Newark *Evening News*, Apr. 2, 1941,
          p. 14.

          Argues that the strength of LH's "stirring stage
          story is in its restrained but thorough indictment
          of undercover methods."

IIID15.   Freedley, George. "The Stage Today; Miss Hellman's
          'Watch on the Rhine' a Timely Drama at the Martin
          Beck," New York *Morning Telegraph*, Apr. 3, 1941, p. 2.

          Maintains that the play is "unbearably moving for the
          half hour ... which climaxes the last act, but Miss
          Hellman has cluttered her play with sub-plots and
          extraneous action to such an extent [as] to obscure
          what might have been her best play."

IIID16.   Gibbs, Wolcott. "The Theatre; This is It," *New
          Yorker*, XVII (Apr. 12, 1941), 32.

          Reports that *WR* is "the best serious play of the year,
          and perhaps of several years."

IIID17.    Gilder, Rosamond.  "Prizes That Bloom in the Spring;
           The Broadway Season in Review;  *Watch on the Rhine*,"
           *Theatre Arts*, XXV (June 1941), 409-411.  Reprinted in
           "War Plays; 'There Shall Be No Night'; 'Watch on
           the Rhine.'"  *Theatre Arts Anthology:  A Record and
           a Prophecy.*  Edited by Rosamond Gilder, Hermione
           Rich Isaacs, Robert M. MacGregor, and Edward Reed.
           New York:  Theatre Arts Books, 1950, pp. 649-651.

           Notes in a summary review that *WR* is "more faulty in
           structure" than LH's previous efforts.

IIID18.    Kronenberger, Louis.  "*Watch on the Rhine*--The Best
           Play of the Season;  A Melodrama of Anti-Nazism,"
           *PM* (New York), Apr. 2, 1941, p. 23.

IIID19.    ————.  "A Melodrama of Anti-Nazism," *PM* (New York),
           Apr. 13, 1941, p. 42.

           Maintains that *WR* is a "remarkable play."  LH has
           given us a meaningful melodrama.

IIID20.    Krutch, Joseph Wood.  "Drama;  No Such Animal," *The
           Nation*, CLII (Apr. 12, 1941), 453.

           Proclaims LH to be "a playwright of unusual resource
           and skill.  The present work is being widely hailed
           as the best anti-Nazi drama, and there is, at least,
           no doubt that it is vastly superior to most."

IIID21.    Lockridge, Richard.  "The New Play;  Lillian Hellman's
           *Watch on the Rhine* Opens at the Martin Beck," New
           York *Sun*, Apr. 2, 1941, p. 20.

           Suggests there is little in the play's beginning to
           suggest that it will ultimately be successful.  LH
           ends the play writing with "burning intensity and
           great compassion."

IIID22.    ————.  "The Stage in Review;  Miss Hellman Hews the
           People, and Lets Abstractions Fall Where They Will,"
           New York *Sun*, Apr. 12, 1941, p. 26.

           Maintains that *WR* "is better organized than either of
           its compelling predecessors, but it shows Miss Hellman
           is still struggling with her problems."

IIID23.    Mantle, Burns.  "*Watch on the Rhine* Stirring Drama
           of a Family of Refugees," New York *Daily News*, Apr.
           2, 1941, p. 59.

Points out that LH has shown us "noble passion, noble conviction in motive, and determination to keep characterization human."

IIID24.    ———. "The Gestapo Tangles With the Drama," New York *Sunday News*, Apr. 13, 1941, p. 70.

Argues that *WR* is a serious Critics' Circle Award contender because it has "warmth and sympathy" which LH's other plays lack.

IIID25.    "Message Without Hysteria; *Watch on the Rhine* Presents Subtle Indictment of Nazis," *Newsweek*, XVII (Apr. 14, 1941), 70.

Welcomes *WR* "to a season that hasn't been distinguished for its dramatic offerings. As propaganda ... the production is eloquent; as drama it lacks craftsmanship and definition of characters...."

IIID26.    "New Broadway Hit; 'Watch on the Rhine,' Brings Nazi Danger Close to Home," *Life*, X (Apr. 14, 1941), 81-84.

Claims that in *WR*, LH "shows less of her usual sting, her tight craftsmanship. Her first act dawdles, some of her characters are routine." However, *WR* "stacks up as a superior play because it states the current crisis in simple, human terms."

IIID27.    "New Play in Manhattan; *Watch on the Rhine*," *Time*, XXXVII (Apr. 14, 1941), 64.

Reports LH "has written an uneven play about Nazism, but it is by far the best thing on the subject to date."

IIID28.    Vernon, Grenville. "The Stage and Screen; *Watch on the Rhine*," *Commonweal*, XXXI (Apr. 25, 1941), 15-16.

Maintains *WR* is "poorly constructed" with "strained and unreal" dialogue. "Moreover many of the characters seemed equally unreal, and the author's knowledge of how American people of tradition act and speak seemed, to say the least, peculiar."

IIID29.    Warner, Ralph. "*Watch on the Rhine*; Poignant Drama of Anti-Fascist Struggle," *Daily Worker* (New York), Apr. 4, 1941, p. 7.

Reports the play has "carefully created and believable characters, a plot which is interwoven to form a

recognizable reproduction of life ... deftness of
line ... swiftness of scene...."

IIID30.    ————. "Audiences Want Plays That Point the Way
Out," *Sunday Worker* (New York), Apr. 20, 1941, p. 7.

Claims LH's *WR* is confusing because it does not
clearly define the "Communist Party as the hope for
world peace."

IIID31.    "*Watch on the Rhine*, Lillian Hellman's New Play,
Opens at the Martin Beck Theatre--Excellent Cast
Headed by Lucille Watson, Paul Lukas, Mady Christians,
and George Coulouris," Brooklyn *Citizen*, Apr. 2,
1941, p. 19.

Includes a positive review.

IIID32.    Watts, Richard, Jr. "The Theater; Portraits of a
German," New York *Herald Tribune*, Apr. 2, 1941, p.
20.

Evaluates *WR* as a "moving and beautiful play, filled
with eloquence and heroic spirit."

IIID33.    ————. "The Theater;  A New Heroic Drama," New
York *Herald Tribune*, Apr. 13, 1941, Sect. 6, p. 1.

Argues that LH has developed the characters in *WR* to
a "depth which is generally only found in novels."
The slow pace of plot development allows this rapid
character development to occur.

IIID34.    Whipple, Sidney B. "Theater; *Watch on the Rhine*
Avoids the Soap Box," New York *World-Telegram*, Apr.
2, 1941, p. 30.

Concludes that *WR* is a "sturdy and moving discussion
of the conflict between totalitarian and democratic
ideals ... a play and not a soap box."

IIID35.    ————. "Hellman Play Gains Power," New York *World-
Telegram*, May 12, 1941, p. 9.

Reports that "rigorous cutting" of the last act has
intensified the effect of the entire play.

IIID36.    Wright, Basil. "The Theatre; *Watch on the Rhine*,"
*The Spectator*, CLXVIII (May 1, 1942), 419.

Proclaims that LH "has made of it [*WR*] the richest and
most moving play we have seen since *Thunder Rock*."

IIID37.   Wyatt, Euphemia van Rensselaer.  "The Drama; *Watch on the Rhine*," *Catholic World*, CLIII (May 1941), 215-216.

Suggests that LH has "reversed the order of procedure and instead of taking for her theme the Nazi's wickedness, she has written a study of a liberal German. *Watch on the Rhine* is designed to remind us not only of our own blessings but of the proximity of menace to them."

IIID38.   Young, Stark.  "*Watch on the Rhine*," *New Republic*, CIV (Apr. 14, 1941), 498-499.

Reports that WR "binds the attention of the audience to the stage, and very often binds it tight.  A great deal of that is due to the expert stage craft of the melodrama itself.  But a great deal, also, comes from the author's remarkable gift for character."

*London Production*
*Aldwych Theatre*
*1942*

IIID39.   Darlington, W.A.  "*Watch on the Rhine*;  Miss Hellman's Play Provides London with Another Smash Hit," New York *Times*, May 3, 1942, Sect. 8, pp. 1-2.

IIID40.   Martin, Kingsley.  "A Fine Play; *Watch on the Rhine* at the Aldwych," *New Statesman and Nation*, XXIII (May 2, 1942), 288.

Calls WR a "harrowing, truthful, and satisfying play."

IIIE.   Reviews of *The Searching Wind*

*Baltimore Opening*
*Ford's Theatre*
*Apr. 3, 1944*

IIIE1.    Kanour, Gilbert.  "For Theater Goers," Baltimore *Evening Sun*, Apr. 4, 1944, p. 14.

Proclaims that the play is melodramatic and that its political conclusions are not clear.

IIIE2.   Kirkley, Donald.  "'Searching Wind,'" Baltimore *Sun*,
         Apr. 4, 1944, p. 12.

         Criticizes the lack of clarity at the end of the play.
         Notes that the political conflict seems to be unre-
         solved.

                              *Broadway Opening*
                               *Fulton Theatre*
                               *Apr. 12, 1944*
                               *77 Performances*

IIIE3.   Allen, Kelcey.  "*The Searching Wind*," *Women's Wear
         Daily*, Apr. 13, 1944, p. 28.

         Notes that the LH–Shumlin combination has "again hit
         the bull's eye with a new play." It "includes effec-
         tive dialogue written with rare control of the lan-
         guage."

IIIE4.   Barnes, Howard.  "Perception and Poetry," New York
         *Herald Tribune*, Apr. 13, 1944, p. 16.

         Points out that LH "has brought back a full measure
         of dignity, perception and beauty to the theatre."

IIIE5.   ————.  "The Theater;  Eloquence, Art in 'The Search-
         ing Wind,'" New York *Herald Tribune*, Apr. 23, 1944,
         Sect. 4, p. 1.

         Concludes that in *SW* LH "is writing with passionate
         intensity and the production has been armed with fine
         acting and sensitive staging."

IIIE6.   Chapman, John.  "'The Searching Wind' a Forceful Drama
         About World Appeasers," New York *Daily News*, Apr. 13,
         1944, p. 35.

         Suggests that *SW* is a "strong and measured indictment
         of appeasers who eventually caused WW II." It is
         "grimly and forcefully written ... eloquently and
         sincerely played...."

IIIE7.   ————.  "A Drama Finally Appears;  'The Searching
         Wind' Is Not the Best Hellman, But Better Than Any-
         thing Else," New York *Daily News*, Apr. 24, 1944, p. 62.

         Discusses the fact that *SW* is not the best by LH
         "because it lacks excitement; but it is better than

any of the other few plays about the wartime world
which have come our way this season."

IIIE8.    Field, Rowland. "New Hellman Play Richly Satisfying,"
          Newark *Evening News*, Apr. 13, 1944, p. 14.

          Claims that *SW* is a "provocative achievement" filled
          with "stunning craftsmanship."

IIIE9.    Freedley, George. "The Stage Today; Lillian Hellman'
          New Play Gives Season Stature, Rates with Best," New
          York *Morning Telegraph*, Apr. 14, 1944, p. 2.

IIIE10.   Garland, Robert. "*Searching Wind* on the Fulton Stage,
          New York *Journal American*, Apr. 13, 1944, p. 10.

          *SW* is "vivid, vital, world-minded drama."

IIIE11.   Gibbs, Wolcott. "The Theatre; 'Miss Hellman Nods,'"
          *New Yorker*, XX (Apr. 22, 1944), 42-44.

          Criticizes *SW* for being "loose as a haystack.... It
          is a play alternating or combining, or perhaps just
          mixing up, love and politics, but I am far from sure
          that Miss Hellman has anything especially new or
          valuable to say about either one."

IIIE12.   Gilder, Rosamond. "Search for a Play; The Sum of
          the Season; *The Searching Wind*," *Theatre Arts*,
          XXVIII (June 1944), 331-333.

          Explains that LH's *WR*, a successful war play, aroused
          hopes for her new play, *SW*. Unfortunately, *SW* "did
          not fulfill them."

IIIE13.   "Hellman's Blue Ribbon," *Newsweek*, XXIII (Apr. 24,
          1944), 86, 88.

          Notes that with *SW* the Broadway season finally
          "achieved distinction. The author has something
          pointedly significant to say and a way of saying it
          that is given to very few of this country's play-
          wrights."

IIIE14.   Ibee. "Plays on Broadway; *The Searching Wind*,"
          *Variety*, Apr. 19, 1944, p. 46.

          Calls *SW* "the outstanding drama of the season."

IIIE15.   "It's a New Hit Because...," *Vogue*, CIII (June 1944),
          110.

Briefly reports that *SW* has a confusing theme but
predicts that it will be a "hit."

IIIE16.   Kronenberger, Louis.  "A Drama with Teeth to It,"
          *PM* (New York), Apr. 13, 1944, p. 20.

          Praises LH for her expository skill in depicting
          history;  however, notes that the love triangle in
          the play is not well balanced.  The political plot
          and the personal plot never merge into a unified play.

IIIE17.   Marshall, Margaret.  "Drama," *The Nation*, CLVIII
          (Apr. 22, 1944), 494-495.

          Claims that in *SW*, LH "plunges into a discussion of
          what are known as vital issues.  She is an experienced
          craftsman, and there is some deft writing....  But
          the play fails for lack of clarity of thought and
          feeling essential to both art and political analysis."

IIIE18.   Morehouse, Ward.  "The New Play -- Lillian Hellman's
          Play, 'The Searching Wind,' Eloquent and Powerful,"
          New York *Sun*, Apr. 13, 1944, p. 17.

          Argues that LH "writes with discernment and consider-
          able bitterness of a generation that saw and sensed
          the rise of Fascism and stood by and let it happen."

IIIE19.   Nathan, George Jean.  "George Jean Nathan's Theatre
          Week; What a Year (in Plays) for Female Buzzards,"
          New York *Journal American*, Apr. 24, 1944, p. 13.

          Points out that *SW* is not as good as LH's usual work,
          but it is better than most of the plays of the year
          written by other playwrights with established repu-
          tations.

IIIE20.   "New Plays in Manhattan;  *The Searching Wind*," *Time*,
          XLIII (Apr. 24, 1944), 72.

          Praises *SW* for "its genuine bite;  its worst weakness
          [is] that it bites off more than it can chew.  It is
          more like two plays--and two very unequal ones."

IIIE21.   Nichols, Lewis.  "The Play;  *The Searching Wind*,"
          New York *Times*, Apr. 13, 1944, p. 25.

          Suggests that LH "is exploring the current state of
          the world and the causes which brought about its
          miserable condition....  She is not preaching a ser-
          mon but writing a play for the theatre, and it is a
          good one...."

IIIE22.  ————.  "'The Searching Wind'; Lillian Hellman's
         Latest Play a Study of Appeasement and Love," New
         York *Times*, Apr. 23, 1944, Sect. 2, p. 1.

         Reports that LH "is offering a play which is a good
         one on its own merits and one which because of the
         way it is performed gives Broadway an evening out of
         its top drawer." It is clearly, however, "not
         Hellman's best."

IIIE23.  Norton, Elliot.  "'Searching Wind' New Hellman Play
         is Disappointing," Boston *Post*, May 21, 1944, Sect.
         A, p. 7.

IIIE24.  Phelan, Kappo.  "The Stage and Screen; *The Searching
         Wind*," *Commonweal*, XL (Apr. 28, 1944), 40.

         Discusses melodramatic elements in *SW*. "Employing
         the dangerous device of surpise, the author deliber-
         ately allows the relationship between the two women
         to atomize increasingly during the period involved,
         deliberately equivocates their separate dramatic
         identities as heroine and villainess and then quite
         suddenly, at the last gasp, allows one to admit to
         the basest motives for reasons which are small,
         startling, unclear, and unproved."

IIIE25.  Pollock, Arthur.  "'The Searching Wind,' Season's
         Best Play by Country's Best Dramatist," Brooklyn
         *Daily Eagle*, Apr. 16, 1944, p. 25.

         Proclaims that the play is "tense and stirring."
         Calls it the best play of the season.

IIIE26.  Price, Edgar.  "Lillian Hellman's *The Searching Wind*,
         One of the Outstanding Plays of the Season Opens at
         the Fulton — Excellent Cast Headed by Cornelia Otis
         Skinner, Dennis King and Dudley Digges," Brooklyn
         *Citizen*, Apr. 13, 1944, p. 18.

IIIE27.  Rascoe, Burton.  "Theater; *The Searching Wind* by
         Miss Hellman, One of the Finest Dramas in Many Years,"
         New York *World-Telegram*, Apr. 13, 1944, p. 14.

         Claims that *SW* is a "beautiful, powerful, and touching
         drama."

IIIE28.  ————.  "New Hellman Drama More Than Triangle," New
         York *World-Telegram*, Apr. 15, 1944, p. 6.

         Argues that most critics have not understood that the
         love triangle in *SW* is a "profound study of feminine
         psychology."

IIIE29.  Sherborne, E.C.  *"The Searching Wind*," *Christian Science Monitor*, Apr. 13, 1944, p. 6.

Notes that *SW* is "stimulating in a season that has few new serious plays."

IIIE30.  Sokosky, George E.  "These Days;  The Battle of the Generations," New York *Sun*, Apr. 15, 1944, p. 9.

Maintains that *SW* "tries to say something about the conflict of the generations over the circumstances leading to war and the consequence of war but becomes so entangled in a Freudian triangle ... that what I saw ... seemed to be a dramatized ... debate."

IIIE31.  *"The Searching Wind*," *Life*, XVI (May 1, 1944), 43-48.

Calls *SW* "an unflinching indictment of appeasers whose do-nothing diplomacy helped bring on Munich and World War II.  Because the play utters profound and disturbing truth it belongs with Miss Hellman's most consequential work."

IIIE32.  Waldorf, Wilella.  "Two on the Aisle -- 'The Searching Wind' a Mild Blast at Compromise and Appeasers," New York *Post*, Apr. 13, 1944, p. 22.

Criticizes *SW* for being a "pretentious, well-meaning drama that always seems on the verge of saying something, but never does."

IIIE33.  Winchell, Walter.  "'The Searching Wind' Is New Lillian Hellman Hit," New York *Daily Mirror*, Apr. 13, 1944, p. 10.

Includes favorable review.

IIIE34.  Wyatt, Euphemia van Rensselaer.  "The Drama;  *The Searching Wind*," *Catholic World*, CLXIX (May 1944), 170-171.

Praises LH's *SW* for "drawing no conclusions.  She holds up the frame;  it is for us to judge if it holds a mirror.  The characters, all of them down to the waiters, are drawn to perfect scale."

IIIE35.  Young, Stark.  "Beyond the Beyond," *New Republic*, CX (May 1, 1944), 604.

Asserts that *SW*'s historical scenes are well written. "They hold our attention, however, not through any

historical distinction or vision, but through their
topicality."

IIIE36.   Zunser, Jesse.  "The World's Conscience," *Cue*, XXIV
          (Apr. 22, 1944), 11-12.

          Discusses the political ramifications of *SW*.  The
          rise of fascism in Europe and American neutrality are
          considered as they relate to the play.


          IIIF.  Reviews of *Another Part of the Forest*


                    *Baltimore Opening*
                    *Maryland Theatre*
                    *Nov. 4, 1946*

IIIF1.    Kirkley, Donald.  "New Play at the Maryland," Balti-
          more *Sun*, Nov. 5, 1946, p. 14.

          Hails *APF* as LH's "finest play."  It has been given
          a "letter perfect, polished performance."


                    *Broadway Opening*
                    *Fulton Theatre*
                    *Nov. 20, 1946*
                    *182 Performances*

IIIF2.    "*Another Part of the Forest*," *Life*, XXI (Dec. 9,
          1946), 71-74.

          Praises *APF* by calling it a play that is "sometimes
          melodramatic but always convincing and entertaining.
          The acting of all the cast and directing, which was
          done by playwright Hellman herself, is as good as
          has been on Broadway for years."

IIIF3.    Atkinson, Brooks.  "The Play in Review," New York
          *Times*, Nov. 21, 1946, p. 42.

          Maintains LH's "fury makes her play as a whole look
          like the deluxe edition of a dime novel, she can
          [nonetheless] write individual scenes of great theatri
          cal intensity."

IIIF4.    ————. "Eating the Earth;  Lillian Hellman Tracks
          Down More 'Foxes,'" New York *Times*, Dec. 1, 1946,
          Sect. 2, p. 1.

          Argues that "by piling one lurid situation on another"
          LH has turned *APF* "into a lurid show."

IIIF5.    Barnes, Howard. "The Theaters;  At Home with the
          Foxes," New York *Herald Tribune*, Nov. 21, 1946, p.
          25.

          Suggests that in *APF* "honest appraisal of human be-
          havior has been traded for somewhat lurid melodrama."
          LH's "new play is disappointing."

IIIF6.    ————. "The Predatory Hubbards of Miss Hellman's
          Play," New York *Herald Tribune*, Dec. 1, 1946, Sect.
          6, pp. 1, 3.

          Reassesses *APF* claiming that it "is written with ruth-
          less insight into human weaknesses;  enacted with
          savage excitement.  In all justice to a very fine
          dramatist, her present work stands on its own.  It
          has an absorbing rhythm and entity."

IIIF7.    Beyer, William. "Reports;  The State of the Theatre:
          Midseason Highlights," *School and Society*, LXV (Apr.
          5, 1947), 251.

          Maintains that "it is regrettable that in writing *The
          Little Foxes*, the playwright did not let well enough
          alone."

IIIF8.    "Big Week in Manhattan; *Another Part of the Forest*,"
          *Time*, XLVIII (Dec. 2, 1946), 56.

          Claims that *APF* has "vivid characters" and a "caustic
          angry tone."  Though it is powerful, it is "not quite
          large size drama."

IIIF9.    Brown, John Mason. "And Cauldron Bubble," *Saturday
          Review*, XXIX (Dec. 14, 1946), 20-23.

          Reports that LH's "script deals with too special a
          case for its own dramatic well-being.  What it gains
          in immediate thrills, it loses in abiding validity.
          It is so overfilled with climaxes and confrontations
          that it has little relationship to life.  But it is
          uncommonly effective theatre...."

IIIF10.    Chapman, John.  "*Another Part of the Forest* Makes
           *The Little Foxes* a Mere Warmup," New York *Daily News*,
           Nov. 21, 1946, p. 67.

           Claims that *APF* gives us "a good stiff dose of pure
           hellishness.... It will release all those emotions
           pent within you and you won't go around picking so
           many fights."

IIIF11.    ———.  "The Family Tree in the Hellman Forest Gets
           a Bit Twisted," New York *Daily News*, Nov. 26, 1946,
           p. 53.

           Calls *APF* "the most exciting piece of dramatic pulp
           fiction on Broadway."  It is "a bang-up, well-directed
           well-acted melodrama...."

IIIF12.    Coleman, Robert.  "New Hellman Play Magnetic Hit,"
           New York *Daily Mirror*, Nov. 22, 1946, p. 24.

           Predicts that *APF* will be a "sensational hit.  It
           grips your interest like a vise at the start and
           never relaxes its hold the entire three acts."

IIIF13.    "Foxes in the Forest," *Newsweek*, XXVIII (Dec. 2,
           1946), 94.

           Suggests that *APF* is likely to be LH's "best play to
           date."

IIIF14.    Freedley, George.  "The Stage Today; *Another Part of
           the Forest* Fine Melodrama;  Has Excellent Acting,"
           New York *Morning Telegraph*, Nov. 22, 1946, p. 2.

           Notes that "the first night audience was carried
           away by the electric quality of the play."

IIIF15.    Garland, Robert.  "At Fulton -- *Another Part of the
           Forest*," New York *Journal American*, Nov. 21, 1946, p. 1

           Includes a positive review noting that *APF* is "tops
           in town."

IIIF16.    Gilder, Rosamond.  "New Year, New Plays; *Another
           Part of the Forest*," *Theatre Arts*, XXXVI (Jan. 1947),
           17-18.

           Claims that the play "raises the audience's blood
           pressure" but ultimately fails in the last scene as
           the "verbal struggle between father and son" is too
           long.

IIIF17.   Gibbs, Wolcott. "The Theatre; Ladies Day," *New Yorker*, XXII (Nov. 30, 1946), 58-60.

Suggests that LH "has ornamented this material with secret documents ... comic retainers ..., and a musical accompaniment of sorts. I can only say that it seems too bad to me that she has neglected to write a play." The "tightness, intensity," and "impeccable construction" are missing from the play.

IIIF18.   Hawkins, William. "*The Forest*, a Modern Theater Classic," New York *World-Telegram*, Nov. 21, 1946, p. 10.

Labels *APF* "one more classic of the modern theatre."

IIIF19.   Ibee. "Plays on Broadway; *Another Part of the Forest*," *Variety*, Nov. 27, 1946, p. 60.

Reports *APF* is the "dour drama it was cracked up to be, but it is splendidly acted and produced."

IIIF20.   Kronenberger, Louis. "Lillian Hellman Writes Another Compelling Drama," *PM* (New York), Nov. 22, 1946, p. 17.

Notes *APF*'s "tension and striking power ... monstrous force of villainy redoubled."

IIIF21.   Krutch, Joseph Wood. "Drama," *The Nation*, CLXIII (Dec. 7, 1946), 671.

Summarizes *APF* as "the story of four scoundrels, two half wits, one insane woman, and a whore...." LH's "ability to imagine dirty tricks and nasty speeches is unrivaled in the contemporary theatre...."

IIIF22.   Morehouse, Ward. "The New Play; Hellman's *Another Part of the Forest* Is a Fascinating and Powerful Drama," New York *Sun*, Nov. 21, 1946, p. 20.

IIIF23.   Nathan, George Jean. "False Alarm Clocks Also Start Ringing," New York *Journal American*, Dec. 2, 1946, p. 14.

Claims that *APF* is a "play which is overwrought by melodrama."

IIIF24.   Phelan, Kappo. "The Stage and Screen," *Commonweal*, XLV (Dec. 6, 1946), 201-202.

Maintains that *APF* "makes for a good evening, but I
think that is all. Miss Hellman does not appear to
be interested in the root or cause of her family's
evil, but rather in particularizing, or melodramatiz-
ing, them and their action. And I think this is
Americanly wrong."

IIIF25.  Watts, Richard, Jr. "Two on the Aisle; Lillian
         Hellman's New Play is Fascinating Drama," New York
         *Post*, Nov. 21, 1946, p. 40.

         Enthusiastically claims LH "has written her most
         fascinating play." It "surpasses [her previous
         dramas] with its sheer overwhelming intensity."

IIIF26.  ————. "Two on the Aisle; What if Miss Hellman's
         Play is Filled with Melodrama," New York *Post*, Nov.
         30, 1946, p. 12.

         Asserts that despite being melodramatic, *APF* is "one
         of the most fascinating works of modern theatre."

IIIF27.  Wyatt, Euphemia van Rensselaer. "The Drama; *Another
         Part of the Forest*," *Catholic World*, CLXIV (Jan.
         1947), 360-361.

         Summarizes *APF* noting that "despite the title, Miss
         Hellman's *Little Foxes* are in the same vineyards but
         the time is 1880 and they are young but maturing
         rapidly in the evil radiated by Mr. Hubbard, Senior,
         the prime sinner in this melodramatic study of
         villainy."

IIIF28.  Young, Stark. "Theatre; Ambitious Plays," *New
         Republic*, CXV (Dec. 16, 1946), 822.

         Points out that "the general fault and failure of the
         play is that all the raging violence and blast and
         lurid vehemence does not proceed sufficiently from
         within the characters. More and more Miss Hellman
         piles things on from the outside, heaps it up into
         rank melodrama, and with an innate lack of essential
         dignity and thrust."

*London Production*
*Liverpool Playhouse*
*1953*

IIIF29.   "The Arts;  The Liverpool Playhouse;  *Another Part*
          *of the Forest* by Lillian Hellman," London *Times*,
          Sept. 4, 1953, p. 10.

          Concludes that *APF* is "a melodrama which runs an in-
          geniously contrived course ... skirting the edge of
          absurdity...."

*New York Production*
*1956*

IIIF30.   Geor.  "*Another Part of the Forest*," *Variety*, Nov.
          28, 1956, p. 58.

          Claims that "due to faulty casting and leisured direc-
          tion the present revival seldom realizes the pungency
          of the drama."

IIIG.   Reviews of *Montserrat*

*Pre-Broadway Opening*
*Philadelphia*
*Playhouse Theatre*
*Oct. 13, 1949*

IIIG1.   Martin, Linton.  "Historical Drama;  Comedy Poles
         Apart in Playhouse," Philadelphia *Inquirer*, Oct. 16,
         1949, p. 20.

         Praises the adaptation noting, however, that the sub-
         ject may limit audience appeal.

IIIG2.   Murdock, Henry T.  "'Montserrat' Opens as a Tense
         Drama," Philadelphia *Inquirer*, Oct. 14, 1959, p. 58.

         Reports the play to be a "tense, moving, and literate
         drama."

IIIG3.   Sensenderfer, R.E.P.  "Living Theatre;  'Montserrat,'"
         Philadelphia *Bulletin*, Oct. 14, 1949, p. 44.

         Maintains that "technically the play ... is magnificent."
         LH has provided us with "her own terse dialogue" and

combining it with her characters has "woven them into
a tour de force of dramatic suspense."

IIIG4.    Waters.  "Play Out of Town," *Variety*, Oct. 18, 1949,
          p. 60.

          Predicts that *Montserrat* will not be a commercial suc-
          cess on Broadway because it "lacks what it takes."


                        *Broadway Opening*
                         *Fulton Theatre*
                          *Oct. 29, 1949*
                         *63 Performances*

IIIG5.    Atkinson, Brooks.  "First Night at the Theatre;
          *Montserrat* Adapted from the French of Emmanuel Robles
          by Lillian Hellman," New York *Times*, Oct. 31, 1949,
          p. 21.

          Claims that the play should be "devastating but the
          effects it achieves are mechanical."  LH's direction
          is on the "monotonous side."

IIIG6.    Barnes, Howard.  "The Theaters; Brilliant Adaptation,"
          New York *Herald Tribune*, Oct. 31, 1949, p. 10.

          Lauds LH for having "written a brilliant adaptation of
          a French drama which tries to decode the imponderables
          of the present day in terms of an 1812 revolution."

IIIG7.    Beyer, William.  "Reports;  The State of the Theatre;
          The Strindberg Heritage," *School and Society*, LXXXI
          (Jan. 14, 1950), 25-26.

          Suggests that *Montserrat* was "difficult to stage," and
          LH "was not very helpful to her actors who, aside from
          [Emlyn] Williams, consequently only gave adequate per-
          formances."

IIIG8.    Beaufort, John.  "Three New Plays on Broadway,"
          *Christian Science Monitor*, Nov. 5, 1949, p. 4.

          Criticizes LH's direction of *Montserrat* as being
          "stilted," thus making the play "ineffective."

IIIG9.    Bolton, Whitney.  "*Montserrat*, Not Quite Perfect," New
          York *Morning Telegraph*, Nov. 1, 1949, p. 2.

          Suspects that LH "has such love for her play that she
          wished to cut away all that interfered with it, such
          as movement, deep exploration of character through the
          medium of direction and, possibly, even setting."

IIIG10.  Brown, John Mason.  "With and Without Music," *Saturday Review*, XXXII (Nov. 19, 1949), 53-55.

Disparagingly reports that "instead of being suspensive, *Montserrat* ... is so repetitious and static that one can hardly wait to have its victims shot."

IIIG11.  Chapman, John.  "*Lost in Stars* Is a Work of Art; *Montserrat* a Brutal Melodrama," New York *Daily News*, Oct. 31, 1949, p. 34.

Calls LH "the most uncompromising and hardest-headed of women dramatists."  The play is "brutal and rebellious."

IIIG12.  Clurman, Harold.  "Theatre;  Robles, Hellman, Blitzstein," *New Republic*, CXXI (Dec. 5, 1949), 21-22.

Proclaims that "the original text required the completion of fully rounded acting and staging.  But Miss Hellman has become the victim of the heresy which maintains that words intelligibly conveyed are all that the stage demands.  Thus, she has not only added unnecessary words, but miscast her play ... and her direction makes neither shape, sense nor good red excitement."

IIIG13.  Coleman, Robert.  "*Montserrat*, Well Acted But Script is Bumpy," New York *Daily Mirror*, Oct. 31, 1949, p. 27.

Criticizes the play for being "uneven and insufficiently motivated.  Between its dramatic peaks lie valleys of stereotyped verbosity."

IIIG14.  Currie, George.  "Theatre;  *Montserrat* at Fulton Theater," Brooklyn *Daily Eagle*, Oct. 31, 1949, p. 8.

Speculates that the play "may have lost something in the translation," for it is an "overworked possibility."

IIIG15.  Dash, Thomas R.  "*Montserrat*;  Fulton Theatre," *Women's Wear Daily*, Oct. 13, 1949, p. 53.

Maintains that *Montserrat* is "a real soul-searching adaptation ... packed with trenchant and remorseless power ... penetration of writing...."

IIIG16.  Field, Rowland.  "'Montserrat,' Grim Tragedy," Newark *Evening News*, Oct. 31, 1949, p. 17.

Calls the play "a tense experience phrased with eloquent social significance." The action, however,
drags and is repetitious.

IIIG17.  Garland, Robert. *"Montserrat* and *Lost in the Stars*:
The 1st is Grim, and 2nd Ornate," New York *Journal
American*, Oct. 31, 1949, p. 8.

A positive review.

IIIG18.  Gassner, John. "The Theatre Arts," *Forum*, CXII (Dec.
1949), 338-339.

Suggests that "the play itself falls short of the
potentialities of the story because it is so largely
taken up with a sequence of scenes in which each of
the hostages goes through an agony of his own....
The effect is too repetitive."

IIIG19.  Gibbs, Wolcott. "The Theatre;  The End and the
Means," *New Yorker*, XXV (Nov. 5, 1949), 62.

Suggests that LH's "adaptation ... is an interminable
repetitive, and I'm afraid, an occasionally eloquent
debate...."

IIIG20.  Hawkins, William. "Theatre; *Lost in the Stars* Has
Zulu Theme; *Montserrat* Hits Like Quake;  Hideous
Tension in Hellman Play," New York *World-Telegram*,
Oct. 31, 1949, p. 10.

Labels *Montserrat* "a theatrical experience not easy
to forget ... a shattering, emotional drama...."

IIIG21.  Hobe. "Plays on Broadway; *Montserrat*," *Variety*,
Nov. 2, 1949, p. 60.

Criticizes the play's "lack of movement" noting that
it "appears to be aggravated by Miss Hellman's rigid,
unimaginative staging."

IIIG22.  Marshall, Margaret. "Drama," *The Nation*, CLXIX (Nov.
12, 1949), 478.

Claims that although "'Montserrat' is contrived as
well as dated, the adaptation shows the hand of an
experienced and skillful worker in the theatre...."

IIIG23.  Morehouse, Ward. "The New Play; *Montserrat*," New
York *Sun*, Oct. 31, 1949, p. 10.

Suggests the drama is "well played by an excellent
cast but it is not a drama of sustained impact ...
disappointing."

IIIG24.   Nathan, George Jean.  "Still Another Stage Battling
for Freedom," New York *Journal American*, Nov. 7,
1949, p. 24.  Reprinted in *The Theatre Book of the
Year 1949-50*.  New York:  Alfred A. Knopf, 1950,
pp. 63-71.

Analyzes the theme of *Montserrat* noting that it is
"altogether too familiar to stimulate the curiosity
of audiences."

IIIG25.   "New Play in Manhattan, *Montserrat*," *Time*, LIV (Nov.
7, 1949), 79-80.

Criticizes the play's lack of "simple intensity ...
it shares its villain's love of tricks, and is too
full of jagged effects to provide a sustained emotion."

IIIG26.   "New Plays; *Montserrat*," *Newsweek*, XXXIV (Nov. 7,
1949), 80-81.

Claims that "even the adaptation of a drama, coming
as this one does from the typewriter of one of America's most successful playwrights, would be an exciting event in any season.  Unfortunately, *Montserrat*
falls considerably short of its promise, and its
faults appear to be inherent in the original."

IIIG27.   Phelan, Kappo.  "The Stage and Screen; *Montserrat*,"
*Commonweal*, LI (Nov. 18, 1949), 179-180.

Maintains that "the author is attempting to deal in
characters--that is, with people of more or less
moral dimension--and therefore he must present us
with a non-persuading hero.  *Montserrat* has nothing
to say.  Or, and this is even more unfortunate, he
has a little to say.  He has a kind of arpeggio of
anguish--gestures, moans, groans, mutterings, and
screams.  But this is *human* arpeggio, not a theater
one."

IIIG28.   Pollock, Arthur.  "Theatre Time; *Montserrat* is Thrilling, but Suffers in Casting," New York *Daily Compass*,
Oct. 31, 1949, p. 18.

Labels *Montserrat* "a thrilling play with little
speeches here and there that cut like knives and reach
the bone."

IIIG29.   Shipley, Joseph.  "On Stage," *New Leader*, XXXII
          (Nov. 26, 1949), 15.

          Suggests *Montserrat* "has a heavy beginning, and a
          sagging end."

IIIG30.   "The New Plays;  *Montserrat*," *Theatre Arts*, XXXIV
          (Jan. 1950), 10.

          Notes that "in the teeth of such unhappy casting and
          direction it is not easy to judge Miss Hellman's
          script."

IIIG31.   Watts, Richard, Jr.  "Weekend Brings in Two Tragic
          Dramas," New York *Post*, Oct. 31, 1949, *Home News*,
          p. 22.

          Argues that *Montserrat* has "striking philosophical
          interest, [yet] it is oddly less powerful in its emo-
          tional impact than its deeply tragic theme would have
          suggested and its strength is curiously hampered by
          monotony that has crept into it."

IIIG32.   ————.  "Two on the Aisle," New York *Post*, Nov. 6,
          1949, Magazine, p. 5.

          Suggests that although "'Montserrat' is to us a
          thoughtful and interesting play, it somehow lacks the
          stunning and emotional power it should have possessed."

IIIG33.   Wyatt, Euphemia van Rensselaer.  "Theatre;  *Montser-
          rat*," *Catholic World*, CLXX (Dec. 1949), 227-228.

          Proclaims that "the punishment of the audience seems
          the chief purpose of this two act horror drama by
          Emmanuel Robles.  The playwright's pleasure has evi-
          dently been to study six diverse reactions to sudden
          death.  This he has done with meticulous enjoyment
          but, strange to say, even with Lillian Hellman's
          collaboration on the English version, as a play,
          *Montserrat* has no structural strength."

                        *London Production*
                         *Lyric Theatre*
                             *1952*

IIIG34.   Darlington, W.A.  "London Letters;  Critics Divided
          on Play About Villain -- Guiness Hailed in Spewack
          Drama," New York *Times*, May 11, 1952, Sect. 2, p. 3.

          A negative review.

IIIG35. "The Lyric Theatre, Hammersmith, *Montserrat* by
Lillian Hellman, Based on the French of Emmanuel
Robles," London *Times*, Apr. 9, 1952, pp. 6, 10.

Proclaims that "there are plenty of theatrical shocks;
yet the means taken to produce them are so superfi-
cially dramatic that they tend with repetition to
lose force."

*New York Production*<br>
*Barbizon Plaza*<br>
*1954*

IIIG36. S[hanley], J[ohn] P. "Theatre; *Montserrat*: Lillian
Hellman Drama at Barbizon Plaza," New York *Times*,
May 26, 1954, p. 34.

Recalls that "on Broadway in 1949 the play failed,
despite a cast that included Emlyn Williams and
Julie Harris. The passage of time and the transfer
to a more intimate showcase have not improved *Montserrat*."

*New York Revival*<br>
*Gate Theatre*<br>
*1961*

IIIG37. Aston, Frank. "'Montserrat' Revived at Gate Theatre,"
New York *World-Telegram and Sun*, Jan. 9, 1961, p. 17.

Calls the play "a gripping tumble of furious emotions."

IIIG38. Balliett, Whitney. "Off Broadway; Martyrs and Mys-
tery," *New Yorker*, XXXVI (Jan. 21, 1961), 68-70.

Labels LH's play "one of those Gallic seminars in
which a moral question is talked to death, with occa-
sional time outs for illustrative but ineffectual
action."

IIIG39. Hammel, Faye. "'Montserrat,'" *Cue*, XLI (Jan. 21,
1962), 9.

Notes briefly that the revival is "first rate."

IIIG40. Herridge, Frances. "Vivid 'Montserrat' Revived at
Gate," New York *Post*, Jan. 9, 1961, p. 43.

Recalls that *Montserrat* "fared indifferently in
1949," but "it comes through as surprisingly vital
theatre" in this revival.

IIIG41.  Kali. "Off Broadway Reviews; *Montserrat*," *Variety*,
         Feb. 1, 1961, p. 74.

         Points out that the play was "never a commercial
         success, [but it] has provocative intellectual con-
         tent."

IIIG42.  Kupferberg, Herbert. "First Night Report; *Montser-
         rat*," New York *Herald Tribune*, Jan. 9, 1961, p. 12.

         Notes that *Montserrat* "provides an intense and almost
         agonizingly suspenseful experience."

IIIG43.  Lewis, Theophilus. "Theatre; *Montserrat*," *America*,
         CIV (Jan. 28, 1961), 577.

         Suggests that "the original French *Montserrat* is an
         historical drama with a religious slant. In Miss
         Hellman's translation it is essentially an intellec-
         tual horror play."

IIIG44.  McClain, John. "'Montserrat' Compels," New York *Jour-
         nal American*, Jan. 9, 1961, p. 17.

         Claims that the play is "compelling theatre, even
         though it seems the premise is beaten to death before
         the final curtain falls."

IIIG45.  R.I.A. "'Montserrat' Movingly Revived at Gate Thea-
         tre," *Women's Wear Daily*, Jan. 11, 1961, p. 110.

IIIG46.  Savino, Guy. "Fine Revival; 'Montserrat' Given
         Superb Treatment Off-Broadway," Newark *Evening News*,
         Jan. 9, 1961, p. 20.

IIIG47.  Tallmer, Jerry. "Theatre; 'Montserrat,'" *Village
         Voice*, Jan. 12, 1961, p. 9.

         Calls *Montserrat* "one of the two or three most power-
         ful and most uncompromising dramas that has been
         written in many recent years."

IIIG48.  Taubman, Howard. "Theatre; *Montserrat*; Lillian
         Hellman Play Revived at the Gate," New York *Times*,
         Jan. 9, 1961, p. 30.

Argues that "in its tight plotting and sharp thrust of characterization, *Montserrat* bears the stamp of Miss Hellman's craftsmanship ... deserves a rehearing."

IIIH. Reviews of *The Autumn Garden*

*Pre-Broadway Opening*
*Philadelphia*
*Feb. 24, 1951*

IIIH1. Martin, Linton. "Miss Hellman's New Drama Keen in Characterization," Philadelphia *Inquirer*, Feb. 25, 1951, Society, p. 25.

Maintains that LH "indisputably established herself as our American Ibsen among contemporary playwrights" with *AG*.

*Broadway Opening*
*Coronet Theatre*
*Mar. 7, 1951*
*101 Performances*

IIIH2. Atkinson, Brooks. "First Night at the Theatre; Lillian Hellman Dramatizes Middle-Aged People in the *Autumn Garden*," New York *Times*, Mar. 8, 1951, p. 36.

Suggests that *AG* "is a little platitudinous. Like the characters whom it admirably describes, it is boneless and torbid." (See Item IVF2.)

IIIH3. ————. "*Autumn Garden*--Lillian Hellman Puts the Emphasis on Characters in a Well-Acted Play," New York *Times*, Mar. 18, 1951, Sect. 2, p. 1.

Notes that *AG* is LH's "most discerning drama."

IIIH4. Beaufort, John. "*The Autumn Garden*," *Christian Science Monitor*, Mar. 17, 1951, p. 6.

Recalls that LH "frequently exercises her gift for pungent dialogue and sharp character observation. But motivations are obscure, certain scenes are clumsily written, and instead of solving stated issues the playwright manages to confuse them."

IIIH5.  Bolton, Whitney.  "Hellman's 'Autumn Garden' Fascina-
        ting, Brilliant Study," New York *Morning Telegraph*,
        Mar. 9, 1951, p. 2.

        Views *AG* as "one of the most fascinating and occasion-
        ally one of the most puzzling plays ... brilliantly
        written...."

IIIH6.  Brown, John Mason.  "A New Miss Hellman," *Saturday
        Review*, XXXIV (Mar. 31, 1951), 27-29.

        Praises LH for trying "a different form of playwriting.
        Although she may not as yet have completely mastered
        it ... she has gone a long way towards doing so.  The
        result is one of the season's most adult and rewarding
        plays."

IIIH7.  Chapman, John.  "Hellman's 'Autumn Garden' Meaty Comedy
        Played by Flawless Cast," New York *Daily News*, Mar.
        8, 1951, p. 75.

        Labels the play "an excellent piece by a resourceful
        dramatist ... a flawless and extraordinarily interest-
        ing cast.  The play is worth quite a lot."

IIIH8.  ————.  "Two Good New Comedies;  Miss Hellman's
        'Autumn Garden' is Seriously Funny;  Herbert's 'The
        Moon is Blue' is Frankly Giddy," New York *Daily News*,
        Mar. 18, 1951, Sect. 2, p. 3.

        Maintains that LH "writes trenchantly, and with all
        those people in it, her play is a full one.  You will
        not find a better play anywhere on Broadway."

IIIH9.  Clurman, Harold.  "Lillian Hellman's *Garden*," *New
        Republic*, CXXIV (Mar. 26, 1951), 21-22.  Reprinted in
        "Lillian Hellman, 1951."  *Lies Like Truth*.  New York:
        Macmillan Co., 1958, pp. 47-49.

        Claims that *AG* is "the most deftly constructed, the
        most maturely thought, the most scrupulously written
        play produced here in a long time...."

IIIH10. Coleman, Robert.  "The Theatre —— 'Autumn Garden'
        Harps on Depressing Theme," New York *Daily Mirror*,
        Mar. 8, 1951, p. 32.

        Criticizes LH for pulling "the strings a little too
        obviously and futilely.  Her people at times appear to
        be puppets....  We think Miss Hellman might do well to
        pay a visit to the new South, which boasts a good many
        happy, prosperous, and moral people."

IIIH11.  Dash, Thomas R.  "*The Autumn Garden*, Coronet Theatre,"
         *Women's Wear Daily*, Mar. 8, 1951, p. 40.

         Argues that "the philosophical discursive play" is
         not LH's "forte ... a rambling, discursive, and
         blurred work...."

IIIH12.  Field, Rowland.  "'Autumn Garden' -- New Hellman Drama,
         Study of Turmoil, Stars Frederic March and Wife!,"
         Newark *Evening News*, Mar. 8, 1951, p. 30.

         Notes that *AG* "finds a gifted author regrettably off
         form."

IIIH13.  Gassner, John.  "Entropy in the Drama," *Theatre Arts*,
         XXXV (Sept. 1951), 16-17, 73.

         Proclaims that LH "makes her point deftly and surely."

IIIH14.  Guernsey, Otis L., Jr.  "The Theatres; *The Autumn
         Garden*;  Some Leaves are Golden," New York *Herald
         Tribune*, Mar. 8, 1951, p. 18.

         Reports that "a distinguished cast creates a lot of
         good theater within a scattered script.... Her work
         is rounded, diffuse and sometimes almost shallow, but
         it provides a suitable gallery for a company of fine
         actors."

IIIH15.  Hawkins, William.  "'Autumn Garden' is Rich and
         Mellow," New York *World-Telegram and Sun*, Mar. 8,
         1951, p. 26.

         Suggests that *AG* is "a play of unusually rich texture
         ... complex themes woven into tapestry."

IIIH16.  Hobe.  "Play on Broadway;  *The Autumn Garden*," *Variety*,
         Mar. 14, 1951, p. 50.

         Notes that *AG* "is a quietly intense, consistently
         interesting drama that doesn't quite equal the sum of
         its considerable assets."

IIIH17.  Kerr, Walter.  "The Stage;  *Autumn Garden*," *Common-
         weal*, LIII (Apr. 6, 1951), 645.

         Reports that "the production is in every way first
         rate.  I don't think you will be altogether exhilarated
         by this play; but I think you will find it interest-
         ing."

IIIH18.   Lardner, John.  "The Theatre; The First Team Takes
          Over," *New Yorker*, XXVII (Mar. 17, 1951), 52-54.

          Argues that "the first two acts ... abound in seeming-
          ly unrelated problems and relationships.  At the end
          with two or three quick movements, Miss Hellman
          braids them all together.  She remains, in short, one
          of the most expert reporters and technicians in the
          theatre business."

IIIH19.   McClain, John.  "Play at Coronet Beautifully Set,"
          New York *Journal American*, Mar. 8, 1951, p. 16.

          Includes a favorable review.

IIIH20.   Marshall, Margaret.  "Drama," *The Nation*, CLXXII (Mar.
          17, 1951), 257.

          Maintains that "the main interest lies in the charac-
          terizations and the probing of relationships, and
          here, Miss Hellman's shrewdness, competence, and
          ruthless humor stand her in good stead."

IIIH21.   Nathan, George Jean.  "Miss Hellman Buries the
          Middle-Aged," New York *Journal American*, Mar. 19,
          1951, p. 14.  Reprinted in *Theatre Book of the Year,
          1950-51*.  New York:  Alfred A. Knopf, 1951, pp. 241-
          244.

          Criticizes *AG*, noting that it "has no big moments."

IIIH22.   "New Plays in Manhattan; *The Autumn Garden*," *Time*,
          LVII (Mar. 19, 1951), 51.

          Argues that the play "offers along with the assorted
          and vital gift of an experienced playwright, the
          wavering and uncertain movement of a transitional
          play."

IIIH23.   "New Plays; *The Autumn Garden*," *Newsweek*, XXXVII (Mar.
          19, 1951), 84.

          Points out that LH "has written about people for
          their own sake, without any 'message' in the conven-
          tional sense.  The result has considerably less drive
          and definition than the shows which established her
          as one of the theater's noisiest dramatists."

IIIH24.   Pollock, Arthur.  "Theater Time; *The Autumn Garden* is
          Miss Hellman in a Pessimistic Mood," New York *Daily
          Compass*, Mar. 9, 1951, p. 12.

Maintains that the play "kicks you in the teeth....
It is not one of the Hellman plays the playwright's
admirers will be happiest in remembering."

IIIH25.  Sheaffer, Louis. "Curtain Time; Hellman's *The
Autumn Garden* Superbly Played at the Coronet,"
Brooklyn *Daily Eagle*, Mar. 8, 1951, p. 4.

Notes that *AG* is "her most mature play to date."

IIIH26.  Shipley, Joseph T. "On Stage--Hellman Drags, Herbert
Soars," *New Leader*, XXXIV (Mar. 19, 1951), 25.

Reports LH's *AG* "is earnest and increasingly boring
... it succumbed to an early frost."

IIIH27.  "The New Plays; *The Autumn Garden*," *Theatre Arts*,
XXXV (May 1951), 18.

Notes that the play does not have a character who can
"leave us with a glimmer of hope." This is the fund-
amental fault in the play, though it "does contain
superb writing."

IIIH28.  Watts, Richard, Jr. "Two on the Aisle; Lillian
Hellman's Latest Drama," New York *Post*, Mar. 8, 1951,
p. 43.

Suggests that *AG* "is a thoughtful and interesting
drama.... It is impossible not to have great respect
for its maturity and integrity."

IIIH29.  ———. "Two on the Aisle; Lillian Hellman's
Chekhovian Mood," New York *Post*, Mar. 18, 1951, p. 12.

Claims LH's usual "dramatic dynamite" is missing from
*AG*.

IIIH30.  Wyatt, Euphemia van Rensselaer. "Theater; *The
Autumn Garden*," *Catholic World*, CLXXIII (Apr. 1951),
67-68.

Reports that LH "has written a play on which actors
are happy to expend themselves because she has given
them real people to study ... this study of that critical period, when middle-age begins to be intrusive
and the present ceases to be timeless becomes an
acrid reality once the curtain is lifted."

*New York Off-Broadway Production*
*1956*

IIIH31.   Geor.  "*The Autumn Garden*," *Variety*, May 9, 1956,
          p. 58.

          Complains of *AG*'s length.  "If this play had kept
          this schedule during its main stem run, it would have
          been rugged on commuter trade.  Despite the competence
          of the current revival of *The Autumn Garden*, there
          seems no need for its 8:40–11:40 running time."

*London Production*
*1960*

IIIH32.   "*The Autumn Garden*," London *Times*, Mar. 2, 1960, p.
          13.

          Suggests that "the performance was in fact perfectly
          adjusted to its context, but the fact perhaps supports
          a defect in the play, which was constantly interest-
          ing but somehow too smooth, too neat, too insulated
          from life."

*Boston Production*
*Charles Playhouse*
*1962*

IIIH33.   Durgin, Cyrus.  "'The Autumn Garden' at Charles Play-
          house," Boston *Globe*, Apr. 26, 1962, p. 13.

          Argues that *AG* "stands as one of Lillian Hellman's
          best plays, even when acted unevenly...."  LH has a
          "felicitous mastery of drawing character in quick
          effective strokes of speech."

IIIH34.   Hughes, Elinor.  "'The Autumn Garden' Lucid, Interest-
          ing," Boston *Herald*, Apr. 26, 1962, p. 41.

          Claims that *AG* "is a study of self-deception and the
          sadness that follows when a group of men and women
          have to face up to the fact that they have wasted
          their lives...."  It is easy to understand why the
          play has been called Chekhovian.

*New Haven, Conn. Production*
*1976*

IIIH35.   Kerr, Walter.   "This 'Garden' Is Nearly Perfect,"
New York *Times*, Nov. 28, 1976, Sect. 11, pp. 3, 42.

Argues that *AG* is LH's "very best."  Praises the acting and direction.  Melodrama in the blackmail scene
is avoided by skillful direction.


IIIi.   Reviews of *The Lark*


*Broadway Opening*
*Longacre Theatre*
*Nov. 17, 1955*
*226 Performances*

IIIi1.   "A Joan with Gumption," *Newsweek*, XLVI (Nov. 28,
1955), 110.

Reports that LH and "actress Julie Harris make the
heroine a crop-haired, sensible little warrior who
leads an army to victory because she has more gumption
and go than the men of her time."

IIIi2.   Atkinson, Brooks.   "Theatre; Saint Joan with Radiance;
Julie Harris Stars in *Lark* at Longacre," New York
*Times*, Nov. 18, 1955, p. 20.

Praises *The Lark* noting that it is "lighted by the
radiance of Julie Harris."  LH's "adaptation has
solid strength in the theatre....  The scheme of the
production is bold and grand."

IIIi3.   ————.   "New Joan of Arc; Julie Harris Plays Her in
*The Lark*," New York *Times*, Nov. 27, 1955, Sect. 2, p.
1.

Calls *The Lark* "sublime."  It is "an intelligent
drama ... a great performance."

IIIi4.   Beaufort, John.   "Julie Harris Starring in Role of
Joan of Arc," *Christian Science Monitor*, Nov. 26,
1955, p. 14.

Reports that play has "great dramatic thrust."
Praises LH's adaptation and Harris' acting.

IIIi5.    Bentley, Eric.  "Theatre," *New Republic*, CXXXIII
          (Dec. 5, 1955), 21.

          Reports that "the New York production is a really
          good show.... Anyone interested in the theatre will
          enjoy it, especially those who are not interested
          in Joan of Arc, history in particular, or truth in
          general."

IIIi6.    Bolton, Whitney.  "All Hands Contribute Superbly to
          Stunning Beautiful 'Lark,'" New York *Morning Tele-
          graph*, Nov. 19, 1955, p. 3.

          LH "has adapted with overwhelming sensitivity and
          perception...."

IIIi7.    Chapman, John.  "Julie Harris Simply Magnificent in
          Beautiful Drama, *The Lark*," New York *Daily News*,
          Nov. 18, 1955, p. 75.

          Reports that "the play is produced in simple splendor.
          ... Miss Harris is electrifying."

IIIi8.    ————.  "Beautiful Performance in a Fine Play; Julie
          Harris Reaches Acting Peak as St. Joan in 'The Lark,'"
          New York *Daily News*, Nov. 27, 1955, Sect. 2, p. 3.

          Notes that the drama has been adapted by LH "and it
          has the inestimable blessing of Julie Harris' acting
          in the title role."  LH "has contributed much to the
          play in the way of theatrical clarity."

IIIi9.    Coleman, Robert.  "*The Lark* Proves Spellbinding,
          Witty," New York *Daily Mirror*, Nov. 18, 1955, p. 36.

          Calls *The Lark* "an excellent adaptation.... If Anouil
          has not achieved the stature of Shaw, he has neverthe-
          less managed to write an intelligent and absorbing
          drama."

IIIi10.   Dash, Thomas R.   "'The Lark,'" *Women's Wear Daily*,
          Nov. 18, 1955, p. 32.

          Proclaims that the play's dialogue combines "honesty
          and intelligence."  It is a play of "stature and mag-
          nitude."

IIIi11.   Field, Rowland.  "Joan Lives Again," Newark *Evening
          News*, Nov. 18, 1955, p. 62.

          Labels *The Lark* "a superior play."  Little critical
          material is included.

IIIi12.  Gibbs, Wolcott. "The Theatre; Miss Sullavan and
         Miss Harris." *New Yorker*, XXXI (Dec. 3, 1955), 112-
         118.

         Comments on the excellent performance of Julie Harris
         as Joan and on the impressive direction and stage
         effects. A plot summary is given.

IIIi13.  Griffin, Alice. "Books of a Different Feather; Fry
         Translation and Hellman Adaptation of *The Lark*,"
         *Theatre Arts*, LX (May 1956), 8-10.

         Reveals that LH's adaptation, "while doubtless more
         appealing to the average American theatre goer, lacks
         the spirit and tone of Anouilh's original, while Fry
         has captured those qualities."

IIIi14.  Hatch, Robert. "Theater and Films," *The Nation*,
         CLXXXI (Dec. 3, 1955), 485-486.

         Claims that *The Lark* is "a clever and deeply felt work
         of theatei craft."

IIIi15.  Hawkins, William. "Julie Harris Captures Inner
         Beauty of Joan," New York *World-Telegram and Sun*,
         Nov. 18, 1955, p. 22.

         Calls *The Lark* "a crisp and new version of the Joan
         of Arc story...."

IIIi16.  Hayes, Richard. "The Stage; *The Lark*," *Commonweal*,
         LXIII (Dec. 23, 1955), 304-305.

         Explains play's title. "And it is as the lark that
         Joan takes her place in the company of Anouilh's
         celebrated heroines--young girls of a fantastic,
         lyrical purity and bloom--virgins all: doomed to vio-
         lation by the grossness of the world's body."

IIIi17.  Hobe. "*The Lark*," *Variety*, Nov. 23, 1955, p. 56.

         Predicts that "this new drama about Joan of Arc is
         likely to prove a sleeper. Because of its heavy
         hookup and the probably limited appeal of the subject
         matter, it's by no means an assured payoff."

IIIi18.  "Julie as a Memorable Joan," *Life*, XXXIX (Dec. 12,
         1955), 113-116.

         Reviews pictorially Harris' performance in *The Lark*.

IIIi19.    Kerr, Walter.  "Theater; *The Lark*," New York *Herald
           Tribune*, Nov. 18, 1955, p. 12.

           Suggests that "Joan has been given a stimulating new
           face; familiar events seem freshly lived, and Julie
           Harris is the cock of the walk."

IIIi20.    ————.  "Theater; A Brisk New Joan," New York *Herald
           Tribune*, Nov. 27, 1955, Sect. 4, pp. 1, 3.

           Notes that LH's "lines do not allow for plainsong.
           They are barbed, bracing and wholly contemporary.
           Joan of Arc has been given yet another new voice, and
           it has a resounding ring to it."

IIIi21.    Lewis, Theophilus.  "Theatre; *The Lark*," *America*,
           XCIV (Dec. 24, 1955), 363-364.

           Proclaims that whatever changes LH made to Anouilh's
           original, they were improvements, "for the drama
           faithfully reflects the mystery and glory of Joan's
           career, the tragedy of her trial, and the integrity
           of her character."

IIIi22.    McClain, John.  "Julie Depicts a Vital Joan; Earthi-
           ness Adds to Dramatic Impact in Flashback Pattern,"
           New York *Journal American*, Nov. 18, 1955, p. 20.

           Labels *The Lark* "a tremendously vital and moving
           version of the Joan of Arc legend...."

IIIi23.    Mannes, Marya.  "Three Playwrights Complement Their
           Audiences; Joan," *The Reporter*, XIII (Dec. 29, 1955),
           31.  Reprinted in *The Passionate Playgoer: A Personal
           Scrapbook*.  Edited by George Oppenheimer.  New York:
           Viking Press, 1958, pp. 592-595.

           Reports that "writers, actors and producers" have
           given *The Lark* "their highest powers of attention."

IIIi24.    Nathan, George Jean.  "George Jean Nathan's Theatre
           Week; Hark, Hark," New York *Journal American*, Dec. 3,
           1955, p. 16.

           *The Lark* "while intelligently considered and eminently
           practical ... misses the valuable lyrical flavor of
           the Christopher Fry translation...."  If you see the
           play, however, you will be "amply rewarded."

IIIi25.    O'Connor, Frank.  "Theater; Saint Joans, from Arc to
           *Lark*," *Holiday*, XIX (Mar. 1956), 77.

Suggests that "Shaw, being in his own eyes free of all such limitations, showed that she was a Protestant Nationalist. Now in *The Lark*, M. Anouilh turns her into a member of the French Underground and I nearly jumped out of my seat when the Inquisitor described Joan as an example of 'Natural Man.' That, I am sure, must be Miss Hellman chiming in. The lesson is plain. We all read ourselves into the part of Joan."

IIIi26. Watts, Richard, Jr. "Two on the Aisle; A Stirring Play About Joan of Arc," New York *Post*, Nov. 18, 1955, p. 44.

The play is "a rare acid exciting occasion.... A brilliant alliance of the dramatic arts.... A moving dramatic experience."

IIIi27. ————. "Two on the Aisle; Random Notes on This and That," New York *Post*, Nov. 22, 1955, p. 33.

Exclaims approval of the play noting that "when anything as exciting as 'The Lark' comes along, a reviewer can see how foolish it is to waste enthusiastic adjectives on works that are just pretty good."

IIIi28. ————. "Two on the Aisle; Notes on a Brilliant Stage Event," New York *Post*, Nov. 27, 1955, p. 20.

Reports that "no one seems disposed to deny that 'The Lark' is a superb example of all-around theatrical craftsmanship and a moving and beautiful drama."

IIIi29. Wyatt, Euphemia van Rensselaer. "Theater; *The Lark*," *Catholic World*, CLXXXII (Jan. 1956), 308-309.

Points out several discrepancies between Joan of Arc's life and the play. Wyatt makes no mention that LH has been the adaptor. Includes plot summary.

IIIJ.   Reviews of *Candide*

*Broadway Opening*
*Martin Beck Theatre*
*Dec. 1, 1956*
*73 Performances*

IIIJ1.   Atkinson, Brooks.  "The Theatre; *Candide*," New York
         *Times*, Dec. 3, 1956, p. 40.

         Labels *Candide* "a brilliant musical satire."

IIIJ2.   ————.  "Musical *Candide*; Lillian Hellman and Leonard
         Bernstein Turn Voltaire Satire into Fine Play," New
         York *Times*, Dec. 9, 1956, Sect. 2, p. 5.

         Exclaims that "*Candide* is full of splendor and variety
         ... a musical feast."

IIIJ3.   Beaufort, John.  "'Candide' Set to Music," *Christian
         Science Monitor*, Dec. 8, 1956, p. 14.

         Criticizes LH's adaptation for being repetitious and
         humorless.  Praises Bernstein's score.

IIIJ4.   Bolton, Whitney.  "*Candide*, Brilliant Compelling Show,"
         New York *Morning Telegraph*, Dec. 13, 1956, p. 2.

         Discusses LH's treatment of Voltaire's original work.
         She "has preserved the best of the fruit she has picked
         and has thrown away what was not of use or value."

IIIJ5.   "*Candide*," *Theatre Arts*, XLI (Feb. 1957), 17–18.

         Briefly notes LH's work on *Candide*.  "When we come to
         the libretto we are on swampier ground ... there is no
         blinking at the fact that she [LH] lost a good deal of
         the satirical bite of Voltaire...."

IIIJ6.   "*Candide*, Indeed!," *Newsweek*, XLVIII (Dec. 10, 1956),
         77.

         Soundly criticizes the play, noting that "some classics
         are best left between book covers and *Candide* seems to
         be one of them."

IIIJ7.   Chapman, John.  "*Candide* an Artistic Triumph, Bern-
         stein's Score Magnificent," New York *Daily News*, Dec.
         3, 1956, p. 44.

Praises *Candide*, noting that it is "a truly notable
event in the musical theatre ... an evening of un-
common quality and a great contribution to the richness
of the American musical comedy stage."

IIIJ8.    ————. "'Candide' a Fine Musical; A Wonderful Score
Is Only Part of Its Many Enjoyments," New York *Daily
News*, Dec. 9, 1956, Sect. 2, p. 1.

Suggests that *Candide* "is the most stimulating theatre
piece of this or several previous seasons...."

IIIJ9.    Coleman, Robert. "Musical *Candide* is Distinguished
Work," New York *Daily Mirror*, Dec. 3, 1956, p. 32.

Labels the play "a colorful and cynical musical."
LH's "libretto is fairly true to the [Voltaire] original."

IIIJ10.   Dash, Thomas R. "*Candide*; Martin Beck Theatre,"
*Women's Wear Daily*, Dec. 3, 1956, p. 28.

Suggests that LH and Bernstein "were groping for a new
form. It is dubious whether they have altogether
succeeded."

IIIJ11.   Donnelly, Tom. "Best Musical News of Year Is Found in
New *Candide*," New York *World-Telegram and Sun*, Dec. 3,
1956, p. 16.

Maintains that *Candide* "doesn't hang together very
well, but the bits and pieces of it are invariably
fascinating, and the whole business is charged with
the excitement that arises when gifted artists come
close to achieving the all but impossible."

IIIJ12.   Driver, Tom F. "On the Run," *Christian Century*, LXXIV
(Feb. 6, 1957), 171-172.

Argues that "as a piece of theatre *Candide* encounters
difficulty because it requires its hero to travel
through too much of the world in order to discover its
final truth. The result is there is too much of
everything and the spectator comes away with a degree
of indigestion."

IIIJ13.   Field, Roland. "*Candide*, Tedious, Much of Voltaire
Satire Lost in Intricately Composed, Elaborately
Staged Operetta," Newark *Evening News*, Dec. 3, 1956,
p. 46.

IIIJ14.   Gibbs, Wolcott. "Voltaire Today," *New Yorker*, XXXII
          (Dec. 15, 1956), 52-54.

          Criticizes the "artists" who created *Candide* for
          creating a work that is "only intermittently satis-
          factory." The work is called as "unlikely a musical
          operation as we are apt to see...."

IIIJ15.   Hayes, Richard. "The Stage; Mr. Bernstein Cultivates
          His Garden," *Commonweal*, LXV (Dec. 25, 1956), 333-
          334.

          Maintains that LH has not been able to "mesh *Candide*
          happily into the sentimental conventions of the musi-
          cal stage; its tone is irrefrangibly moral. Nor can
          she impose a dramatic progression on either its per-
          sonages or its rapid succession of malicious episodes

IIIJ16.   Hewes, Henry. "Broadway Postscript; 'Free' Pose and
          Free Fall," *Saturday Review*, XXXIV (Dec. 22, 1956),
          34-35.

          LH's "comedy seems labored, her attitude toward the
          total work unclear. One suspects she sides with
          Martin in his statement that we live in the worst of
          all possible worlds, for she takes delight in attack-
          ing such old enemies as aristocracy, injustice,
          racial discrimination, and British Imperialism."
          But this is not as Voltaire intended nor is it in the
          "musical comedy spirit."

IIIJ17.   Keating, John. "'Candide,'" *Cue*, XXXVI (Dec. 15,
          1956), 8-9.

          Reports that LH's inability to preserve the humor of
          Voltaire's satire is the major fault of the play.

IIIJ18.   Kerr, Walter. "Theater; *Candide*," New York *Herald
          Tribune*, Dec. 3, 1956, p. 10.

          Reports that LH, Bernstein, and Guthrie "have joined
          hands to transform *Candide* into a really spectacular
          disaster."

IIIJ19.   ———. "Voltaire's 'Candide' As a Light Opera,"
          New York *Herald Tribune*, Dec. 23, 1956, Sect. 4, pp.
          1, 4.

          Notes that LH's "precise talents do not lie in the
          vein of elegant vaudeville." LH's libretto is com-
          pared to "a blind elephant stalking a treadmill."

IIIJ20.  Kolodin, Irving.  "Candied *Candide*," *Saturday Review*,
         XL (Feb. 23, 1957), 49.

         Briefly reviews the musical score.  "I attempt no
         diagnosis of the dramatic values in the adaptation
         (generally agreed to be inferior to the score), but,
         so far as the music is concerned ... the score is
         deficient in melodic content, padded out by formula
         instead of creative impulse, constantly trying to
         live beyond its musical means."

IIIJ21.  McCarthy, Mary.  "The Reform of Dr. Pangloss," *New
         Republic*, CXXXV (Dec. 17, 1956), 30-31.

         Argues that "what the present authors have forgotten
         or failed to see [is] ... *Candide* [as] a dangerous
         work.  It is really and truly subversive.  A fuse
         burns in it; that is why it is exciting.  There are
         many things wrong with the present production--cos-
         tumes, scenery, music--but the chief and essential
         failure is a failure of nerve."

IIIJ22.  McClain, John.  "*Candide*; Fine, Bright--But Operetta
         Lacks Spark," New York *Journal American*, Dec. 3, 1956
         p. 12.

         Praises *Candide* for being "ambitious and brilliant."
         Regrettably notes that "it didn't quite score."

IIIJ23.  M[ajeski], F.M., Jr.  "Bernstein Writes Operetta
         Score," *Musical America*, LXXXVI (Dec. 15, 1956), 26.

         Praises *Candide*'s score.  "Many musicians from the
         concert and opera world are featured in the work which
         is based on Voltaire's satire, and the music proved
         an excellent vehicle for them to display their varied
         talents ... a tuneful delightful score."

IIIJ24.  Mannes, Marya.  "News and Reviews; New Shows; Three
         Runs, Three Hits, Whose Error?"  *The Reporter*, XVI
         (Jan. 24, 1957), 35.

         Claims that "*Candide* has definite faults, most of
         which lie in its lagging pace and solemn periods,
         but it has the best new music and the wittiest lyrics
         and the handsomest production in town."

IIIJ25.  "New Musical Version of *Candide*," London *Times*, Dec.
         12, 1956, p. 5.

         Suggests that *Candide* is "an artistic triumph ...
         [filled with] witty ... pungent satire."

IIIJ26.   "New Operetta in Manhattan; *Candide*," *Time*, LXVIII
          (Dec. 10, 1956), 70.

          Points to differences between Voltaire's and LH's
          works. "Where Voltaire is ironic and bland, she [LH]
          is explicit and vigorous. Where he is diabolical ...
          she is humanitarian."

IIIJ27.   Oppenheimer, George. "On Stage; All for the Best,"
          *Newsday*, Dec. 14, 1956, Sect. C, p. 7.

          Maintains that "in all departments *Candide* has aimed
          high. As a result even its misses are well above the
          norm and musically and visually it is better than
          anything of the current season."

IIIJ28.   Taubman, Howard. "Broadway and TV; Both Sources Pre-
          sent Music of Stature," New York *Times*, Dec. 16, 1956,
          Sect. 2, p. 9.

          Reports that "an exhilarating score [has been] pro-
          duced for *Candide*."

IIIJ29.   Watts, Richard, Jr. "Two on the Aisle; Voltaire's
          'Candide' as an Operetta," New York *Post*, Dec. 3,
          1956, p. 64.

          Lauds Bernstein's score and criticizes LH's libretto
          for failing to "cope with the tremendous problem of
          reducing Voltaire's savage and free-wheeling satire."

IIIJ30.   ————. "Two on the Aisle; Random Notes on This and
          That," New York *Post*, Dec. 5, 1956, p. 74.

          Reports that it is hard to believe Atkinson and Kerr
          were in the same theatre when they viewed the play.
          (See Items IIIJ1, IIIJ18.)

IIIJ31.   ————. "Two on the Aisle; Notes on 'Candide' and
          'Li'l Abner,'" New York *Post*, Dec. 16, 1956, p. 22.

          Suggests that LH "faced what may well be an impossible
          task in trying to capture the letter and the spirit
          of Voltaire in libretto [and] with all my admiration
          for her, I can't believe she has succeeded."

IIIJ32.   Wyatt, Euphemia van Rensselaer. "Theater; *Candide*,"
          *Catholic World*, CLXXXIV (Feb. 1957), 384-385.

          Argues that "to dramatize Voltaire's picaresque satire
          is very much like trying to chart a straight course

through New York traffic. With sanguine temerity,
Miss Hellman has appropriated the characters appear-
ing in Part I of *Candide*.... She has woven a story
with a continuity only those who remember the ram-
blings of the original can remember."

*London Production*
*Saville Theatre*
*Apr. 1959*

IIIJ33.   Brien, Alan. "The Patient Should Live," *The Spectator*, CCII (May 8, 1959), 649-650.

Calls the lyrics and music "glittering" and claims
that the play does not deserve the bad reviews it has
received.

IIIJ34.   "*Candide* Made Musical," London *Times*, May 1, 1959,
p. 6.

Claims that *Candide* is well done but "not entirely
successful." The music is well suited, but the over-
all production is "heavy handed." Voltaire's irony
is lost.

*Salt Lake City Production*
*1976*

IIIJ35.   Barber, Clint. "*Candide*--Bernstein at his Best,"
*Deseret News*, June 26, 1976, Sect. W, p. 5.

Notes in a positive review that "when the musical
*Candide* opened on Broadway in 1956, it was not very
successful. One reason was the writers treated it
too seriously and the public didn't know how to
accept it."

IIIK.   Reviews of *Toys in the Attic*


*Pre-Broadway Opening*
*Boston*
*1960*

IIIK1.   Hughes, Elinor.   "The Theater; *Toys in the Attic*,"
         Boston *Herald*, Feb. 4, 1960, p. 24.

         Maintains that "time has not blunted the edge of Miss
         Hellman's keen observation of humanity...."

IIIK2.   ————.   "*Toys in the Attic*; Rich Absorbing," Boston
         *Herald*, Feb. 7, 1960, Sect. 3, p. 10.

         Summarizes *TIA* calling it "a fine play."


*Broadway Opening*
*Hudson Theatre*
*Feb. 25, 1960*
*110 Performances*

IIIK3.   "A Drama of Disastrous Love," *Life*, XLVII (Apr. 4,
         1960), 53–54.

         Pictorially reviews *TIA* calling it "an excellent
         Broadway play."

IIIK4.   Aston, Frank.   "*Toys in the Attic* Takes Apart Lives of
         Five," New York *World-Telegram and Sun*, Feb. 26, 1960,
         p. 18.

         Proclaims that LH's play is "brilliant ... [the] text
         operated like strokes of a surgical blade."

IIIK5.   Atkinson, Brooks.   "Theatre; Hellman's Play *Toys in
         the Attic* in Bow at the Hudson," New York *Times*, Feb.
         26, 1960, p. 23.

         Notes that though *TIA* "is not the greatest play in the
         world, it is head and shoulders above the level of the
         season, and it provides some opportunities for some
         extraordinary acting."

IIIK6.   ————.   "One Revue; One Play; *Thurber Carnival* and
         *Toys in the Attic*," New York *Times*, Mar. 6, 1960,
         Sect. 2, p. 1.

Reports that "all seven of the newspaper reviews" of *TIA* were "favorable. Here the enthusiasm for her new play is moderate."

IIIK7.  Bolton, Whitney. "Hellman Welcome with *Toys in the Attic*," New York *Morning Telegraph*, Feb. 27, 1960, p. 2.

Claims that *TIA* is "almost certainly the best play of the season."

IIIK8.  ————. "Theatre," New York *Morning Telegraph*, Mar. 1, 1960, p. 2.

Calls *TIA* "brilliant," bringing life to the theatre season.

IIIK9.  Brustein, Robert. "The Play and the Unplay," *New Republic*, CXLII (Mar. 14, 1960), 22-23.

Suggests that because of the tightening of the play's form, *TIA* "never seems more than moderately interesting. One is too aware of contrivance and manipulated action, and the characters ... do not have much life beyond dramatic functions."

IIIK10. Chapman, John. "Miss Hellman's *Toys in the Attic* Vigorous and Absorbing Drama," New York *Daily News*, Feb. 20, 1960, p. 45.

Reports that LH "jolted the theatre out of its childishness with a smacking virogous drama, *Toys in the Attic....*"

IIIK11. ————. "One of the Season's Best; Miss Hellman, an Old Pro, Writes Another Absorbing Drama," New York *Daily News*, Mar. 13, 1960, Sect. 2, p. 1.

IIIK12. Clurman, Harold. "Theatre," *The Nation*, CXC (Mar. 19, 1960), 261-262.

Argues that "the play is congested by irrelevantly melodramatic turns in plot, implausibilities and jags of lurid violence."

IIIK13. Coleman, Robert. "*Toys in the Attic*, Sure Fire Hit," New York *Mirror*, Feb. 27, 1960, p. 29.

Proclaims that *TIA* "has restored real theatre to the Rialto. It's the best shocker since Tennessee Williams' *Sweet Bird of Youth*."

IIIK14.  Dash, Thomas R.  "*Toys in the Attic* Should Bring One
         Playtime Thrill," *Women's Wear Daily*, Feb. 26, 1960,
         p. 24.

         Notes that *TIA* "should add considerable stature to a
         thus far disappointing season. It is an honest
         searching play of revelation...."

IIIK15.  Driver, Tom F.  "Puppet Show," *Christian Century*,
         LXXVII (Apr. 17, 1960), 511-512.

         Maintains that "most of the characters here, as in so
         many of Miss Hellman's plays, are the very embodiment
         of greed. Those who aren't greedy for money are
         greedy for love of one kind or another. All in all,
         they are a despicable lot...."

IIIK16.  Field, Rowland.  "New Hellman Play Incisive," Newark
         *Evening News*, Feb. 26, 1960, p. 18.

         Praises *TIA* noting that "with almost surgical genius,
         she plunges deeply beneath and around throbbing inner
         turmoil."

IIIK17.  Gassner, John.  "Broadway in Review," *Educational
         Theater Journal*, XII (May 1960), 43-45. Reprinted in
         *Dramatic Soundings: Evaluations and Retractions
         Culled from 30 Years of Dramatic Criticism*. New York:
         Crown, 1968, pp. 481-484.

         Claims that LH demonstrates her usual strong talent
         for writing sharp dialogue. She gives us characters
         with compassion.

IIIK18.  Hewes, Henry.  "Love in the Icebox," *Saturday Review*,
         XLIII (Mar. 12, 1960), 71-72.

         Reports that LH "has reluctantly but generously given
         us another glimpse of her tough naked attitudes and
         literate dialogue in *Toys in the Attic*. Exhibiting a
         hard boldness that she reserves for her own plays,
         Miss Hellman uncovers the nasty spectacle of one re-
         pressed woman who is ruining the lives of five people
         around her."

IIIK19.  Hobe.  "Shows on Broadway," *Variety*, Mar. 2, 1960,
         p. 70.

         Labels *TIA* a "gripping melodrama" that returns to the
         "unhealthy family relationships" theme found in *LF*.
         The characters are "predatory."

IIIK20.  Kerr, Walter.  "First Night Report; *Toys in the Attic*," New York *Herald Tribune*, Feb. 26, 1960, p. 12.  Reprinted in "Conventional Theater; Miss Hellman." *The Theater in Spite of Itself*.  New York: Simon and Schuster, 1963, pp. 235-238.

Points out that "for all the acidity that is in the nature of the beast called *Toys in the Attic*, there is the splendor of straightforward, uncompromised writing."

IIIK21.  ———.  "Lillian Hellman Whets Her Knife of Language," New York *Herald Tribune*, Mar. 6, 1960, Sect. 4, p. 1.

Suggests that *TIA* "binds us with a cold serpentine grace, that is born of a clear head, a level eye, and a fierce respect of the unchanging color of the precisely used word."

IIIK22.  Lewis, Theophilus.  "Theatre; *Toys in the Attic*," *America*, CIII (May 28, 1960), 323.

Calls *TIA* "a gallimaufry of twisted characters and relationships one expects to encounter in a Tennessee Williams play.  Miss Hellman, however, is a playwright who never fails to respect the dignity of drama or the maturity of the audience.  While Miss Hellman handles her material with circumspection and taste, her new play remains a tawdry tale without either the dramatic drive or social illumination of some of her earlier works."

IIIK23.  McClain, John.  "*Toys in the Attic*, Top Writing--Top Acting," New York *Journal American*, Feb. 26, 1960, p. 23.

Predicts that *TIA* will be "a hit."  It is "solidly constructed drama, acted with excellent effect by a brilliant cast."

IIIK24.  Mannes, Marya.  "Miss Hellman's Electra," *The Reporter*, XXII (Mar. 31, 1960), 43.

Reports that in *TIA* "you hang on to every word ... one of the few evenings this winter when theater becomes experience."

IIIK25.  "New Plays on Broadway; *Toys in the Attic*," *Time*, LXXV (Mar. 7, 1960), 50.

Lauds *TIA* noting that it "slaps a slumped, lethargic theater season into awareness. The reason is not just that *Toys* has a sense of tartness, insight, and power; it also has a pervasive sense of playwriting."

IIIK26.  Oppenheimer, George.  "On Stage; Mann from Hellman," *Newsday*, Mar. 9, 1960, Sect. C, p. 4.

Maintains that "it has taken Lillian Hellman, one of our major American playwrights to inflict this sick season with a shock treatment. The patient may not have fully recovered from its manifold ills, but it is at least sitting up, wondering what hit it. For Miss Hellman has written a drama with an impact as great as her *Little Foxes*."

IIIK27.  Savery, Ronald.  "Lillian Hellman in the Deep South," *The Stage*, XXXVII (Apr. 13, 1960), 21.

Suggests that in *TIA* LH displays her "fine skill in developing situation, story line, and character."

IIIK28.  "Theater Triumph for Starkness; *Toys in the Attic*," *Newsweek*, LV (Mar. 7, 1960), 89.

Objectively notes that *TIA* demonstrates LH's "acute sense of chracterization," but it is not among her best plays.

IIIK29.  Tynan, Kenneth.  "The Theatre; Deaths and Entrances," *New Yorker*, XXXVI (Mar. 5, 1960), 124-125.

Views *TIA* with thankful relief. *TIA* is, "in the context of this benighted season, an experience rather like setting foot on dry land after wading through a swamp. One feels relieved, reassured, and disposed to give thanks."

IIIK30.  Watts, Richard, Jr.  "Two on the Aisle; Lillian Hellman's Striking Drama," New York *Post*, Feb. 26, 1960, p. 48.

Reports that *TIA* "is at once stunning in its frank theatrical power, disturbing in its ugly candor, and brutally alive."

IIIK31.  ————.  "Two on the Aisle; Random Notes on This and That," New York *Post*, Mar. 1, 1960, p. 48.

Argues that "the ailing theatre season apparently needed ... a woman's touch.... [LH] certainly brough it back to life" with *TIA*.

IIIK32.    ————."Two on the Aisle; The High Skill of Lillian
           Hellman," New York *Post*, Mar. 6, 1960, p. 21.

           Claims that LH's "new drama is stunning, absorbing,
           engrossing, powerful, dynamic, fascinating, striking,
           and any other similar words in what is no doubt my
           limited vocabulary of expressions of enthusiasm."

*London Production*
*1960*

IIIK33.    Brien, Alan.  "The Bathetic Fallacy," *The Spectator*,
           CCV (Nov. 18, 1960), 782-783.

           Calls the play "an anthology of bathos" because the
           characters "whine" and attempt to make tragedy out
           of the problems of a Georgia suburb.

IIIK34.    Terwin, J.C.  "The World of the Theatre; Deep Down,"
           *The Illustrated London News*, CCXXXVII (Nov. 26,
           1960), 964.

           Notes that *TIA* "has been overcharged and overwritten.
           One comes from the theatre remembering little but a
           clutter of theatrics: Deep South stuff...."

IIIK35.    "The Arts; English Fineness in an American Play,"
           London *Times*, Nov. 11, 1960, p. 16.

           Calls *TIA* "an intensely American play and perhaps
           requires American players."  The review is primarily
           a plot summary.

IIIK36.    Tynan, Kenneth.  "Bumpy Crossing," London *Observer*,
           Nov. 13, 1960, p. 10.

           Criticizes *TIA* production for being unevenly directed
           and miscast with unconvincing actors.  It is not LH's
           best.

*Chicago Production*
*1961*

IIIK37.    Henahan, Donald.  "*Toys in the Attic*; Holiday Package
           of Horror Opens," Chicago *Daily News*, Dec. 26, 1961,
           p. 13.

           Criticizes dragging portions of *TIA*.  "Elimination of
           half an hour's worth of padding and tiresome reitera-

tion would have made this a more absorbing play, but
for all its creaking ... it is worth your time."

*Washington, D.C. Production*
*National Theatre*
*1961*

IIIK38.    Coe, Richard L.  "One on the Aisle; A 'Best Play' on
E Street," Washington *Post*, Oct. 10, 1961, Sect. B,
p. 11.

Claims that "it is a pleasure to attend a play so
richly, firmly made."

*Houston Production*
*1962*

IIIK39.    "Houston Preview," Houston *Post*, July 29, 1962, *Now*,
p. 2.

Calls *TIA* an "effective play" which "suitably focuses
its power."

*Long Island Production*
*1963*

IIIK40.    Abrams, Arnold.  "*Toys in the Attic* Isn't Worth Drive
Out to Gateway Theatre," *Newsday*, July 17, 1963,
Sect. C, p. 3.

Calls the play "stale watered-down Tennessee Williams
.... This production is just plain dreary."

IIIL.    Reviews of *My Mother, My Father and Me*

*Broadway Opening*
*Plymouth Theatre*
*Mar. 21, 1963*
*17 Performances*

IIIL1.    Bolton, Whitney.  "*My Mother, My Father and Me* Disappointing Play by Hellman," New York *Morning Telegraph*, Mar. 26, 1963, p. 2.

Calls the play "more frail than robust, more overt
than audacious, more sprawling than is her custom."

IIIL2.    Chapman, John.  *New York Theatre Critics' Reviews,
          1963*.  Volume 24, p. 302.

          Calls the play "flimsy."  The second half of the play
          is so desperate that it "falls completely apart."
          (Chapman, the reviewer for the New York *Daily News*,
          wrote the review during New York newspaper strike.
          His entire review was published here.)  (See Item
          IIIL3.)

IIIL3.    ————.  "What Happened on Stage; Summary of Plays
          and Musicals Which Opened During Strike," New York
          *Daily News*, Apr. 7, 1963, Sect. 2, pp. 1, 6.

          Recalls his unpublished review.  "I called it a
          flimsy whimsey.  Miss Hellman is a notable playwright
          but this wasn't her dish."

IIIL4.    Coe, Richard L.  "Hellman Play is Letdown," Washington
          *Post*, Mar. 26, 1963, Sect. B, p. 4.

          Evaluates the first two acts as funny and "brilliantly
          played"; however, the action is not drawn together in
          Act Three.

IIIL5.    Coleman, Robert.  "The B'Way Theatre Scene; New York's
          Alive Again; Lillian Hellman Play is Depressing
          Farce," New York *Daily Mirror*, Apr. 1, 1963, p. 28.

          Includes very negative review.  "As Samuel Goldwyn
          is supposed to have once said, 'Include me out!'"

IIIL6.    Clurman, Harold.  "Theatre," *The Nation*, CXCVI (Apr.
          20, 1963), 334.

          Disappointedly criticizes the play.  "I regret I
          cannot praise *My Mother, My Father and Me*, for despite
          everything I was 'on its side.'  Its production was
          almost symbolic of our whole lopsided theatre."

IIIL7.    Cooke, Richard P.  "The Theater; Miss Hellman's
          Comedy," *Wall Street Journal*, Mar. 25, 1963, p. 14.

          Suggests that the play has "several scenes which are
          curiously flat.  Every so often the early mood is
          restored, but in between times the playwright changes
          her wavelength."

IIIL8.   "Family Gargoyles," *Newsweek*, LXI (Apr. 8, 1963), 85.

Chides *MMMF&M* calling it "a sort of soul sick farce
which starts out like a vehicle for Gertrude Berg
and winds up something in the mad environs of the
Theater of the Absurd.  Although the play is as fascinating as it is funny, it travels a course that
leaves most playgoers either straggling or lost."

IIIL9.   "Gathering Toadstools; *My Mother, My Father and Me*,"
*Time*, LXXXI (Apr. 5, 1963), 56.

Maintains that LH had difficulty in writing the play.
"This catalogue of latter-day evils presumably calls
for the wrath of Jeremiah.  Unfortunately Lillian
Hellman only manages to turn bile into bilgewater."

IIIL10.  Gottfried, Martin.  "Tough -- an Hour Riddle -- New
Play by Lillian Hellman," *Women's Wear Daily*, Mar.
25, 1963, p. 16.

Notes that LH has "a very good title.... She should
have stopped while she was ahead.  Having no sense of
humor, she was foolhardy to try and write comedy ...
a disaster."

IIIL11.  Hewes, Henry.  "Last Laugh and Last Tapes," *Saturday
Review*, XLVI (Apr. 27, 1963), 27.

Concedes that LH "contrived some outrageously funny
moments, and created an accurate image of the monstrous insanity we accept as a substitute for pur-
poseful action.  Yet the cumulative effects of her
play were an unpleasantness and unconcern grimly
suffered by the audience to no apparent dramatic
purpose."

IIIL12.  Hipp, Edward Sothern.  "House of Cards; *My Mother,
My Father and Me* Staged," Newark *Evening News*, Mar.
25, 1963, p. 16.

Includes LH's effort among other disappointing plays
of the season.  "Since such playwriting giants as
Tennessee Williams, William Inge and Sidney Kingsley
have fallen on their faces during this Broadway season, it should not come as shattering news that
Lillian Hellman got into the stumbling act last Saturday night."  Argues that the play fails because it
tries to combine "domestic comedy with nihilism."

IIIL13.   Hobe. "Shows on Broadway; *My Mother, My Father and Me*," *Variety*, Mar. 27, 1963, p. 64.

Severely criticizes the play, labeling it "an appalling botch, a hard, cruel, sordid, tasteless, unfunny play about odious people."

IIIL14.   Kerr, Walter. *New York Theatre Critics' Reviews, 1963*. Volume 24, p. 302.

Suggests that the play "attempts to mate extravagant satirical incoherence of the Theatre of the Absurd with homier, milder, and more plausible nonsense of *You Can't Take It with You* ... they are quite incompatible." (Kerr, of the New York *Herald Tribune*, wrote this during New York newspaper strike. It was published only here.)

IIIL15.   Lewis, Emory. "'My Mother, My Father and Me,'" *Cue*, XLIII (Apr. 6, 1963), 13.

Notes that LH's theme is similar to themes found in Albee's "The American Dream." Argues that Gower Champion's direction fails to "capture the humor" in LH's script.

IIIL16.   McCarten, John. "The Theatre; Domestic and Foreign," *New Yorker*, XXXIX (Mar. 30, 1963), 108.

Points out that LH is "a playwright of consequence, but I'm afraid that the sort of domestic comedy she essays here is not her forté; the play deals with a Jewish resident in Manhattan, and while some of Miss Hellman's observations are amusing, the work as a whole is disjointed and at times incoherent and vulgar."

IIIL17.   McClain, John. *New York Theatre Critics' Reviews, 1963*, Volume 24, p. 303.

Maintains that *MMMF&M* is a "far cry from Miss Hellman's usual product, but it reveals her as an experienced writer in the field of straight comedy. I believe it will succeed." (McClain, the New York *Journal American* reviewer, wrote this during the New York newspaper strike. The entire review was not published in the newspaper.

IIIL18.   ———. "What Happened to the Theatre During the News Blackout," New York *Journal American*, Apr. 3, 1963, p. 24.

Enthusiastically praises *MMMF&M* for being "a wild
and utterly outlandish romp which kids the britches
off the U.S. establishment ... a series of vignettes
which lay out everything from sex and psychoanalysis
to the plight of the American Negro."

IIIL19.   Maddocks, Melvin. *"My Mother, My Father and Me,"*
          *Christian Science Monitor*, Mar. 26, 1963, p. 4.

          Maintains that LH "probably ... should not have
          attempted to frame her large miscellany of social
          opinions within the convention ... of a Broadway
          play." LH is out of her element.

IIIL20.   Mannes, Marya. "The Half World of American Drama,"
          *The Reporter*, XXVIII (Apr. 25, 1963), 48-50.

          Evaluates the play's problems. "It could be said
          of Lillian Hellman's recent short-lived savagery,
          *My Mother, My Father and Me*, that satire and love
          are by nature incompatible, and certainly her often
          funny and always brutal scatter shots at what she
          understandably hates in our society left little room
          for compassion."

IIIL21.   Nadel, Norman. *New York Theatre Critics' Reviews,*
          *1963*.  Volume 24, p. 304.

          Sharply criticizes LH's play noting that "whatever
          her purpose, nothing succeeds.... distasteful,
          dismal, and dull." (Nadel, the New York *World-
          Telegram and Sun* reviewer, wrote this during the New
          York newspaper strike.)

IIIL22.   Oppenheimer, George. "On Stage; I Dismember Mamma,"
          *Newsday*, Mar. 27, 1963, Sect. C, p. 3.

          Labels *MMMF&M* "a satire comedy, which has failed."

IIIL23.   Pryce-Jones, Alan. "Openings/New York: *My Mother,
          My Father and Me*," *Theatre Arts*, XLVII (May 1963),
          69-70.

          Notes LH's playwriting problems. She "is not a
          comedy writer, and, when a joke fails she is liable
          to insert a surprising note of commonness in an
          attempt to bolster it up.  But the result is neither
          scatty enough to make a farce, nor sufficiently
          thought out to offer a valid comment on what is
          basically a perfectly serious theme."

IIIL24. Smith, Michael. "Theatre Uptown," *Village Voice*, Mar. 28, 1963, p. 1.

Maintains that *MMMF&M* "goes embarrassingly wrong in several ... scenes, and it lacks the book's extravagance of horror...."

IIIL25. Taubman, Howard. "Theatre; Hellman Satire; Life in Middle Class Home is Mirrored," New York *Times*, Mar. 25, 1963, p. 5.

Reports that "there is not much mirth ... in Miss Hellman's laughter. Nor is her play conventionally engaging or charming. It is too busy speaking some furious truths."

IIIL26. Watts, Richard, Jr. "Two on the Aisle; Angry Comedy by Lillian Hellman," New York *Post*, Mar. 25, 1963, p. 36.

Proclaims *MMMF&M* to be "relentlessly bitter, angry, and sardonic.... If the whole is not altogether successful, the parts are often brilliantly compounded."

IIIL27. ————. "Two on the Aisle; Family Comedy With a Difference," New York *Post*, Apr. 7, 1963, p. 15.

Suggests that audiences go to see *MMMF&M* despite its weaknesses.

*London Production*
*1965*

IIIL28. "The Arts; Most Novel Play of the New York Season," London *Times*, Apr. 22, 1965, p. 16.

Praises *MMMF&M* calling it "both biting and funny.... the most novel play of the season."

IV.  SCHOLARLY ARTICLES, BOOKS, AND SURVEYS
OF HELLMAN'S WORKS


IVA.  Scholarly Articles, Books, and Surveys
-- *The Children's Hour*

IVA1.  Armato, Philip M.  "Good and Evil in Lillian Hellman's
*The Children's Hour*," *Educational Theatre Journal*, XXV
(Dec. 1973), 443-447.

Ponders whether *CH* is melodramatic or not.  The juxta-
position of good and evil within the play is considered
in detail.  Concludes by stating that the play is
"within the limits of a wholly successful moral play.
Hellman suggests that adults are too often 'children.'"

IVA2.  Block, Anita.  *The Changing World in Plays and Theatre*.
New York: Da Capo Press, 1971, pp. 120, 122-126.

Notes that LH's *CH* frankly deals with homosexuality.
The play is "not flawless, but the playwright deals
with a subject of grave human import," giving it
"deepest meaning and significance."

IVA3.  Boulton, Marjorie.  *The Anatomy of Drama*.  London:
Routledge & Kegan Paul, 1960, pp. 10, 50.

Maintains in a discussion of censorship and artistic
merit that *CH* is a powerful and disturbing drama which
should be for adults only.  States that the play could
be rated X as "in the film industry" to protect young
people from sights and thoughts which might be disturbing and could even lead to vice or crime.  Notes, however, that adults profit from serious, thought-provok-
ing themes in drama.

IVA4.  Lawson, John Howard.  "The Obligatory Scene."  *Theory
and Technique of Playwriting*.  New York: G.P. Putnam's
Sons, 1936, pp. 262-267.

Discusses the relationship between the obligatory
scene, "the close of the second act," and the climax
of the play. Maintains that the link between the two
acts in *CH* is "weak."

IVA5.  Nathan, George Jean. "The Playwrights; Lillian Hellman."
*The Theatre of the Moment*. Rutherford, Madison,
Teaneck, N.J.: Fairleigh Dickinson U. Press, 1936, pp.
248-250.

Includes a short critical piece on *CH* calling it a
"material contribution to American Playwriting." Discusses the "faulty" last act of the play.


IVB.  Scholarly Articles, Books, and Surveys
-- The Hubbard Family: *LF* and *APF*


IVB1.  Beyer, William. "The State of the Theater; The
Strindberg Heritage," *School and Society*, LXXI (Jan.
14, 1950), 23-28.

Maintains that Strindberg's "neurotic hatred of women"
and LH's use of hatred throughout her plays are similar. Discusses *LF* in comparison to Blitzstein's opera
*Regina*.

IVB2.  Collinge, Patricia. "Another Part of the Hubbards or
When They Were Even Younger," *New Yorker*, XXIII (Mar.
15, 1947), 29-30.

Includes a satirical dialogue by Collinge using LH's
characters from *APF*, sequel to *LF*. She satirically
makes the characters younger than they appear in *APF*.

IVB3.  Dusenbury, Winifred L. "In the South." *The Theme of
Loneliness in Modern American Literature*. Gainesville:
U. of Florida Press, 1960, pp. 134-154.

Considers themes in *LF* and *APF*. The condemnation of
the Hubbard family, "an up-and-coming" Southern family,
is clear. They are contrasted with the "ruined aristo-
cracy" of the South without explicitly condemning the
pre-Civil War South. The plays illustrate the tragedy
of "belonging to nothing but business. The devotion
of the Southern gentry to a way of life brings grief,
but a deeper loneliness may be in store for those 'who
eat the earth' than for those who stand around and watch.

IVB4.   Freedman, Morris. "Toward an American Tragedy." *American Drama and Social Context*. Carbondale and Edwardsville: Southern Illinois U. Press, 1971, pp. 116-117.

Notes the importance of the post-Civil War South as a setting for *LF*. The tragedy of the post-Civil War South of the setting contributed directly to the tragedy and pathos of the evil characters in the play.

IVB5.   Gassner, John. "A Chronology of Modern Theatre." *Directions in Modern Theatre and Drama*. New York: Holt, Rinehart, and Winston, 1966, pp. 387-420.

Calls the 1939 production of *LF* a "social drama with naturalistic, *comedie rossé*, qualities that invite comparison of the play with Becque's *Les Corbeaux*."

IVB6.   Going, William T. "The Prestons of Talladega and the Hubbards of Bowen: A Dramatic Note." *Essays on Alabama Literature*. Tuscaloosa: U. of Alabama Press, 1975, pp. 142-155.

Notes that the most famous plays about Alabama are Augustus Thomas' *Alabama* (1891), *LF*, and *APF*. The South influenced LH significantly because she spent much of her youth in New Orleans. Explains that the Hubbard family is typical of the post-Civil War family discovering the evils of capitalism. Provides plot summaries of the plays.

IVB7.   Halman, Robert. "Dramas of Money," *Shenandoah*, XXI (Summer 1970), 20-33.

Discusses drama with themes concerning money. LH's *LF* "never lets us lose sight of the hard aggressive money-grabbing that animates half the major characters." Numerous other plays are also considered.

IVB8.   Triesch, Manfred. "Hellman's *Another Part of the Forest*," *The Explicator*, XXIV (Oct. 1965), Item 20.

Discusses very briefly the relationship between *APF* and *LF*, the former being a sequel to the second. Points out that the title of the later play came from Shakespeare's *Titus Andronicus* as did the names for the two main characters, Marcus and Lavinia.

        IVC.   Scholarly Articles, Books, and Surveys
               -- The War Plays: *WR* and *SW*

IVC1.   Gagey, Edmond M. *Revolution in American Drama*. New
        York: Columbia U. Press, 1947, pp. 126, 137-138, 142,
        268.

        Suggests that *WR* and "its companion pieces helped pre-
        pare the nation for war."

IVC2.   Gassner, John, ed. *Best Plays of the Modern American
        Theatre: Second Series*. New York: Crown, 1947, pp.
        xxiii-xxvii, 642.

        Discusses briefly the realism of characters in LH's two
        war plays, *WR* and *SW*. The characters were realistic
        rather than melodramatic (as critics have claimed) be-
        cause of their "human nature."

IVC3.   Gilder, Rosamond. "The Kingdom of War; Broadway in Re-
        View; *Watch on the Rhine*." *Theatre Arts*, XXV (Nov.
        1941), 782-793.

        Compares *WR* to other war plays including F.H. Brennan's
        *The Wookey*, Maxwell Anderson's *Candle in the Wind*,
        Robert E. Sherwood's *There Shall Be No Night*, and
        briefly considers other plays of the theatre season.
        Notes that *WR* has a "fighting (anti-fascist) message,"
        just as Sherwood's play does. LH makes her argument
        by implication unlike others who are less subtle in
        attacking Hitler.

IVC4.   Heilman, Robert Bechtold. *Tragedy and Melodrama*.
        Seattle: U. of Washington Press, 1968, pp. 76-81, 85.

        Examines the melodramatic structure in *WR*. The play
        has "easy emotional appeal: giving the audience no
        choice but to hate the Nazis and love everybody else."
        In some respects LH moves away from melodrama in the
        play by "altering stereotypes" to the extent that they
        do not always evoke the conventional response from the
        audience other melodramas do.

IVC5.   Miller, Jordan Y. "Drama; The War Play Comes of Age."
        *The Forties: Fiction, Poetry, Drama*. Edited by Warren
        French. Deland, Fla.: Everett/Edwards, 1969, pp. 69-71,
        75.

        Argues that *WR* is not melodramatic as many critics have
        maintained, but is a play that exposes on a personal

level the evils and terror the Nazis evoke.  The play is not sentimental and thus dodges the melodrama classification.

IVC6.  Nannes, Caspar H.  *Politics in the American Drama.* Washington, D.C.: The Catholic U. of America Press, 1960, passim.

Includes extensive plot summaries of *WR* and *SW*.

IVC7.  Schwarzert, Ernst.  "Notes on the Theatre During War; Authors Have a Vast Problem Keeping Their Plays About Current Events in a Purely Dramatic Form," New York *Times*, May 11, 1941, Sect. 9, pp. 1, 2.

Considers the dramatic problem which playwrights have in containing the action within the three walls of the stage as the world is being blown apart by the war offstage.  Robert E. Sherwood's *There Shall Be No Night*, Clare Boothe's *Margin for Error*, S.N. Behrman's *The Talley Method*, and LH's *WR* are analyzed.  LH has failed in her "struggle between theatre and reality," and thus her play is melodramatic.  Her political message is so "air tight" that the drama suffers.

IVC8.  Sobel, Bernard.  "Propaganda and the Play," *Saturday Review of Literature*, XXV (Mar. 7, 1942), 13.

Gives a history of the play as a medium for propaganda and concludes that these plays succeed only if they are entertaining.  Cites *WR* as an example of a successful propaganda play.


IVD.  Scholarly Articles, Books, and Surveys
-- Early Hellman Plays


IVD1.  Cameron, Gledhill.  "Hellman Defends Her Characters; Surprised at Reaction to Hateful Heroines," New York *World-Telegram*, Dec. 23, 1946, p. 15.

Considers (in an interview with LH) the evil characters she has created in *LF*, *APF*, and *CH*.  The characters' destruction is caused by their own greed and lies.

IVD2.  Clark, Barrett H.  "Lillian Hellman," *College English*, VI (Dec. 1944), 127-133.

Explores the five plays LH had written at this time:
*SW*, *LF*, *DC*, *WR*, and *CH*. Points out that although LH
never belonged to a theatre group, her plays are of
the "propagandist" school. Urges conversion from her
style of plays for reform's sake. Argues that she
should try to "illuminate the world she knows as she
sees it, through the power of her imagination, without
insisting too much on guiding and instructing it. It
is questionable whether the preacher ever did anything
as effectively as the poet."

IVD3.   Egri, Lajos. *The Art of Dramatic Writing*. London: Sir
        Isaac Pitman and Sons, 1950, pp. 13-14, 243, 248.

        Divulges the origins of *CH* and *WR* in a chapter about
        how playwrights find ideas for plays. Portions of the
        Van Gelder interview, New York *Times*, reprinted. (See
        Item IID8.)

IVD4.   Goldstein, Malcolm. "The Playwrights of the 1930's."
        *The American Theatre Today*. Edited by Alan S. Downer.
        New York: Basic Books, 1967, pp. 34-36.

        Considers *CH* and *LF* as plays in which LH "expressed
        the belief that those whose social attitudes she de-
        spised were too tough and too experienced to be swept
        aside...."

IVD5.   Gurko, Leo. *The Angry Decade*. New York: Harper
        Colophon Books, 1947, pp. 272-274.

        Analyzes briefly *LF* and *WR*. Calls *LF* a "penetrating
        study of a rapacious Southern family."

IVD6.   Himelstein, Morgan Y. *Drama Was a Weapon: The Left
        Wing Theatre in New York 1929-41*. New Brunswick, N.J.:
        Rutgers U. Press, 1963, passim.

        Considers briefly *DC*, *LF*, and *WR* as left-wing dramas.

IVD7.   Isaacs, Edith J.R. "Lillian Hellman; A Playwright on
        the March," *Theatre Arts*, XXVIII (Jan. 1944), 19-24.
        Reprinted in *Discussions of Modern Drama*. Edited by
        Walter Meserve. Boston: Heath, 1965, pp. 46-51.

        Discusses *CH*, *LF*, *APF*, *WR*, *The North Star*, and the
        achievements/receptions of each. LH's reaction to
        critics' accusations of "melodrama" is given.

IVD8.   Kernodle, George R. *Invitation to the Theatre*. New
        York: Harcourt, Brace and World, 1967, pp. 12, 59-60,
        572.

        Discusses *CH* and *LF* as examples of realism.  Because
        LH included "subtle detail and variety" she was able
        effectively to depict realism on the stage.  Includes
        excerpt from *LF*.

IVD9.   Krutch, Joseph Wood. *The American Drama Since 1918*.
        New York: Random House, 1939, pp. 130-133.

        Calls *CH* and *LF* "genuine tragedies" and plays that
        earned LH a noteworthy reputation.  *DC*, though unsuc-
        cessful, suggested that the playwright's major inter-
        est was in writing about social forces.  The same
        theme, "adulterated meanness and villainy," appeared
        in all three of the early LH plays.

IVD10.  Lockridge, Richard.  "The Stage in Review; Miss
        Hellman Hews to People, and Lets Abstractions Fall
        Where They Will," New York *Sun*, Apr. 12, 1941, p. 26.

        Maintains that the absence of abstractions in LH's
        plays is one of her "finest attributes" as a drama-
        tist.  LH shows the audience in *WR* that fascism "hurts
        people and makes people hurt one another."  In *CH* and
        *LF* the "sharp appreciation of human personality"
        rather than dialogue containing abstract dogma con-
        demning the lies and greed of the characters is clear.

IVD11.  Mersand, Joseph. *The Drama of Social Significance,
        1930-1940*.  New York: Modern Chapbooks, 1940, pp. 11,
        20.

        Comments on *DC* noting how plays about the labor move-
        ment have not been supported by the public and have
        quickly closed.  Calls *LF* a "serious tragedy."

IVD12.  ————. *Traditions in American Literature: A Study
        of Jewish Characters and Authors*.  Port Washington,
        N.Y.: Kennikat Press, 1939, p. 11.

        Examines briefly *CH* and *LF*.  Notes that *CH* deserved
        the 1934 Pulitzer Prize.

IVD13.  Morehouse, Ward. *Matinee Tomorrow: Fifty Years of
        Our Theatre*.  New York: McGraw-Hill Book Co., 1949,
        pp. 248-249.

Recounts the productions in the 1930's of *CH*, *DC*, and
*LF*.  Tells of Shumlin's anger when *LF* did not win the
Pulitzer Prize.

IVD14.  Nicoll, Allardyce.  *World Drama*.  London: George G.
Harrap and Co., 1949, pp. 829-830.

Maintains in a section on American Realism that in
her first five plays LH stands between those playwrights who deal with social themes and those whose
main concern is character depiction.  She was not
very adept in dealing with only social themes (labor
problems in *DC*); however, her "understanding of human
evil is acute" in her plays.  Notes LH's decline into
melodrama in *WR* and *SW*.

IVD15.  Thorp, Willard.  *American Writing in the Twentieth
Century*.  Cambridge, Mass.: Harvard U. Press, 1960,
pp. 96-97.

Presents a short survey of LH's most famous works including *CH*, *LF*, *APF*, *WR*, *SW*.

IVE.  Scholarly Articles, Books, and Surveys -- *The Lark*
(see also Items VJ1, VJ2, and VIIIB1)

IVE1.  Hewitt, Alan.  "*The Lark*; Theatrical Bird of Passage,"
*Theatre Arts*, XL (Mar. 1956), 63-64.

Compares the Fry, Anouilh, and LH versions of *The
Lark*.  "The differences in national temperament between English, French, and American writers" are
illustrated.

IVE2.  Knepler, Henry W.  "*The Lark*: Translation vs. Adaptation; A Case History," *Modern Drama*, I (May 1958),
15-28.

Compares and contrasts Anouilh's play *The Lark* with
Fry's translation of the work and LH's adaptation.
Shaw's *St. Joan* is also discussed in relation to *The
Lark*.  Concludes that LH has "injected drama" into
many of the scenes.  She has simplified the play's
structure, characters, and language, thus confirming
that LH knows that "in American drama it is better
in the end to settle on the side of furtive tears than

to stray toward self-conscious smiles." Extensive
dialogue comparisons are made. The differences in
the plays' endings are examined.

IVE3.　　─────. "Translation and Adaptation," *Modern Drama*,
IV (Summer 1961), 31-41.

Includes one paragraph noting that Fry's translation
of *L'Alouette* makes use of the flashback found in the
Anouilh original. LH in her adaptation did not use
the device.

IVE4.　　O'Flaherty, Vincent J. "St. Joan Wouldn't Know Herself," *America*, XCV (Apr. 28, 1956), 109-110.

Maintains that the playwrights "don't appear to realize that if one were ever able to separate the Joan
of history from her church and its sacraments and her
true voices, there would be left one of those disagree-
able women who have done nations a considerable lot of
harm and left behind a bad taste of scandal and blood.
There would no longer be a Joan to write about."

IVF.　　Scholarly Articles, Books, and Surveys -- *AG* and *TIA*

IVF1.　　Adler, Jacob H. "Miss Hellman's Two Sisters," *Educational Theatre Journal*, XV (May 1963), 112-117.

Carefully analyzes *TIA* by first comparing it to LH's
earlier work. Notes Ibsenian influences in plays
from *CH* to *APF* and Chekhovian influences in *AG*. A
combination of Tennessee Williams and Ibsen has influenced *TIA*. Maintains that basic material is from
Chekhov's *Three Sisters*. There are unhappy sisters
and a brother in both plays, yet there are only two
sisters in *TIA*. Claims *TIA* bows to Chekhov's play,
but that LH has combined her usual virtues of truth,
detachment, and tremendous dramatic power in her play.

IVF2.　　Clurman, Harold. "Letters Found in the Drama Mailbag,"
New York *Times*, Apr. 22, 1951, Sect. 2, p. 3.

Explains the role of Sophie in LH's *AG* pursuant to a
critic's admission that he didn't understand the character. Emphasizes that in important plays all aspects
are rarely clear during the first viewing. Sophie's

role in the play is important in depicting the "European point of view." Sophie is philosophically shal-
low and her ideals are not substantiated by her
actions. (See Item IIIH2.)

IVF3.    Felheim, Marvin. "'The Autumn Garden'; Mechanics and
         Dialectics," *Modern Drama*, III (Sept. 1960), 191-195.

         Argues that in *AG*, LH has moved away from the well-
         made play style found consistently in her previous
         works. *AG* is Chekhovian in terms of its dialogue and
         character development. It is a play about people who
         are bored, and yet the play retains its vitality.

IVF4.    Gassner, John. "Ebb Tide; Lillian Hellman; *The Autumn
         Garden*." *Theatre at the Crossroads*. New York: Holt,
         Rinehart, and Winston, 1960, pp. 132-139.

         Reminisces about the initial reaction by critics to
         *AG* on Broadway, noting that it was not greeted favor-
         ably. LH "presents a hard doctrine [stating] that our
         little weaknesses pile up like calcium in the body
         and end in a bursitis of character." Maintains that
         LH failed in her attempt to write as Chekhov did be-
         cause she lacked his "oblique style and bizarre humor."
         Considers other LH plays in relationship to *AG*. Calls
         *TIA* a "mordant" drama.


         IVG.  Scholarly Articles, Books, and Surveys
         -- Assessment of Several or All Hellman Plays


IVG1.    Adler, Jacob H. "The Rose and the Fox: Notes on the
         Southern Drama." *South: Modern Southern Literature
         in its Cultural Setting*. Edited by Louis D. Rubin,
         Jr., and Robert Jacobs. Garden City, N.Y.: Dolphin
         Books, 1961, pp. 349-375.

         Along with numerous plays by other Southern playwrights,
         briefly considers and summarizes LH's *LF*, *APF*, *AG*,
         *TIA*, *WR*, and *SW*. "In listing the dramatists of the
         South I am convinced Miss Hellman deserves second
         place [to Tennessee Williams]."

IVG2.    ————. *Lillian Hellman--Southern Writers Series*,
         Number 4. Austin, Texas: Steck, Vaughan, 1969.

Includes in a pamphlet (44 pp.) biographical information (through 1969) and considerations of all LH's
plays.  Includes a lengthy discussion of *CH*.  Maintains that faulty plot and lack of unified construction caused *DC* to fail.  In analyzing *APF*, considers
the literary relationship between Ibsen and LH.  "Her
discipleship is clear; she is the single most important American Ibsenian outside of Arthur Miller."
Notes that LH presents issues of social significance.
LH's "lapse into melodrama" in *WR* and *SW* and her reaction to critics' assertions that her plays are melodramatic are discussed.  Points to the significant
Chekhovian influence present in *AG*.  Includes numerous quotations from the "Introduction" to *Four Plays
by Lillian Hellman* as well as a bibliography of works
by LH and checklist of seventeen works about LH.  Concludes by saying that LH's "methods are viable methods,
and of them she is a minor master."

IVG3.   Blum, Daniel.  *A Pictorial History of the American
        Theatre: 1900-1956*.  New York: Greenberg, 1956,
        passim.

        Includes photographs of scenes taken from LH's Broad-
        way productions.  All plays, *CH* through *The Lark*, re-
        presented.

IVG4.   Clark, Barrett H., and George Freedley, eds.  *A History
        of Modern Drama*.  New York and London: D. Appleton
        Co., 1947, pp. 728-729.

        Includes critiques of several LH works.  States that
        *CH* is "an effective study in evil....  It is pure
        theatre."  Of *DC* notes that LH maintained an attitude
        of aloofness, unable to decide "whether to preach or
        simply to reveal" the social struggle being waged.
        This results in a radical approach to the problem.
        *LF* is "the most completely satisfying" of LH's plays.
        Labels it a "brilliant picture of greed," giving us
        characters without scruples or conscience, "in the
        final stages of degeneracy."  *WR* and *SW* are discussed
        as plays in which LH continues to "preach," conveying
        ideas that the critics call "communist."  In spite of
        her bias and her "moral tones," LH "promises to write
        plays that may be even more effective and moving than
        any she has yet given us, ... she is learning that
        social criticism is useful largely to the extent to
        which it is not added to, but inherent in, the works
        which attempt to drive it home."

IVG5.   Downer, Alan S. *Fifty Years of American Drama 1900-
        1950*. Chicago: Henry Regnery Company, 1951, pp. 60-61,
        139-141.

        Discusses briefly *WR*, *SW*, *LF*, and *AG*. Of *WR* and *SW*:
        "Miss Hellman was so caught up in contemporary issues
        that the structure of the drama in each case is faulty
        and the impact weakened." *AG* "was the most promising
        play of the year."

IVG6.   Geisinger, Marion. *Plays, Players, and Playwrights*.
        New York: Hart Publishing, 1971, pp. 548-553.

        Contains biographical information on LH and surveys
        *CH* to *TIA*.

IVG7.   Gottfried, Martin. *A Theatre Divided*; *The Post-War
        American Stage*. Boston: Little, Brown, 1967, pp. 160,
        191.

        Discusses the 1967 Repertory Theatre at Lincoln Center
        stating that "a revival of Lillian Hellman's very
        right wing *Little Foxes* is to be produced by the right
        wing Broadway producer Saint Subber and directed by
        Mike Nichols." Calls LH's libretto for *Candide* "im-
        possibly heavy handed," and classifies it as "a left
        wing musical."

IVG8.   Herron, Ima Honaker. *The Small Town in American
        Drama*. Dallas: Southern Methodist U. Press, 1969, pp.
        237-238, 342-344, 442-444.

        Reveals that *LF* and *APF* are dramas with "disagreeable
        and dangerous" characters. *CH*, *TIA*, and *AG* are also
        briefly considered.

IVG9.   Holmin, Lorena Ross. *The Dramatic Works of Lillian
        Hellman*. Stockholm: Acta Universitatis Upsaliensis,
        Studia Anglistica Upsaliensis, 1973. (178 pp.)

        Includes detailed analysis of LH's *CH*, *DC*, *LF*, *WR*, *SW*,
        *APF*, *AG*, *TIA*. LH's development of character and struc-
        ture within each play is discussed. Each analysis is
        broken into the following sections: statement of
        thesis; plot summary; analysis of characterization,
        plot, and dialogue; critical evaluation of the play.
        Also included are biographical notes about LH, pro-
        duction information about her plays on Broadway, a list
        of LH play productions in Nordic countries, and a bib-
        liography of works by and about LH.

IVG10.  Kronenberger, Louis, ed. *The Best Plays of 1952-1953*.
        New York: Dodd, Mead, 1954, passim. (See Item IIA47.)

IVG11.  Laufe, Abe. *Anatomy of a Hit*. New York: Hawthorne
        Books, 1966, pp. 138-141, 293-297.

        Appraises *CH* and *TIA*. *CH* is "a forceful drama" which
        illustrates the tragedy caused "by malicious gossip
        and lies." In *TIA*, LH's "rigorous dialogue and action
        hold audience interest."

IVG12.  Lewis, Emory. *The Fifty Year Child of the American
        Theatre*. Englewood Cliffs, N.J.: Prentice-Hall, 1969,
        passim.

        Pays particular attention to the war plays and to LH's
        appearance before the HUAC. Included are several
        pages on *MMMF&M* calling it "a hilarious satire of un-
        common merit."

IVG13.  Maney, Richard. *Fanfare, the Confessions of a Press
        Agent*. New York: Harper and Brothers, 1957, passim.

        Includes numerous passing references to LH and her
        plays. Surveys *CH*, *LF*, *DC*, *The Lark*, and includes
        some biographical historical material on LH and her
        productions.

IVG14.  Moody, Richard. *Lillian Hellman, Playwright*. New
        York: Pegasus, 1972.

        In a 361-page volume, considers the life and works of
        LH. The book is more biographical than critical and
        is primarily drawn from *UW*. All the plays and several
        movies are discussed. The HUAC and McCarthy confron-
        tation are also treated. Included is a five-page
        selective bibliography of works by and about LH. A
        very positive view of LH is found throughout the
        volume: "The theatre needs her tough mind, her stout
        heart that never turns spongy soft, her stinging in-
        dignation, her passion for uncovering evil, her
        troubled and troubling characters, her infallible
        command of authentic dialogue, her sure instinct for
        theatrical excitement, her clear eye for scenes and
        characters that can find their only true life on the
        stage." (See Item VM7.)

IVG15.  Morris, Lloyd. *Curtain Time*. New York: Random House,
        1953, p. 337.

Includes short reviews of *CH*, *LF*, *APF*, *WR*, and *SW*.
Calls *CH* "melodrama." Includes no critical material.

IVG16.   Nathan, George Jean. *Theatre Book of the Year, 1943-
         1944.* New York: Alfred A. Knopf, 1944, passim.

         Includes numerous references to LH.

IVG17.   ————. *Theatre Book of the Year, 1946-1947.* New
         York: Alfred A. Knopf, 1947, passim.

         Includes several references to LH.

IVG18.   Phillips, John, and Anne Hollander. "The Art of the
         Theatre; Lillian Hellman; An Interview," *Paris Review*,
         XXXIII (Winter-Spring 1965), 64-65. Reprinted in
         "Lillian Hellman." *Writers at Work; "The Paris Review"
         Interviews, Third Series.* New York: Viking Press,
         1967, pp. 115-140.

         Reveals in this interview with LH that she likes *AG*
         best of all her plays. Comments on her *CH*, *LF*,
         Hammett, and play-writing theories. Includes LH's
         feelings about Pete Seeger, Faulkner, and numerous
         other topics as well as a copy of the letter to Con-
         gressman John S. Wood, Chairman of HUAC, dated May 19,
         1952.

IVG19.   Stern, Richard G. "Lillian Hellman on Her Plays,"
         *Contact* #3 (1959), 113-119.

         Includes an interview with LH on her plays. The entire
         tape of the original interview is available at Harper
         Library, University of Chicago. *WR* and *LF* are the
         primary concerns of the article.

IVG20.   Taubman, Howard. *The Making of the American Theatre.*
         New York: Coward McCann, Inc., 1965, pp. 236, 250-251,
         294, 313, 326-327.

         Surveys all of LH's plays. Notes that *CH* established
         LH as a tough, uncompromising writer. She continued
         the trend by showing life without any sentimentality
         or illusion. LH "did not soften her portraits or ob-
         servations to please a public unaccustomed to such
         unyielding truths; such was the measure of her disci-
         pline and integrity as an artist." The critique of
         LH's war plays notes that the "characters and con-
         flicts" do not hold up. The moving struggles against

Nazism found in *SW* and *WR* are "not quite as moving
two decades after the war." *AG*, perhaps LH's "subtlest
and finest play," was not "charged with the electri-
city" found in other plays. *TIA* was "second rate."
The careful descriptions of Southern decadence in *LF*
appeared "routine" in *TIA*. The LH of the sixties
appeared to have "enlisted in an alien milieu."

IVG21.  Triesch, Manfred.  "Lillian Hellman: A Selective Bib-
        liography," *American Book Collector*, XIV (June 1964),
        57.

        Includes a twenty-five-entry checklist citing criti-
        cal material/reviews of plays by LH.

IVG22.  ————. "The Lillian Hellman Collection," *Library
        Chronicle of the University of Texas*, VIII (Jan. 1965),
        17-20.

        Describes briefly the cataloging of the University of
        Texas collection done by Triesch. (See Item IVG24
        for summary.)

IVG23.  ————. "Modern Drama; Library Collections," *Modern
        Drama*, VII (Feb. 1965), 374.

        Announces the collection of LH material held by the
        University of Texas: notebooks, rough drafts of plays,
        filmscripts, and letters are included in the collec-
        tion.

IVG24.  ————. *The Lillian Hellman Collection at the Uni-
        versity of Texas*. Austin: U. of Texas, 1966.

        Describes, in a 167-page volume, the collection at
        the University of Texas containing: (1) autographed
        manuscripts and typescripts; (2) contributions and
        letters. It also lists secondary sources about LH.

IVG25.  Weales, Gerald. *American Drama Since World War II*.
        New York: Harcourt, Brace, and World, 1962, pp. 89-
        92, 151-152.

        Notes that the dramatic roots of *AG* and *TIA* can be
        seen in LH's earlier works, *CH* and *LF*. Character
        development and dramatic impact are very similar
        despite the long timespan between LH's early and re-
        cent dramas. On *Candide*: "Lillian Hellman's book,
        which came in for heavy criticism when the show opened,
        does its job well."

IVG26.   ————. *The Jumping-Off Place*. London: The Macmillan
         Co., 1969, pp. 1-3.

         Comments on the success of the revival of *LF* in 1967
         and the failure of *MMMF&M* in 1963.

IVG27.   Whitney, Frank M. "Modern Drama; Odets and Social
         Protest." *An Introduction to the Theatre*. New York:
         Harper and Brothers, 1961, p. 122.

         Considers briefly *CH*, *LF*, *APF*, *Candide*, and *TIA*.


                IVH. Scholarly Articles, Books, and Surveys
                -- Assessments of LH as Playwright


IVH1.    Atkinson, Brooks. *Broadway*. New York: Macmillan,
         1970, pp. 258-262, 298-300, 357, 392.

         Notes that LH was "the most clearheaded and the best
         organized of the writers" who were "opposed to the
         status quo." Numerous other passing references to LH
         and her plays are made.

IVH2.    Bradbury, John M. *Renaissance in the South*. Chapel
         Hill: U. of North Carolina Press, 1963, pp. 190-192.

         Compares LH to Tennessee Williams. Maintains that
         outwardly there is little difference between her mil-
         itant liberalism and the exposure of greed and evil,
         and his "romantic treatment of twisted lives." Both,
         however, are able to achieve an "untarnished ... ro-
         mantic idealism which speaks silently of its outrage
         at what it is compelled to portray."

IVH3.    Brandon, Henry. "A Conversation with Arthur Miller,"
         *World Theatre*, XI (Autumn 1962), 229-240.

         Reveals Miller's view of LH. She has "a remorseless
         rising line of action in beautifully articulated
         plays." Deals with current developments in drama
         from Miller's perspective.

IVH4.    Brockett, Oscar G., and Robert R. Findlay. *Century of
         Innovations: A History of European and American
         Theatre and Drama Since 1870*. Englewood Cliffs, N.J.:
         Prentice-Hall, 1973, pp. 459, 524-526, 567.

Included is a survey of LH's work. Characterizes LH as "a moralist preoccupied with the evil in man, usually within the individual, but sometimes that in society."

IVH5.   Brustein, Robert. "Why Plays are Not Literature," *Harpers*, CCXIX (Oct. 1959), 166-172. Reprinted in *Writing in America*. Edited by John Fisher and Robert B. Silvers. New Brunswick, N.J.: Rutgers U. Press, 1960, pp. 46-60.

Maintains in an article on the poor quality of American drama that standards of "intellectual ferment" provided by LH and others are "non-existent today."

IVH6.   Gassner, John, ed. *Best American Plays: Third Series -- 1945-1951*. New York: Crown, 1952, pp. xii, xx-xxi, xxvi, 206.

Notes that LH has comfortably made the transition from writing plays with social themes to writing serious Chekhovian-style dramas. *AG* and *APF* are examples.

IVH7.   Hersey, John. "Lillian Hellman," *New Republic*, CLXXV (Sept. 18, 1976), 25-27. See also excerpt reprinted in Los Angeles *Times*, Sept. 26, 1976, Sect. 2, p. 1.

Includes an interpretive biographical article pointing to LH's "rebelliousness" as the "essence of her vitality." It demonstrates the "rebelliousness" in several biographical and textual examples from her plays.

IVH8.   Knelman, Martin. "Starring ... the Writer," *Atlantic*, CCXL (Nov. 1977), 96-98.

Examines "Turtle," a chapter from *Pentimento*. It is unexpected that LH is popular today, not for her plays (*CH*, *LF*, *WR*), but for her memoirs and the movie *Julia*. Information about the movie is presented. "Like the turtle that rose from the dead, she [LH] has become an icon of survival with honor."

IVH9.   Lewis, Alan. "The Survivors of the Depression--Hellman, Odets, Shaw." *American Plays and Playwrights of the Contemporary Theatre*. New York: Crown Publishers, 1965, pp. 99-115.

Discusses all LH plays. Points to LH's ability to come out of the Depression era and still write popular viable plays while other dramatists who were also prominent before 1929 could not.

IVH10.  Miller, J. William. *Modern Playwrights at Work: Volume
        I*. New York: Samuel French, 1968, passim.

        Maintains that LH and Arthur Miller have numerous
        similarities. Both seem to imitate the Chekhovian and
        Ibsenian methods. Makes numerous other passing ref-
        erences to LH and her plays.

IVH11.  Nathan, George Jean. "Playwrights in Petticoats,"
        *American Mercury*, LII (June 1941), 750-755.

        Maintains that "*Watch on the Rhine* proves two things:
        It proves again that Lillian Hellman is the best of
        our American Women playwrights, and it proves that
        even the best of our women falls immeasurably short
        of our best masculine. The generic feminine inability
        or perhaps disinclination to hold the emotions within
        bounds has been responsible in Miss Hellman's case for
        the unwitting excess of melodrama in *The Children's
        Hour*, *The Little Foxes*, and the latest, *Watch on the
        Rhine*."

IVH12.  Sievers, W. David. "Freudian Fraternity of the Thir-
        ties: Lillian Hellman." *Freud on Broadway*. New
        York: Hermitage House, 1955, pp. 279-289.

        Reveals that LH underwent psychoanalysis as did other
        playwrights of the thirties. LH absorbed the "themes
        of rapacity, human evil, Fascism, blackmail, and
        diplomatic duplicity" by living during that era.
        Deals with LH's ability to avoid sensationalism when
        treating lesbianism in *CH*. Labels *CH* a "daring step
        forward in the theatre's humanizing power to create
        understanding and empathy" for deviation from the
        norm. Discusses failure of *DC*. Considers *LF* as a
        psychological study of evil. *WR*, *SW*, *AG*, *TIA*, are
        also considered using LH's knowledge of psychoanalysis
        as a focal point of the discussion.

IVH13.  Spacks, Patricia Meyer. "Free Women," *Hudson Review*
        XXIV (Winter 1971-1972), 559-573.

        Discusses Lessing, Nin, de Beauvoir, Charlotte Brontë,
        LH and others as women writers seeking identity in
        their work. "All autobiography must rest on a founda-
        tion of self-absorption; men as well as women indulge
        in self-manufacture and self-display. What is perhaps
        peculiarly feminine about the autobiographic writing
        of Lillian Hellman is the obsessiveness of its impli-
        cit or explicit concern with the question of freedom,

psychic and social, and the nature of its revelations about freedom's limitations for women."

IVH14.  Wien, Florence Von. "Playwrights Who Are Women," *Independent Woman*, XXV (Jan. 1946), 12-14.

Maintains that LH is the outstanding woman playwright "She is keenly perceptive and has an awareness of the sick anxieties of humanity, intellectual indignations and technical skill to say what she wants to say."

# V.  REVIEWS OF DRAMA IN BOOK FORM

### VA.  *The Children's Hour*

VA1.  C[anby], H[enry] S[eidel].  "Drama: *The Children's Hour*,"
       *Saturday Review*, XI (Mar. 2, 1935), 523.

       Recalls that "twenty or thirty years ago Miss Hellman's
       play, enthusiastically received in New York, would
       doubtless have been stopped by the police.  As it is
       both engrossing drama and a serious and sincere study
       of abnormal psychology, this change may imply a certain
       progress in the public discernment."

VA2.  Eaton, Walter Prichard.  "New Plays for Reading," New
       York *Herald Tribune*, Mar. 10, 1935, Sect. 7, p. 20.

       Concerns the publication of several plays, among them
       *CH*: "if not the best play of the winter, it is assuredly
       the most painful."

VA3.  Gilder, Rosamond.  "Theatre Arts Bookshelf," *Theatre
       Arts*, XIX (May 1935), 392.

       Briefly notes that *CH* is a "psychological drama."

VA4.  Hammond, Percy.  "The Theatres," New York *Herald Tribune*,
       Dec. 2, 1934, Sect. V, p. 1.

       Suggests that those potential playgoers who may be
       offended by the lesbian theme in *CH* might read the pub-
       lished version before attending.

VA5.  Vernon, Grenville.  "The Play," *Commonweal*, XII (May
       31, 1935), 134.

       Calls *CH* one of the best plays of the year; however,
       its theme lacks "universal interest or applicability."

VB. *Days to Come*


VBI.  Eaton, Walter Prichard.  "New Plays to Read," New York
      *Herald Tribune*, June 20, 1937, Sect. 10, p. 7.

      Reviews several plays.  *DC* has "a complete lack of tech-
      nical ease of directness of purpose and clear con-
      struction."

VB2.  "The World of Books; *Days to Come*; Lillian Hellman's
      Drama of Labor Strife," Springfield *Daily Republican*,
      June 16, 1937, p. 12.

      Praises *DC* calling it "a play full of drama--emotion
      and action.  Moreover its story has a message...."

VB3.  "Strike Breakers," *Literary Digest*, CXXII (Dec. 26,
      1936), 22-23.

      Points out that *DC* production was a failure.  There was
      potential for a good play, but the theme became confused
      and lost by the character Mrs. Rodman.



VC. *The Little Foxes*


VC1.  Anderson, John.  "The Season's Theater," *Saturday Review
      of Literature*, XX (Apr. 29, 1939), 14-15.

      Reviews the past Broadway season by examining published
      versions of the plays.  Calls *LF* "overplotted and melo-
      dramatic."  The exposition and characterization are
      "superb."

VC2.  *Booklist*, XXXV (May 1, 1939), 287.

      Calls *LF* an "effective but unpleasant drama."

VC3.  Eaton, Walter Prichard.  "Some Modern Plays in Print,"
      New York *Herald Tribune*, July 23, 1939, Sect. 4, p. 11.

      Notes that *LF* has "compact well-knit construction com-
      bined with its poignant picture...."

VC4.  Robertson, T.H.B.  "Two Big Town Hits for Stay-at-Home,"
      Boston *Evening Transcript*, Apr. 22, 1939, Sect. 4, p. 1.

Asserts that *LF* "is as brilliant and incisive a play as the current season is apt to produce."

## VD.   *Watch on the Rhine*

VD1.   *Booklist*, XXXVIII (June 15, 1941), p. 488.

Concludes that the "appeal of the characters heightens the tragedy."

VD2.   Eaton, Walter Prichard.  "Stage Plays in Print," New York *Herald Tribune*, Oct. 5, 1941, Sect. 9, p. 28.

Praises play as "another example of the writer's ability to inject new vitality in the formula of the well made play."

VD3.   Freedley, George.  "New Book Summary; Adult Book Selection; *Watch on the Rhine*," *Library Journal*, LXVI (May 15, 1941), 462.

Predicts that *WR* will be "much in the public prints because it discusses the impact of World War II on America. It is highly readable and the characters are readily understandable."

VD4.   "'Read but Not Seen' Condemns Most Plays, but Not This One," New York *Herald Tribune*, June 22, 1941, Sect. 6, p. 2.

Praises *WR* publication.

## VE.   *Four Plays by Lillian Hellman*

VE1.   Anderson, John.  "Preface Sheds Light on Hellman Plays; Author Examines Charge of Critics That Her Plots are Too Well-Made," New York *Journal American*, Mar. 25, 1942, p. 12.

Reviews the Library Journal Edition containing *CH*, *LF*, *DC*, and *WR* noting that it "contains an interesting and candid introduction."

VE2.   *Booklist*, XXXVIII (Apr. 1, 1942), 241.

      Announces the publication. No critical material included.

VE3.   Freedley, George. "New Book Appraisals; Plays in Print; *Four Plays*," *Library Journal*, LXVII (Apr. 1, 1942), 320.

      Cites the "illuminating introduction" by LH.

VE4.   Gilder, Rosamond. "Theatre Arts Bookshelf; Hellman on Playwrighting; *Four Plays by Lillian Hellman*," *Theatre Arts*, XXVI (May 1942), 346.

      Includes a summary review.

VE5.   Tinker, Edward Larocque. "New Editions, Fine and Otherwise," *New York Times Book Review*, June 14, 1942, p. 19.

      Praises LH's introduction noting that it "delights, surprises, and confounds many enthusiasts whose admiration for her critical discriminations is unlimited."

## VF.   *The Searching Wind*

VF1.   *Booklist*, XLI (Sept. 1944), 14.

      Asserts that "there is some good dialogue, but the ideas are confused and plot and characters lack compelling interest."

VF2.   Eaton, Walter Prichard. "Plays That Can Be Read; *The Searching Wind*," New York *Herald Tribune*, Aug. 6, 1944, Sect. 6, p. 11.

      Points out that LH's "characters are literate and alive ... and the drama is charged with emotional overtones which makes it rich and rewarding."

VF3.   Freedley, George. "Current Library Literature; Plays in Print; *The Searching Wind*," *Library Journal*, LXIX (Sept. 15, 1944), 762.

      Evaluates *SW* as "not ... top-drawer ... [however] it is head and shoulders above most recent plays. [It] deals with the causes of America's participation in World War II as reflected in an upper-class family."

VF4.  *Kirkus*, XII (May 1, 1944), 209.

Includes summary of *SW*.


VG.  *Another Part of the Forest*

VG1.  *Booklist*, XLIII (May 1, 1947), 269.

Claims that "the picture of almost unrelieved villainy
is almost incredible."

VG2.  Eaton, Walter Prichard.  "Plays That Can Be Read," New
York *Herald Tribune*, May 25, 1947, Sect. 7, p. 27.

Hopes that LH has now had enough of "these unsavory
people [the Hubbards].  There doesn't seem to be much
more to be gained by a contemplation of them."

VG3.  Freedley, George.  "New Books Appraised; The Theatre;
*Another Part of the Forest*," *Library Journal*, LXXII
(May 15, 1947), 811.

Suggests that LH's second play "about the Hubbard family
is less dramatically believable than *The Little Foxes*.
Nonetheless it is recommended for all drama collections."

VG4.  *Kirkus*, XV (Jan. 15, 1947), 56.

Includes plot summary.

VG5.  Terry, C.V.  "Broadway Bookrack," *New York Times Book
Review*, Apr. 6, 1947, p. 12.

Argues that in *APF* LH has committed "self-plagiariza-
tion" by rearranging the characters and setting of *LF*
without saying anything new about them.

VG6.  "The New Books," San Francisco *Chronicle*, July 27, 1947,
*This World*, p. 12.

Calls *APF* a "tightly plotted melodrama... [written with]
taste and skill."

VH.  *Montserrat*


VH1.  Freedley, George.  "The Theatre," *Library Journal*, LXXV
       (Mar. 15, 1950), 496.

       Favorably reviews publication.



Vi.  *The Autumn Garden*


Vi1.  *Booklist*, XLVII (June 15, 1951), 360.

       Maintains that *AG* has "little action but good dialogue."

Vi2.  F.J.  "Among the New Books," San Francisco *Chronicle*,
       Sept. 30, 1951, *This World*, p. 25.

       Reveals that *AG* contains "uncanny brilliant dialogue,
       a play to be read and re-read."

Vi3.  Freedley, George.  "New Books Appraised; The Theatre;
       *The Autumn Garden*," *Library Journal*, LXXVI (June 15,
       1951), 1030.

       Calls *AG* "one of the author's most penetrating plays
       though not a great box office success."

Vi4.  *Kirkus*, XIX (Mar. 15, 1951), 171.

       Notes that LH has "again [written] a drama of decaying
       Southern gentility."  It comes "from the pen of America's
       most gifted (and voluble) woman dramatist."



VJ.  *The Lark*


VJ1.  Freedley, George.  "New Books Appraised; The Theatre;
       *The Lark*," *Library Journal*, LXXXI (Mar. 1, 1956), 652.

       Asserts that *The Lark* is "superb."  Compares the play to
       the Fry translation and finds the LH version superior.

VJ2.  Griffin, Alice.  "Books--of a Different Feather,"
       *Theatre Arts*, XL (May 1956), 8-10.

Compares Fry's translation and LH's adaptation of Anouilh's play.  LH has made her version more "romantic" while Fry has included more of Anouilh's irony.


## VK.  *Candide*


VK1.  Freedley, George.  "The Theatre," *Library Journal*, LXXXII (Aug. 1957), 1923.

Labels *Candide* book "dull" and recommends it only for those seeking complete collections.


## VL.  *Toys in the Attic*


VL1.  *Booklist*, LVI (July 15, 1960), 677.

Briefly notes that *TIA* has "some sharply insightful dialogue."

VL2.  Freedley, George.  "New Books Appraised; Theatre; *Toys in the Attic*," *Library Journal*, LXXXV (Aug. 1960), 2809.

Maintains that *TIA* is "a deeply absorbing play about possible incest and definite miscegenation in modern New Orleans.  It is as if Miss Hellman were playing with her toys in Tennessee Williams' backyard."


## VM.  *The Collected Plays of Lillian Hellman*


VM1.  Allen, Trevor.  "Books in Brief," *Books and Bookmen*, XVIII (Jan. 1973), 122.

Claims that the book is a "well produced volume," but complains because it has no illustrations.

VM2.  "Arts and Letters," *Saturday Review*, LV (Dec. 2, 1972), 72.

Announces the publication.

VM3.   *Booklist*, LXVIII (June 15, 1972), 880.

       Includes a summary.

VM4.   *Choice*, XI (Sept. 1972), 830.

       Speculates that "perhaps this collection will encourage
       a revival of interest in Hellman's works, especially
       after the recent publication of her memoir, *An Unfin-
       ished Woman.* Since her plays are sometimes presented
       on TV, this work will certainly be welcomed by professors
       and students of American drama, in particular."

VM5.   Harris, Robert R.   "Recent Revised and New Additions;
       Recent Anthologies; *The Collected Plays*," *Library Jour-
       nal*, XCVII (Feb. 15, 1972), 672.

       Points out in a short paragraph that this volume is con-
       sidered a definitive edition of LH's plays because of
       the revisions she made prior to the book's publication.

VM6.   Moers, Ellen.   "Family Theatre," *Commentary*, LIV (Sept.
       1972), 96-99.

       Argues that "all the plays ... are built around two con-
       suming obsessions: family and capital.  Capital is
       power, lust, hate, duty, destiny; like the family it is
       forever.  The world of the Hellman family is as violent
       as a summer thunderstorm, but just as dry and airless,
       and it is absolutely sealed off from strangers."

VM7.   Samuels, Charles Thomas.   "*Lillian Hellman, Playwright*,
       by Richard Moody; *The Collected Plays* by Lillian
       Hellman," *New York Times Book Review*, June 18, 1972, p.
       2.

       Evaluates Moody's book.  "Almost all the biographical
       data ... comes straight from her memoir.... The inter-
       pretations of her plays are equally second hand: new
       thoughts eked out with quotations." LH's book is called
       "the definitive edition of her works."  (See Item IVG14.)

VM8.   Szogyi, Alex.   "*The Collected Plays*," *Saturday Review*,
       LV (Aug. 12, 1972), 51-52.

       Suggests that "when the curtain comes down and a final
       list is made of the most important American plays of our
       time, several Hellman creations will be among them."

VI. REVIEWS OF SCREENPLAYS BY LILLIAN HELLMAN
(Television and Motion Picture Reviews Included)


VIA. *The Dark Angel*


VIA1. "On the Current Screen: *The Dark Angel*," *Literary Digest*, CXX (Sept. 14, 1935), 33.

Reports that the movie has been "skillfully adapted" by LH and Mordaunt Shairp. "The talkie is a more mature and satisfying work than its predecessor." (The previous version was a silent movie.)

VIA2. Sennwald, Andre. "The Screen: Samuel Goldwyn Presents a New Edition of *The Dark Angel* at Rivoli Theatre," New York *Times*, Sept. 6, 1935, p. 12.

Maintains that it is "a highly literate screen adaptation of Guy Bolton's play, skirting all the more obvious opportunities for tear jerking and over emphasis."


VIB. *These Three* (*The Children's Hour*--1936)


VIB1. Nugent, Frank S. "The Screen; Heralding the Arrival of *These Three* at the Rivoli--Charlie Chan at the Circus," New York *Times*, Mar. 19, 1936, p. 22.

Labels *These Three* "an unusual picture and it has been brought to the screen with perception, beauty, and a keen sense of drama."

VIB2. ————. "*These Three*, Those Five; *The Children's Hour* and the Dionnes Alike Have Whispering Campaigns," New York *Times*, Mar. 22, 1936, Sect. 11, p. 3.

Reasserts that "*These Three* emerges as an exception-
ally fine picture, compactly written, splendidly performed, and brilliantly directed and photographed."

VIB3.   "The Story of a Success," Brooklyn *Daily Eagle*, Mar.
15, 1936, Sect. C, p. 5.

Includes a short positive review.

VIB4.   Verschoyle, Derek.  "Stage and Screen; *The Children's
Hour*," *The Spectator*, CLVII (Nov. 20, 1936), 905.

Reports that "*These Three* was recently presented in
this country [Great Britain] in a form weakened by the
bowdlerisation which conventional prejudice against
discussion of its theme imposed.  The play itself has
been refused license."

VIB5.   Watts, Richard, Jr.  "*These Three*," New York *Herald
Tribune*, Mar. 19, 1936, p. 16.

Maintains that it is "a stirring, mature, and powerful
motion picture that is in every way worthy of its cel-
ebrated original...."

## VIC.   *The Spanish Earth*

VIC1.   Barnes, Howard.  "*The Spanish Earth*--Fifty-fifth Street
Playhouse," New York *Herald Tribune*, Aug. 21, 1937, p.
4.

Proclaims that *The Spanish Earth* is "the most powerful
and moving documentary film ever screened."

VIC2.   M[cManus], J[ohn] T.  "The Screen; *The Spanish Earth*
at 55th Street Playhouse, in a Plea for Democracy--
*Gangway at the Roxy*," New York *Times*, Aug. 21, 1937,
p. 7.

Reports that it is "the most rational appeal the screen
thus far has presented for the cause of Spanish demo-
cracy."

## VID. *The Little Foxes*

VID1. Barnes, Howard. "On the Screen; *The Little Foxes*--
Music Hall," New York *Herald Tribune*, Aug. 22, 1941,
p. 8.

Claims that a "fine play has become a finer film."

VID2. Crowther, Bosley. "The Screen in Review; *The Little
Foxes*, Full of Evil, Reaches the Screen in the Music
Hall -- Andy Hardy Becomes a Man at the Capitol -- New
Film at Palace," New York *Times*, Aug. 22, 1941, p. 19.

Points out that the "acidity and sinister nature" of
the play is "preserved in the screen version."

VID3. Ferguson, Otis. "The Man in the Movie," *New Republic*,
XC (Sept. 1, 1941), 278.

Calls *LF* "one of the really beautiful jobs in the whole
range of movie making...."

VID4. HB. "The New Movie; Bette Davis Adds to Her Screen
Laurels in *The Little Foxes* at the Music Hall," New
York *Sun*, Aug. 22, 1941, p. 14.

Calls *LF* "taut, tense ... a thrilling opening...."


## VIE. *Watch on the Rhine*

VIE1. Barnes, Howard. "On the Screen--*Watch on the Rhine*,"
New York *Herald Tribune*, Aug. 28, 1943, p. 6.

Proclaims that LH's play "has fared brilliantly on the
screen."

VIE2. Crowther, Bosley. "The Screen; 'Watch on the Rhine'
a Fine Screen Version of the Lillian Hellman Play,
Opens at the Strand--New Bill at Rialto," New York
*Times*, Aug. 28, 1943, p. 15.

Suggests that "it is meagre praise to call it one of
the fine adult films of these times." The action at
the play's beginning is characterized as "somewhat
stale, but it turns out to be lucid, and surely con-
ceived."

VIE3.  ———.  "Reflections of Passing Events in the Screen
       World; *Watch on the Rhine*," New York *Times*, Sept. 5,
       1943, Sect. 2, p. 3.

       Maintains that "the magnificence of Miss Hellman's drama
       lies in the fortitude and compassion of her leading
       characters."


                    VIF.  *The North Star*


VIF1.  "Cinema; The New Picture; *The North Star*," *Time*, XLII
       (Nov. 8, 1943), p. 54.

       Claims that "*North Star* tries to be a work of art.  It
       is not.... it does effectively bring experience of
       modern war to U.S...."

VIF2.  Crowther, Bosley.  "The Screen in Review; *The North
       Star* Invasion Drama, with Walter Huston, Opens in Two
       Theatres Here--*Claudia* at Music Hall," New York *Times*,
       Nov. 5, 1943, p. 23.

       Argues that "*North Star* has so much in it that is
       moving and triumphant that its sometime departures
       from reality may be generally overlooked."


                  VIG.  *The Searching Wind*


VIG1.  Crowther, Bosley.  "The Screen in Review; *The Searching
       Wind*, Paramount Film Based on Stage Play by Lillian
       Hellman, Opens Here--Robert Young in Top Role," New
       York *Times*, June 27, 1946, p. 29.

       Reports that *SW* is a "disappointing job ... the struc-
       ture of the drama is weak...."

## VIH.   *Another Part of the Forest*

VIH1.   Barnes, Howard.   "On the Screen--'Dynastic Skulduggery,'"
        New York *Herald Tribune*, May 19, 1948, p. 17.

> Argues that "the stage production was disappointing be-
> cause it stressed the lurid aspects of the family
> strife.  The film does not mute them...."

VIH2.   Hatch, Robert.  "Movies; Broadway in Hollywood," *New
        Republic*, CXVIII (June 7, 1948), 29.

> Notes that "despite its weakness" *APF* "is a field day
> for actors, and this Universal International Production
> is well cast."

VIH3.   "Movies of the Week; *Another Part of the Forest*," *Life*,
        XXIV (May 31, 1948), 63-64.

> Includes a positive pictorial review of the movie.

VIH4.   T.M.P.  "The Screen--*Another Part of the Forest*, More
        About Hubbard Family, New Film at the Rivoli," New
        York *Times*, May 19, 1948, p. 30.

> Recalls that "while the new picture definitely does not
> have the stature of *The Little Foxes*, it is ... com-
> pelling entertainment."


## VIi.   *The Children's Hour* (1962)

VIi1.   "Admirable Film of Hellman Play; Odeon Cinema; The
        Loudest Whisper," London *Times*, Aug. 17, 1962, p. 11.

> Summarizes *CH* plot.

VIi2.   Berkley, Paul V.  "The New Movies--'The Children's
        Hour,'" New York *Herald Tribune*, Mar. 15, 1962, p. 19.

> Argues that "the film is characterized by a stagelike
> order of events ... failing to arouse the imagination."

VIi3.   Crowther, Bosley.  "The Screen; New *Children's Hour*,
        Another Film Version of Play Arrives; Shirley MacLaine
        and Audrey Hepburn Star," New York *Times*, Mar. 15,
        1962, p. 28.

Reports that "there is nothing about this picture of which he, Mr. Wyler [the director], can be proud."

VIi4.  Winston, Archer.  "Reviewing Stand--'The Children's Hour' in Dual Bow," New York *Post*, Mar. 15, 1962, p. 63.

Criticizes *CH* film for being melodramatic. "This version now feels that Modern American Society has advanced enough to face the facts, but the ensuing huff, puff, and blow the emotional house down melodramatics are strictly from the 30's."


VIJ.  *Toys in the Attic*


VIJ1.  Christ, Judith.  "Tarnished *Toys in the Attic*," New York *Herald Tribune*, Aug. 1, 1963, p. 6.

Reports that *TIA* is "marked by two fine performances by two fine actresses." *TIA* "emerges on the screen as another Grand Guignol, of crazy mixed-up folk in the Deep South."

VIJ2.  Crowther, Bosley.  "The Screen; *Toys in the Attic* Opens," New York *Times*, Aug. 1, 1963, p. 17.

Points out that "somebody out there in Hollywood has made even more of a wreck of *Toys in the Attic*, than was made of it on the stage."

VIJ3.  Winston, Archer.  "Reviewing Stand; *Toys in the Attic* at Astor, Cinema I," New York *Post*, Aug. 1, 1963, p. 22.

Includes a mixed review stating that the movie has "contrived action" and "brilliance."


VIK.  *The Chase*


VIK1.  Crowther, Bosley.  "The Screen; *The Chase*; Overheated Western is Served at Two Theatres," New York *Times*, Feb. 19, 1966, p. 12.

Labels the screenplay "overheated." Cites the "emotional content, the pictorial style, the directing, the acting, the fist fighting, the burning of the junkyard at the end" as all overdone.

VIK2. ————. "The IQ of Hollywood Films," New York *Times*, Feb. 20, 1966, Sect. 2, p. 1.

Labels *The Chase* "a shockingly cheap sensational film ... a cross between *High Noon* and *Peyton Place*."

VIK3. Winston, Archer. "Reviewing Stand--'The Chase' at Victoria and Sutton," New York *Post*, Feb. 20, 1966, p. 49.

Includes a summary.

## VIL. *Montserrat* (TV Version)

VIL1. Gould, Jack. "TV; Of War and Hostages but Lacking Persuasion," New York *Times*, Mar. 2, 1971, p. 71.

Satirically notes that "*Montserrat* evokes the tension of watching a metronome."

## VIM. *Another Part of the Forest* (TV Version)

VIM1. O'Connor, John J. "TV Review; Culture's Key to Public Broadcasting Season," New York *Times*, Oct. 3, 1972, p. 91.

Suggests that the center of LH's drama "may be hollow." *APF* "is not one of her more convincing efforts."

VII.   REVIEWS OF HELLMAN AUTOBIOGRAPHIES

VIIA.   Reviews of *An Unfinished Woman*.   1969

VIIA1.   Allen, Trevor.   "Books in Brief," *Books and Bookmen*, XVIII (June 1973), 137.

Announces Penguin paperback edition of *UW* and includes brief summary.

VIIA2.   *American Jewish Archives*, XXIII (Apr. 1971), 105.

Notes that LH's autobiography is filled with a "melancholic strain."

VIIA3.   Bailey, Paul.   "Beyond the Veil; *An Unfinished Woman*," *The Listener*, LXXXII (Oct. 23, 1969), 567-568.

Characterizes LH as "a generous and ferociously dignified woman."   Does not like LH's plays, but *UW* receives a favorable review here.

VIIA4.   Barkham, John.   "The Literary Scene," New York *Post*, June 30, 1969, p. 18.

Points out that LH "has never lived a conventional life" and thus her autobiography is unconventional. "Those who have waited years to read it will not be disappointed."

VIIA5.   Beam, Alvin.   "The Memoirs of Dramatist Lillian Hellman," Cleveland *Plain Dealer*, July 6, 1969, Sect. H, p. 4.

Criticizes *UW* for being incomplete.   "One puts the book down wishing there were more to it...."   Characterizes LH as a "fascinating woman."

VIIA6.   Beaufort, John.   "Not Least on Herself," *Christian Science Monitor*, July 24, 1969, p. 7.

Criticizes LH for not including information about the
theatre, films, or any of the actors and collaborators
who helped her achieve fame. "Yet perhaps no snub
[of those in the theatre] was intended. Perhaps it
was merely part of the paradox of her life that one
so intolerant of any artifice should have achieved
her reputation with the aid of those who lived by
artifice."

VIIA7.   Blakestone, Oswell. "In Love with Books," *Books and
         Bookmen*, XV (Jan. 1969), 48-49.

         Proclaims that *UW* is "alive, absorbing, inspiring and
         legend making ... written by someone who is truthful
         and courageous as well as gifted." Books for LH are
         "the best of life."

VIIA8.   *Booklist*, LXVI (Sept. 1, 1969), p. 25.

         Labels *UW* an "unsentimentalized, sometimes penetrating,
         and often frustrating self-portrait."

VIIA9.   Brien, Ann. "Personal Document," Chattanooga *Times*,
         June 29, 1969, Sect. B, p. 2.

         Calls LH's autobiography "far more a personal than a
         professional document.... The whole book's good."

VIIA10.  Campbell, Mary. "Book Corner; Christine to Tell All,"
         San Francisco *Examiner*, July 10, 1969, p. 35.

         Concludes that LH may perceive herself as "unfinished"
         but she is nevertheless "not so very unfinished, and
         fascinating to read about."

VIIA11.  *Choice*, VII (Apr. 1970), 246.

         Maintains that *UW* is "disappointing" because despite
         its occasional eloquence, "allusion annoyingly re-
         places definition, the tone is often that of gossip,
         and the organization is essentially personal and
         chaotic." Praises anecdotes about Dorothy Parker,
         Hemingway, and others.

VIIA12.  Derrickson, Howard. "'Dash' Hammett Her Man, After
         All--Lilly Hellman's War and Peace," St. Louis *Globe-
         Democrat*, June 28-29, 1969, Sect. C, p. 5.

         Argues that LH's "unerring ear for dialogue makes
         this autobiography come alive on every page. Cadence
         and tone are always authentic, whether representing

Dorothy Parker's brittle wit or Hemingway's desperately masculine rodomontade."

VIIA13.   Duffy, Sister M. Gregory, OP. *Best Sellers*, XXIX (July 1, 1969), 132-133.

Calls *UW* intelligent and imaginative in a positive review.

VIIA14.   Epstein, Joseph.  "No Punches Pulled; *An Unfinished Woman: A Memoir*," *New Republic*, CLXI (July 26, 1969), 27-29.

Points out that LH has been an exceptional playwright, she "has known the love of an extraordinary man," and "has gotten through more than sixty years with only minimum rations of self-deception.  She may consider herself an unfinished woman, but from here hers appears a remarkably complete life."

VIIA15.   Finlayson, John.  "Among the Literati Life Was Seldom Mild," Detroit *News*, July 6, 1969, Sect. E, p. 3.

The book is filled with "candor.  The looking back is often despairing and bitter."  The compassion in the book does not take the "chill" out.

VIIA16.   French, Philip.  "A Difficult Woman," *New Statesman*, LXXVIII (Oct. 24, 1969), 580.

Notes that in *UW*, LH "has taken modesty a little too far.  That she apparently doesn't much care for the theatre world or that her political views are not carefully thought through, does not strike me as a good reason for the omission."

VIIA17.   Fuller, Edmund.  "The Bookshelf; Shy Solitary Writer as a Difficult Woman," *Wall Street Journal*, July 9, 1969, p. 16.

Calls *UW* "rewarding ... both as a personal document and for its pictures of people, times, and places....."

VIIA18.   Gardner, Marilyn.  "A Playwright's Life Unfolds in Patches Bright and Somber," Milwaukee *Journal*, July 20, 1969, Sect. 5, p. 4.

Criticizes *UW* for being an "unfinished book."  LH has omitted too much from her autobiography.

VIIA19.   Grant, Annette.   "Lively Lady; *An Unfinished Woman:*
          *A Memoir*," *Newsweek*, LXXIII (June 30, 1973), 89-90.

          Concludes that *UW* "is a peculiar breed of autobio-
          graphy.  Nonconsecutive and erratic, it swings freely
          between chatty anecdote and unsparing self-lacera-
          tion."

VIIA20.   Hipp, Edward Sothern.   "Hellman on Life," Newark
          *Sunday News*, Sept. 14, 1969, Sect. E, p. 23.

          Suggests that *UW* is an "unfinished book."

VIIA21.   *Kirkus*, XXXVII (Apr. 15, 1969), 484.

          Briefly notes that *UW* gives us "roses and thistles,
          and in casual fashion, an intimate and eloquent re-
          miniscence."

VIIA22.   Knight, Al.   "Lillian Hellman's Memoirs Written with
          Candor, Graceful Self-Doubt," Denver *Post*, July 27,
          1969, *Roundup*, p. 16.

          Reports that *UW* is "candid," and is "written with a
          graceful sense of self-doubt that is neither evasive
          nor overwrought."

VIIA23.   Kotlowitz, Robert.   "The Rebel as Writer," *Harper's*,
          CCXXXVII (June 1969), 87-92.

          The volume is "lucid, flirty, and vulnerable."  It
          is filled with "compressed prose" and biting dia-
          logue similar to that found in her plays.

VIIA24.   Lasson, Robert.   "Something Old, Something New,
          Something Borrowed," Chicago *Tribune*, June 22, 1969,
          Sect. 9, p. 5.

          Calls *UW* "disappointing....  It is not ungracious to
          suggest that Lillian Hellman who in her time has fed
          the beast good red meat has chosen to stay out of
          range this time."

VIIA25.   Lehmann-Haupt, Christopher.   "Books of the Times;
          The Incompleat Lillian Hellman," New York *Times*,
          June 30, 1969, p. 37.

          Criticizes *UW* by noting that "by juxtaposing odd
          pieces of her life she has given us a detailed por-
          trait of a person who doesn't want to be portrayed."

VIIA26.   Leigh, Rebecca.   "Books," *Chatelaine*, XLII (Oct. 1969), 6.

Labels *UW* a "fascinating autobiography.   The only criticism, she leaves too much out."

VIIA27.   Malpede, Karen.   "A Woman's Search for Self," St. Louis *Post Dispatch*, July 6, 1969, Sect. B, p. 4.

Suggests that *UW* "is most interesting when it follows the objective style of journalism--made subjective by choice and arrangement of observations.   Her gift is not analytical and her scattered attempts at analysis, usually of herself, are disappointing."

VIIA28.   [Mam].   "A B Trade Reviews," *A B Bookman's Weekly*, V-VI (Aug. 4-11, 1969), 314.

Claims that *UW* is a "rewarding and unpretentious book of partial self-revelation by a creative woman who does not take on about it."

VIIA29.   Menn, Thorpe.   "Books of the Day; Book News & Previews; A Woman of Many Worlds," Kansas City *Star*, July 13, 1969, Sect. D, p. 3.

Includes a short review of *UW* that is primarily informational, calls the book "unpredictable."

VIIA30.   Meserve, Walter J.   "Drama; Bibliographies, Histories, Anthologies, Dissertations," *American Literary Scholarship, 1969*.   Edited by J. Albert Robbins.   Durham, N.C.: Duke U. Press, 1971, p. 299.

Points out that *UW* is "interesting reading ... but disappointing for the person hoping to find comments on her plays or the theatre."

VIIA31.   M[oody], M[innie] H[ite].   "Uninhibited Memoir Is Almost Biography," Columbus *Dispatch*, July 6, 1969, *Tab*, p. 12.

Illustrates LH's "great gift for timing and turn of phrase ... she lays herself bare without self-consciousness, and to useful purpose."   It is "a book to admire."

VIIA32.   Morton, James.   "Lillian Hellman's Memoirs," *Contemporary Review*, CCXVI, (Mar. 1970), 165-166.

Summarizes *UW*.   "Throughout this memoir flit the years of thirties, forties and fifties in kaleidoscopic

fashion shifting page by page, the sad death of
George Gershwin, Hammett's quarrels with Hemingway,
Hammett's championship of Scott Fitzgerald.  Lost
friends, lost opportunities, lost decades are beautifully recalled."

VIIA33.  Nelson, Elizabeth R.  "The Book Review; Biography and
Personal Narrative; *An Unfinished Woman*," *Library
Journal*, XCIV (June 15, 1969), 2461.

Notes that LH's "memoirs may not be to every reader's
taste; the book is at times intensely personal and
again sketchily anecdotal in style."

VIIA34.  "Notable Books of 1969," *American Libraries*, I (Mar.
1970), 277.

Includes *UW* in a list and labels it "warm and honest."

VIIA35.  "Paperbacks," *Publishers Weekly*, CXCVII (May 11,
1970), 42.

Calls *UW* a "candid and understated story of an important life."

VIIA36.  "People; *An Unfinished Woman*," *Saturday Review*, LIII
(Nov. 28, 1970), 39.

Claims that LH's "slightly off-center memoir cuts
less close to the core of her own being than to the
heart of her uncommonly lively circle...."

VIIA37.  Perley, Maie E.  "The Book Scene; Lillian Hellman
Memoirs May Sully Some Images," Louisville *Times*,
July 16, 1969, Sect. A, p. 7.

Maintains that "this astringent piece of autobiography
brims with the richness of experience and also bears
the rugged imprint of truth and honesty.  Compassion
for the human condition runs deep in this woman who,
by confession, is both tempestuous and passionate."

VIIA38.  Pritchett, V.S.  "Stern Self Portrait of a Lady,"
*Life*, LXVI (June 28, 1969), 12.

Suggests that LH's "memoir is not of the long-winded,
self-caressing kind.  It is a good humored but drastic
search for what she has been and is.  She chisels
away at areas of her past, like a sculptor seeking
aspects of the figure hidden somewhere in the stone."

VIIA39. "Probing Without Pattern," *Times Literary Supplement*, Jan. 22, 1970, p. 75.

Concludes that *UW* is "set down with an integrity and courage which surely offers hope for the future."

VIIA40. Pryce-Jones, Alan. "On Books; Author's Autobiography Skies, but Don't Skip It," *Newsday*, June 19, 1969, Sect. C, p. 6.

Notes that LH "has written an unfinished autobiography: a grasshopper of a book, which leaps a decade here and there, tidies no loose ends, and seldom stops to explain. It also enchants. Miss Hellman is an extra-ordinarily good writer. She expresses a totally feminine nature in totally masculine prose, and the result is un-put-downable."

VIIA41. "P W Forecasts," *Publishers Weekly*, CXCV (Apr. 14, 1969), 94.

Notes that *UW* is "one of the most compelling auto-biographies of the season."

VIIA42. Rabinowitz, Dorothy. "Experience as Drama," *Commentary*, XLVIII (Dec. 1969), 95-96.

Claims that *UW* "is a record of personal discovery most of which does not approach the fine emotional conclusions on Hammett.... Some of the details are ordinary, some are not: the feel of all of it is intensity bordering on the exorbitant." LH's "drama-turgical instincts permit no conversation, no word, no twitch of a face, no walk across a room which does not create a scene."

VIIA43. "Recommended," Nashville *Tennessean*, July 20, 1969, Sect. B, p. 6.

Summarizes *UW* and recommends that others read it.

VIIA44. Rogers, W.G. "Personal History," *Saturday Review*, LII (July 5, 1969), 30-31.

Claims that "the whole book is [like] vivid, thrilling theater; the littlest incident is whipped into a dramatic scene. There will be curtain calls galore."

VIIA45. Roth, Russell. "Lillian Hellman Unveils Fading Era in New Book," Minneapolis *Star*, July 7, 1969, Sect. A, p. 14.

Calls *UW* an "almost masochistic autobiography" because of the "depressing" nature of the book.  It
"rambles" with anger.

VIIA46.   Ruggles, Eleanor.  "Reflections from Lillian
          Hellman," Boston *Sunday Globe*, July 6, 1969, Sect.
          A, p. 72.

          Reports that like LH's plays her memoir "has a grim
          humor and a coruscating brilliance."

VIIA47.   Rumley, Larry.  "Miss Hellman Remembers," Seattle
          *Times*, Aug. 3, 1969, Magazine, p. 18.

          Calls *UW* "a remarkably candid memoir" by the "premier
          woman playwright."

VIIA48.   Saal, Rollene W.  "Pick of the Paperbacks," *Saturday
          Review*, LIII (Nov. 28, 1970), 39.

          Briefly notes that *UW* is about LH's friends.  Recom-
          mends it for Christmas giving.

VIIA49.   Tinkle, Lon.  "The Sharp Imprint of Miss Hellman,"
          Dallas *News*, June 29, 1969, Sect. F, p. 8.

          Exclaims that in *UW*, LH has written superb, effort-
          less prose.

VIIA50.   Toomey, Philippa.  "Paperbacks--*An Unfinished Woman*
          by Lillian Hellman," London *Times*, Feb. 22, 1973, p.
          11.

          Calls *UW* a "scrappy and disorganized memoir [with]
          some deep insights into her [LH's] nature."

VIIA51.   Weeks, Edward.  "The Peripatetic Reviewer," *Atlantic*,
          CCXXIV (July 1969), 106.

          Emphasizes that LH "is astringently honest with her-
          self; she does not try to hide her Jewish sensitivity
          --or her indignation at meanness.  I like to read
          about people who lose their temper, and Lillian
          Hellman loses hers with speed and hit-back that are
          a joy to watch."

VIIA52.   Wilds, John W.  "Memories Return Her to a New Orleans
          Fig Tree," New Orleans *Times-Picayune*, June 29, 1969,
          Sect. 3, p. 3.

          Reports that "after 280 pages the reader knows that
          Miss Hellman has been showing off ever since [her

childhood]. And very successfully too.... She has
a mind of her own."

VIIA53.  Williams, Michaela. "Miss Hellman's Personal Frag-
ments Merge into Personality of Beauty," *National
Observer*, July 14, 1969, p. 17.

Includes no critical comment with the exception of
the article's title.

VIIA54.  Young, Stanley. "A Public Person's Portrait of Her
Private Self; *An Unfinished Woman*," *New York Times
Book Review*, June 29, 1969, p. 8.

Predicts that "readers will respond to her book because it not only shows rare imagination and literary
skill but reveals with an almost sad reluctance the
unexpected personal story of a great American playwright."

VIIB.  Reviews of *Pentimento: A Book of Portraits*. 1973

VIIB1.  Alexander, James E. "An Incisive Work from Lillian
Hellman," Pittsburgh *Post-Gazette*, Sept. 15, 1973,
p. 17.

Suggests that "*Pentimento* seems to outdo fiction,
[for it] turns many sharp and fascinating corners as
it goes, and lays bare not only bits of flesh of
others, but gives a biting picture of the author herself."

VIIB2.  Annan, Gabriele. "Professional Portraits; *Pentimento*,"
*The Listener*, XCI (Apr. 25, 1974), 535-536.

Notes that "one expects memoirs to be a bit more
cinema-verité ... her very professionalism and craftsmanship injure her credibility."

VIIB3.  Beam, Alvin. "Brilliantly Hellman," Cleveland *Plain
Dealer*, Oct. 7, 1973, Sect. F, p. 4.

Claims that *Pentimento* "is one of the fine memoirs of
our century, a book to surprise the young and move and
delight their remembering seniors."

VIIB4.    *Booklist*, CXX (Oct. 15, 1973), 204.

          Includes a very brief summary.

VIIB5.    "Books; Flashback," *The Economist*, CCLI (May 25, 1974), 143-144.

          Calls the book a "new successful genre" for LH who claims "she has finished writing drama. It does not matter, if this superb form of flickering autobiography is what she chooses to do instead.... a remarkable form of autobiography."

VIIB6.    "Books; Looking Back," *Chatelaine*, XLIV (Dec. 1973), 4.

          Maintains that "in *Pentimento* ... she attempts to find out what these people meant to her then, and what they mean now, and handles the two levels so well that you are left wishing she had found time to write novels as well as plays."

VIIB7.    Brady, Charles A. "Playwright Pens Series of Portraits," Buffalo *News*, Sept. 15, 1973, Sect. B, p. 8.

          Considers *Pentimento* "an utterly charming book" which has "enormous human depth."

VIIB8.    Carroll, Edward. "Lil Hellman Unlocks Cupboards of Past," *Variety*, Oct. 17, 1973, p. 43.

          Calls *Pentimento* interesting and revealing. LH's family has provided "raw material" for her best plays.

VIIB9.    Cattoi, Louis. "Combing the Past; Lillian Hellman Puts It on Stage," Milwaukee *Journal*, Sept. 9, 1973, Sect. 5, p. 4.

          Suggests that *Pentimento* is "an addendum" to *UW*. It is a "fascinating book."

VIIB10.   *Choice*, X (Jan. 1974), 1718.

          Recalls that "this is a brilliant series of sketches, reminiscences, portraits, almost all of which have been excerpted in *Esquire*, *Atlantic*, and *New Yorker*."

VIIB11.   Cochran, Bess White. "A Treat for the Reader," Nashville *Tennessean*, Sept. 23, 1973, Sect. E, p. 8.

Proclaims that LH "is an accomplished literary craftsman ... [who demonstrates] a deft gift of weaving words so that the separate stories appear seamless."

VIIB12. Cosgrove, Mary Silva. "Outlook Tower," *Horn Book*, L (Feb. 1972), 76.

Describes *Pentimento* as a collection of "fascinating portraits, described with dramatic precision and sparkling dialogue in her own unique style."

VIIB13. Dignan, Josef. "Playwright Trips Down Memory Lane; Brings Back a Deep South Potpourri," Louisville *Times*, Sept. 20, 1973, Sect. E, p. 5.

Notes that the book "offers us a rare glimpse into the mind and heart of one of our foremost theater artists."

VIIB14. Downing, Robert. "Ad Lib," Denver *Post*, Sept. 2, 1973, *Roundup*, p. 2.

Argues that although the book has merit, its "invective and strange sly humor is overproduced and over-priced by its publishers."

VIIB15. Duffy, Martha. "Half Told Tales," *Time*, CII (Oct. 1, 1973), 114.

Criticizes LH for not being more direct in *Pentimento*. She should have written her memoirs "in the same, forthright, energetic fashion as she apparently lived her life. Alas, not so."

VIIB16. Edgerton, Michael. "Miss Hellman Eludes Us Too Much," Chicago *Sun Times*, Sept. 30, 1973, *Showcase*, p. 14.

Maintains that *Pentimento*'s chapters "read like short stories in which she [LH] is a character as often as her friends. The author as short story writer and the author as autobiographer are at odds with one another. The autobiographer is facile ... the short story writer uncraftsmanlike...."

VIIB17. Fremont-Smith, Eliot. "Lillian Hellman; Portrait of a Lady," *New York*, VI (Sept. 17, 1973), 82.

Recalls *UW* and notes that "what seems unfinished or ungenerous in the first book is explored and resolved here."

VIIB18.   French, Philip.  "A Difficult Woman; *Pentimento* by
          Lillian Hellman," London *Times*, Apr. 25, 1974, p. 12.

          Labels *Pentimento* "illuminating."  It is "a book that
          fills the gaps" of *UW*.

VIIB19.   Grossman, Edward.  "The Past Refinished," *Commentary*,
          LXXIV (Feb. 1974), 88-90.

          Claims that *Pentimento* "has its ups and downs, but on
          the whole it is really bad--there's no getting around
          that.  The interesting part is why one wants to try.
          From the beginning, instead of being slight and
          charming, the writing is irritating for several
          reasons, one of them a strange portentousness that
          is so heavy at times it almost passes for preten-
          tiousness."

VIIB20.   Haynes, Muriel.  "More on the *Unfinished Woman*,"
          *Ms.*, II (Jan. 1974), 31-33.

          Calls LH a "scrupulously searching woman" who should
          write more in order to "continue to distill her ex-
          periences."

VIIB21.   Hirsch, Foster.  "*Pentimento: A Book of Portraits*,"
          *America*, CXXIX (Dec. 29, 1973), 508-510.

          Points out that the chapter in *Pentimento* concerning
          LH's plays "is surely the most direct statement we
          will ever have from the playwright herself about her
          own work, and it is therefore of value to the student
          of American drama.  Crisply and unflinchingly, she
          compiles a record of the genesis of each of her
          plays ... and of her frequent dissatisfaction with
          the discrepancy between what she intended to write
          and what she saw, finally, on the stage."

VIIB22.   Horwitz, Carey A.  *Library Journal*, XCVIII (Nov. 15,
          1973), 3369.

          Claims that LH "is not a very accessible individual;
          the same privateness that has given strength to her
          character gives strength to this work, which be-
          comes essentially the battleground upon which the
          dialectic war between the emotional truth of her
          memory and the objective truth of her real past is
          waged.  The struggle is fought, of course, with
          words: and Hellman has never used them better."

VIIB23.   Hutsching, Ed.  "Lillian Hellman; Just Too Honest,"
          San Diego *Union*, Sept. 30, 1973, Sect. E, p. 6.

          Predicts that the book "will not be to everyone's
          taste, but it will delight Hellman fans and students
          of the American language who appreciate its capabil-
          ities as well as its shortcomings."

VIIB24.   Janeway, Elizabeth.  "Passionate, Enigmatic Charac-
          ters," *Newsday*, Sept. 9, 1973, *Books*, p. 1.

          Suggests that LH "has clapped her spectacles over our
          eyes for a moment to let us see as she does."

VIIB25.   Keith, Don Lee.  "A Playwright Sorts, Shares Her
          Memories," New Orleans *Times-Picayune*, Oct. 7, 1973,
          Sect. 3, p. 10.

          Evaluates *Pentimento*: a "successful balance, combin-
          ing the right ingredients in the right proportions
          demands insight, sensitivity, and discipline, and
          this volume is a supreme example of all three in
          tightrope action."

VIIB26.   *Kirkus*, XLI (July 15, 1973), 792.

          Claims that LH's "portraits of people are idiosyncrat-
          ically, palpably, and marvelously real and present."

VIIB27.   Kirsch, Robert.  "Books; Three Authors and Their
          Second Thoughts," Los Angeles *Times*, Sept. 23, 1973,
          *Book Review*, p. 5.

          Maintains that "people painted in *Pentimento* have
          been used before, transformed into characters in her
          plays.  She does not say this explicitly but one
          cannot help feeling that it is so."

VIIB28.   Krome, Margery Loomis.  "An Artist Reworks Her Life,"
          Norfolk *Virginian-Pilot*, Sept. 30, 1973, Sect. C,
          8.

          Criticizes *Pentimento* for lapsing "into the 'little-
          did-I-know-then' kind of mysterious innuendo that
          leaves her story half-told and her reader half-satis-
          fied.  In spite of this irritating style the people
          in her book emerge as motley and colorful."

VIIB29.   Kupferberg, Herbert.  "Hellman Memoir Summons People
          for an Encore," *National Observer*, Oct. 13, 1973, p.
          19.

Praises LH for adding "depth to certain aspects of
the picture of her life, mostly through some remarkable character portrayals."

VIIB30.  Lamson, Pam.  "A Gem by Lillian Hellman," Boston
         *Globe*, Oct. 7, 1973, Sect. A, p. 94.

         Calls *Pentimento* "a splendid, marvelously funny and
         evocative work."  Its contents are "captivating, in-
         cisive, and absorbing."

VIIB31.  Lee, Charles.  "Lillian Hellman's Memoirs Candid,
         Graceful, Tough," Philadelphia *Bulletin*, Sept. 23,
         1973, Sect. 2, p. 8.

         Considers the book a "satisfying fragment; paradoxi-
         cally it's complete in itself, as excellent and ab-
         sorbing as its predecessor," *UW*.

VIIB32.  Lehmann-Haupt, Christopher.  "Books of the Times;
         Seeing Others to See Oneself; *Pentimento*," New York
         *Times*, Sept. 17, 1973, p. 31.  See also Washington
         *Star*, Sept. 28, 1973, Sect. B, p. 6.

         Proclaims that *Pentimento* is a "mysteriously exciting
         and beautiful thing to see in print."

VIIB33.  Leonard, John.  "1973: An Apology and 38 Consola-
         tions," *New York Times Book Review*, Dec. 2, 1973, p.
         2.

         Suggests that *Pentimento* contains "prose as precise
         as an electron microscope."

VIIB34.  Liebrum, Martha.  "More Masterpieces from Hellman,"
         Houston *Post*, Sept. 12, 1973, *Spotlight*, p. 12.

         Argues that the book is "as good as her first work.
         And hopefully it will not be her last because there
         are huge areas she has not covered...."

VIIB35.  McCabe, John.  "Lillian Hellman's Life and Times;
         Bittersweet Memories of a Playwright," Detroit *News*,
         Sept. 16, 1973, Sect. E, p. 5.

         Evaluates *Pentimento* as a "humanizing book ...
         superb."

VIIB36.  McLellan, Joseph.  "Pick of the Paperbacks; 1974,"
         *Book World* (Washington *Post*, Chicago *Tribune*), Dec.
         22, 1974, p. 3.

Announces the Signet publication of *Pentimento* and
claims that LH has had "an uncommonly rich textured
life."

VIIB37. Mather, Bobby. "Lillian Hellman Looks Back--Again,"
Detroit *Free Press*, Oct. 7, 1973, Sect. D, p. 5.

Suggests that LH "gives this rich dower to her
readers, looking back at times that were simultaneously more innocent and more sophisticated than
today. The effect is like a fascinating older aunt,
indulgently letting the youngsters look through her
jewelry."

VIIB38. M[oody], M[innie] H[ite]. "Lillian Hellman Pens
Second Candid Memoir," Columbus *Dispatch*, Oct. 7,
1973, Sect. D, p. 6.

Claims that parts of *Pentimento* are filled with "sheer
excitement and tension.... maintains all the way a
remarkably high literary level."

VIIB39. Morley, Sheridan. "Memories of 'An Unfinished
Woman,'" London *Times*, May 1, 1974, p. 11.

Includes a summary review.

VIIB40. "News in Paperback; *Pentimento*," *New York Times Book
Review*, Oct. 13, 1974, p. 46.

Briefly notes that the book is "engaging, brilliantly
finished."

VIIB41. Nordell, Roderick. "Book Briefings," *Christian
Science Monitor*, Nov. 14, 1973, p. 46.

Points out that LH "recalls herself as a lady on a
train, smuggling money into Hitler's Germany for a
girlhood friend. She recalls later friends like the
rich mercurial lawyer Arthur Cowan--an unlikely
companion of McCarthy-era blacklisting who now cites
dismay not so much at 'the persecutors' as at 'those
who allowed the persecution.'"

VIIB42. "Painted Over," *Times Literary Supplement*, Apr. 26,
1974, p. 440.

Exclaims that *Pentimento* is "a strange, fascinating
book, which attempts to impose the clear structures
of fiction upon the real world, yet gains in artistry
whenever the untidiness of reality breaks in to confuse the pattern."

VIIB43.   Prescott, Peter S.   "Leftover Life," *Newsweek*, LXXXII
          (Oct. 1, 1973), 95-96.

          Argues that LH, as a playwright, "was a remarkably
          strong storyteller; she sustains that difficult art
          throughout this translation into a different, perhaps
          equally demanding genre."

VIIB44.   Poirier, Richard.   "*Pentimento: A Book of Portraits*,"
          *Book World* (Washington *Post*, Chicago *Tribune*), Sept.
          16, 1973, p. 1.

          Notes that *Pentimento* "provides one of those rare
          instances when the moral value of a book is wholly
          inextricable from its immense literary worth...."

VIIB45.   "P W Forecasts," *Publishers Weekly*, CCIV (July 16,
          1973), 106.

          Claims that the book is "a unique sort of human car-
          tography that is part memoir, part portrait, part
          charting of those human unknowns that are eternally
          fascinating and mysterious."

VIIB46.   Rabinowitz, Dorothy.   "Books in Brief; *Pentimento:
          A Book of Portraits*," *World*, II (Aug. 28, 1973), 39.

          Briefly notes that LH's book gives pleasure in a
          "peculiarly sharp way."

VIIB47.   Raphael, Frederic.   "Under Fire," London *Sunday
          Times*, Apr. 28, 1974, p. 38.

          Includes a mixed review.   "My deference blends a
          feeling that she is a little too sure of her own im-
          portance and a bit of a prig.   Under one's 'yes' for
          the book, an underlying 'no' insists on being seen."

VIIB48.   Ross, Jackie.   "The Point Has Aged," Hartford *Courant*,
          Sept. 30, 1973, Sect. F, p. 6.

          Maintains that as an artist with words LH is honest,
          forthright, and demanding.   The book was written, it
          seems, more for herself than for the average reader
          to "take home for a moment's pleasure."

VIIB49.   Roud, Richard.   "What Lillian Left Off Broadway,"
          Manchester *Guardian Weekly*, May 11, 1974, p. 22.

          Harshly criticizes *Pentimento* and LH.   "The trouble
          is that her very best plays aren't masterpieces either.

Seldom has a writer got so much mileage on so little achievement." *Pentimento* is "shop talk," not "totally uninteresting."

VIIB50.  Schorer, Mark. "A Way of Seeing and Then Seeing Again; *Pentimento*," *New York Times Book Review*, Sept. 23, 1973, pp. 1-2.

Forecasts that "it will be a long time before we have a book of personal reminiscence as engaging as this one, and even longer before we have another with a more intriguing title."

VIIB51.  Schoretter, Hilda N. "Lillian Hellman Writes of Life," Richmond *Times Dispatch*, Sept. 23, 1973, Sect. F, p. 3.

Considers *Pentimento* "a remarkably fine piece of writing...." It is "exciting, poignant, completely readable, thoroughly enjoyable."

VIIB52.  Siggins, Clara M., Ph.D. *Best Sellers*, XXXIII (Oct. 1, 1973), 303.

Maintains that LH's strength is in writing drama. "But now that Miss Hellman has recaptured these fine careless raptures twice over, she might as well take her own advice from her Memoirs -- to hell with this memory nonsense -- 'The play's the thing.'"

VIIB53.  Simon, John. "Pentimental Journey," *Hudson Review* XXVI (Winter 1973-1974), 741-752.

Explores each of the seven essays of *Pentimento* in a lengthy review. "Though Miss Hellman is evidently a memory artist, she never gives us the look, the essential characteristics, the feel of a person in one of those rapid sketches that cleaves to a reader's remembrance. There is not one character in *Pentimento* whom, however much I may get to know him or her in other ways, I can clearly visualize despite the painterly title and promise of this memoir."

VIIB54.  Tallmer, Jerry. "Woman in the News; Lillian Hellman," New York *Post*, Oct. 13, 1973, Sect. 3, p. 1.

Claims that *Pentimento* "contains some of the most brilliant talent that goes back to *The Children's Hour* in 1934, and the critics are quite rightfully saying so. In *Pentimento* the shadings and nuances of

*An Unfinished Woman* have deepened and sharpened, in accordance with the meaning of the word that gives the book its name."

VIIB55.   Theroux, Paul. "Dowager Empress," *New Statesman*, LXXXVII (Apr. 26, 1974), 587–588.

Reports that LH "survived an age that killed her friends, ruined her financially and scattered her family; she writes calmly, as a survivor, with her elegance intact, like a dowager empress surveying a lost kingdom from the last throne in the land."

VIIB56.   Thomas, Phil. "In Anger and Happiness; Book Forum," San Francisco *Examiner*, Oct. 18, 1973, *Books*, p. 1.

Claims that *Pentimento* is full of remembrances that are "beautifully evoked, as are all the portraits in this book."

VIIB57.   Walt, James. "An Honest Memoir; *Pentimento: A Book of Portraits*," *New Republic*, CLXIX (Oct. 20, 1973), 27–28.

Labels *Pentimento* "an honest work and because honesty is one of the surest means of keeping a book from hopelessly dating, Hellman's two volumes of memoirs are likely to be read as long as her best plays."

VIIB58.   Warga, Wayne. "Lillian Hellman's Memory Serves Her Correctly," Los Angeles *Times*, Jan. 13, 1974, *Calendar*, p. 1.

Maintains that LH "has said much that is not easy to say, and she will doubtlessly say more. All that she has said is important in that, like all great writers, what she says about herself tells us about ourselves."

VIIC.   Reviews of *Scoundrel Time*.   1976

VIIC1.   Alexander, James E. "McCarthy Era Recalled by Hellman," Pittsburgh *Post-Gazette*, Apr. 24, 1976, p. 17.

Reports that *ST* "contains several scattered memories, some unrelated to the hearings. It seems she wants to get down some recollections before they fade away completely, such as being unable to eat breakfast offered her by Henry Wallace: a poached egg and shreaded wheat. Perhaps three or four autobiographical books on the same person are too many."

VIIC2. Allen, Bruce. "Witness to a Period of Suspicion, Paranoia," Boston *Sunday Globe*, June 13, 1976, Sect. E, p. 16.

Considers *ST* as an "oblique, tantalizing 'history' of the Hollywood blacklist and its long aftermath ... [it is] like Kurt Vonnegut's novel *Slaughterhouse Five*; it had to be written, but its slapdash anecdotal construction, and its confusing mixture of tones and motives, limit its success...."

VIIC3. Beam, Alvin. "Lillian Hellman Recalls the Time of Witch Hunts," Cleveland *Plain Dealer*, Apr. 25, 1976, Sect. 5, p. 26.

Claims that in *ST*, LH is proclaiming that "it is never altogether over, and there are words for our time too in this uniquely individualist book full of private discernments and wit, and flavor."

VIIC4. "Books Briefly," *Progressive*, XL (Aug. 1976), 44.

Praises *ST* for being "vividly alive done with superb time and skill." Includes summary of the book.

VIIC5. *Booklist*, LXXII (Apr. 1, 1976), 1083.

Reports that in *ST* "with typical acerbity, Hellman reveals the ongoings behind the scene of this episode [HUAC hearings]...."

VIIC6. "Books; *Scoundrel Time*," *Economist*, CCLXI (Nov. 20, 1976), 140.

Maintains that "parts of the book are offensively patrician in tone: there is no greater morality in detailed recollection of other people's actions of betrayal, when one is oneself not subject to their stresses, financial or social, than there is by being attacked by the Nixons of the world for one's position."

VIIC7. Brechman, Arnold. "Playwright Lillian Hellman's Memoir; *Scoundrel Time*; Different Value Systems Seen Operating," *Christian Science Monitor*, May 17, 1976, p. 23.

Sharply criticizes LH's negative statements concerning Lionel Trilling and her views on communism.

VIIC8.  Brown, Dennis. "A Struggle for Decency," St. Louis
        *Post-Dispatch*, Apr. 18, 1976, Sect. G, p. 4.

        Emphasizes that *ST* "with its all-too-symbolic red
        dust jacket, is a frightening yet compelling memoir
        of courage during a crisis when there was no time to
        recognize courage."

VIIC9.  Buckley, William F., Jr. *"Scoundrel Time*; & Who is
        the Ugliest of Them All," *National Review*, XXIX
        (Jan. 21, 1977), 101-106.

        Includes scathing and bitter criticism of *ST*. "What
        does one go on to say about a book so disorderly, so
        tasteless, guileful, self-enraptured?  The disposition
        to adore her, feel sorry for her, glow in the vicar-
        ious thrill of her courage and decency ... runs into
        hurdle after hurdle in the obstacle course of this
        little book.  She is elderly, but there is time yet,
        time to recognize that she should be ashamed of this
        awful book."  LH appears on the cover of the issue.

VIIC10. Campenni, Frank. "Hellman Looks Back in Anger,"
        Milwaukee *Journal*, May 16, 1976, Sect. 5, p. 4.

        Suggests that LH "refuses to reach 'historical con-
        clusions' claiming 'it isn't my game.'  But she writes
        her history as a playwright should through vivid scenes,
        some grotesquely comic."

VIIC11. Clemons, Walter. "The Way It Was," *Newsweek*, LXXXVII
        (Apr. 26, 1976), 96-97.

        Reports that *ST* is "about 'an unpleasant part of my
        life' [and] leaves us exhilarated.  The only truth
        Hellman doesn't tell--maybe she's shy about this--
        is what a terrific life she's had."

VIIC12. Coles, Robert. "'Are You Now or Have You Ever Been.
        ...'" *Book World* (Washington *Post*, Chicago *Tribune*),
        May 9, 1976, p. 5.  See also New York *Post*, May 17,
        1976, p. 37.

        Speculates that "Kierkegaard would have loved *Scoun-
        drel Time* for its fine, sardonic humor, its unsparing
        social observation and, not least, the skill of its
        narration."

VIIC13. Cook, Bruce. "Notes on a Shameful Era," *Saturday Re-
        view*, LIX (Apr. 17, 1976), 28-29.

Labels *ST* a "triumph of tone. No writer I know can match the eloquence of her ah-what-the-hell as she looks back over the whole sorry spectacle and tells with restraint and precision just what she sees."

VIIC14. Cushman, Kathleen. "Hellman on HUAC; A Woman's Record of a Terrible Time," *National Observer*, May 1, 1976, p. 19.

Reports that LH "tells the story of those years with plain-spoken vigor, sticking to what she knows, and her version of that slimy episode of our history is necessarily intensely personal."

VIIC15. Edwards, Verne E., Jr. "Book Reviews," *Journalism Quarterly*, LIII (Winter 1976), 751-752.

Notes that "this slim beautifully emotional volume ... should be required reading for America's Bicentennial reflections."

VIIC16. Freeman, James O. "The Lady Refused to Testify," Philadelphia *Bulletin*, Apr. 18, 1976, Sect. 5, p. 18.

Claims that *ST* is "lucid in its controlled passion [as it] sets the record straight on a mean chapter in the life of the American spirit."

VIIC17. Fussell, Paul. "Treason of the Clerks," *Spectator*, CCXXXVII (Nov. 13, 1976), 20.

Calls *ST* full of good anecdotes; however, LH's "fury all but destroys her style." Her long-standing belief that literature influences people's actions seems "naive."

VIIC18. Glazer, Nathan. "An Answer to Lillian Hellman," *Commentary*, CXII (June 1976), 36-39.

Strikingly attacks LH's stand in *ST* for "finding no justification for public concern with communism," and for ignoring the "communist enemy." The introduction to *ST* (by Garry Wills) "disgraces her memoir." (See Items II06-10.)

VIIC19. Goldberg, Shirley. "Russian Roulette," St. Louis *Globe-Democrat*, May 1-2, 1976, Sect. F, p. 4.

Explains that LH "is charitable to members of the committee, seeing them as small men without deep commitments, unable to give up their day in the sun. The

real Hellman vitriol--and she is a very feisty lady
--is aimed at those in the intellectual community
who failed to come to the aid of their stricken
colleagues."

VIIC20.   Goodman, Walter.   "Fair Game; *Scoundrel Time*," *New
          Leader*, LXI (May 24, 1976), 10-11.

          Notes that *ST* "did not excite any desire in me to
          rush out and get hold of the other books.  It is a
          self-celebrating piece of work by a skilled writer
          who knows that the best way to persuade readers of
          one's honesty and right-thinkedness is to concede
          that one has made passing 'mistakes.'"

VIIC21.   Gornick, Vivian.   "Neither Forgotten nor Forgiven,"
          *Ms.*, V (Aug. 1976), 46-47.

          Labels *ST* a "monument to civilized intelligence."

VIIC22.   Gray, Paul.   "Books; *An Unfinished Woman*; *Scoundrel
          Time*," *Time*, CVII (May 10, 1976), 83.

          Reports that it is "a memorable portrait of, in her
          own phrase, 'an unfinished woman,' a polished stylist,
          and an invaluable American."

VIIC23.   Hapjan, Mary Ann.   "Lillian Hellman Recalls Painful
          Moments," Cincinnati *Enquirer*, May 2, 1976, Sect. F,
          p. 9.

          Suggests that "in a year saturated with Bicentennial
          orations [LH's] latest volume ... is not only iron-
          ically appropriate, but acidly refreshing.  It is not
          a pretty story."

VIIC24.   Hartnett, Robert C.   "'Scoundrel Time,' and 'Men
          Against McCarthy,'" *America*, CXXXV (Sept. 4, 1976),
          102-104.

          Argues that *ST*, as a historical/political volume, is
          "superficial and disconnected."  Her purpose is "self-
          revelation," not political analysis.

VIIC25.   Hartt, Susan L.   "Hellman Recalls the 'Scoundrel
          Time,'" Miami *Herald*, May 16, 1976, Sect. E, p. 7.

          Claims that "it could have been a spectacular book,"
          but it is not.  "We have come to expect more of this
          decent, gracious, undeniably courageous woman."

VIIC26.   Homer, Frank X.J.   "Biography," *America*, CXXXV (Nov.
          13, 1976), 336.

          Presents a brief summary of LH's appearance before
          HUAC.   No critical evaluation of *ST* made.

VIIC27.   Hook, Sidney.   "Authors and Critics; Lillian Hellman's
          *Scoundrel Time*," *Encounter*, XLVIII (Feb. 1977), 82-
          91.

          Includes an extremely negative review of *ST*.   "For
          someone like Lillian Hellman, who loyally cooperated
          with members of the Communist Party in all sorts of
          political and cultural enterprises for almost forty
          years, to impugn the integrity of liberal Anti-
          Communists like Lionel Trilling and others of his
          circle is an act of political obscenity."   Claims
          that in *ST*, LH "seems to have duped a generation of
          critics devoid of historical memory and critical
          common sense."   Defends HUAC's subpoena of LH because
          she was a notorious "participant and defender of
          Communist causes."   Examples of LH's involvement are
          provided.   Vigorously attacks her book by citing his-
          torical discrepancies in LH's interpretations of
          McCarthyism and HUAC and Hook's own historical per-
          spective.

VIIC28.   Howard, Maureen.   "*Scoundrel Time*," *New York Times
          Book Review*, Apr. 25, 1976, pp. 1-2.

          Notes that *ST* "is compelling, quite wonderful to
          read."

VIIC29.   Hunt, David.   "Clean Conscience," *Listener*, LXXXIX
          (Nov. 18, 1976), 656-657.

          Considers *ST* "a moving story ... but it must be said
          that, with all her skill in writing, it is not very
          easy reading.   She assumes too much knowledge in the
          reader, and there is too much vagueness about dates
          and places."

VIIC30.   Howe, Irving.   "Lillian Hellman and the McCarthy
          Years," *Dissent*, XXIII (Fall 1976), 378-382.

          Claims that LH's *ST* is "unbalanced and inaccurate."
          Maintains that LH is mistaken when she states that
          domestic Communists did the country no harm.   The
          consequences of their support of Stalin are ignored
          by *ST*.   She attacks liberals who failed to attack

McCarthy (Lionel Trilling and others) and "ignores
the fact that many intellectuals found it possible
to reject both McCarthy and Communism." Very critical of Garry Wills' introduction to *ST*.

VIIC31.   Kempton, Murray. "Witnesses," *New York Review of
Books*, XXIII (June 10, 1976), 22-25.

Proclaims that *ST* "is not quite true."

VIIC32.   *Kirkus*, XLIV (Feb. 15, 1976), 233.

Briefly suggests that *ST* is "eloquent, the more so
for what remains unsaid."

VIIC33.   Kissel, Howard. "Lillian Hellman; Survival and the
McCarthy Era," *Women's Wear Daily*, May 5, 1976, p.
28.

Includes summary review.

VIIC34.   Lardner, Ring, Jr. "Hellman and 'the Toads,'" Chicago
*Sun Times*, Apr. 25, 1976, *Show*, p. 8. See also
Cleveland *Press*, May 28, 1976, *Showtime*, p. 19.

Reports that "the theme [of *ST*] is political but it
isn't politics that make it such an absorbing and
beautiful book. This is a personal story, a contin-
uation" of her memoirs previously written.

VIIC35.   Lehmann-Haupt, Christopher. "Books of the Times;
Going One's Own Way; *Scoundrel Time*," New York *Times*,
Apr. 15, 1976, p. 31.

Includes an informational review, no critical comment.

VIIC36.   Liebrum, Martha. "Rancor from the Attic," Houston
*Post*, May 2, 1976, *Spotlight*, p. 30.

Claims that LH needs to write another book consider-
ing "her life with Dashiell Hammett. One senses
that it will be her most difficult work, and perhaps
her best. This latest one may have been difficult,
but it is not her best."

VIIC37.   Luke, K. McCormick. "Hellman's 'Scoundrel Time' Shows
Rotten Side of Patriotism Abuse," Denver *Post*, May
30, 1976, *Roundup*, p. 13.

Includes an informational review of *ST* that makes no
critical comment except to support LH's stand during
HUAC hearings.

VIIC38. McNally, Owen. "1950's; A Decade to Rue," Hartford
*Courant*, Apr. 25, 1976, Sect. F, p. 14.

Claims that *ST* "is a rather disturbing book; disturbing since it recalls a period in American history that
many would sooner forget."

VIIC39. McWilliams, Carey. "Time is the Scoundrel," *The
Nation*, CCXXII (June 19, 1976), 741-742.

Reports that in *ST*, a fascinating memoir of an encounter with Congressional inquisitors in the 1950's,
LH shrewdly observed that "we are a people who do not
remember much -- and then proceeds to prove her point
by forgetting some things she might have been expected
to remember."

VIIC40. Maloff, Saul. "Jewel Without Price," *Commonweal*,
CIII (July 2, 1976), 438-442.

Includes a summary review; not critical.

VIIC41. Marcus, Greil. "Remembering the Witch Hunt," *Rolling
Stone*, May 20, 1976, p. 97.

Severely criticizes LH's condescending tone in *ST*,
noting that she is unjustified in her conviction of
"nobility and innocence." However, despite "her in-
tolerable superiority," *ST* is recommended because of
the striking story told.

VIIC42. Marvin, John R. *Library Journal*, CI (May 1, 1976),
1110.

Evaluates LH's *ST* "vis-a-vis McCarthyism" as a "milky
suspension of fact and bias, clear headedness, and
distortion, which might well be classified 'PG.'"

VIIC43. Mayne, Richard. "Ishmael and the Inquisitors,"
*Times Literary Supplement*, Nov. 12, 1976, p. 1413.

Concludes that *ST* "prompts misgivings as well as
applause." (See Items II014-16.)

VIIC44. Mee, Charles L., Jr. "A Woman of Courage," *Horizon*,
XVIII (Summer 1976), 104-105.

Maintains that LH "should have known enough about
Stalin's brutality by the later 1930's to have repu-
diated it...." LH has "lived up to her vocation by
showing us how to behave with courage when our dignity
and liberties are threatened."

VIIC45.  Menn, Thorpe.  "Liberals Are Poor Soldiers," Kansas
         City *Star*, Apr. 18, 1976, Sect. D, p. 12.

         Calls LH "forthright and refreshing," but points out
         that Garry Wills' introduction is as valuable as the
         rest of the book.

VIIC46.  Middleton, Harry.  "Hellman Reviews Old Charges
         Against Her," New Orleans *Times-Picayune*, Apr. 25,
         1976, p. 32.

         Reports that *ST* is "not vitriolic pursuit for re-
         venge.  Rather, it is a tightly controlled personal
         history, and, as always, her style is impeccable."

VIIC47.  Miller, Stephen.  "The Legend of *Scoundrel Time*," *The
         Alternative: An American Spectator*, X (Jan. 1977),
         5-9.

         Calls LH a "veritable virtuoso of uncharity."  LH is
         mistaken when she states that American Communists
         "did no harm" because some of them were "truly sub-
         versive."  Her response to the McCarthy era is
         "hysterical."

VIIC48.  M[oody], M[innie] H[ite].  "Lillian Hellman Memoir
         Recalls Unhappy Years," Columbus *Dispatch*, May 30,
         1976, Sect. J, p. 16.

         Notes that *ST* is "compressed like a play, never de-
         viating from its course, and professionally precise
         in its particular kind of drama."

VIIC49.  Nash, Alanna.  "A Woman of Consequence in a Time of
         Scoundrels," Louisville *Courier Journal*, July 25,
         1976, Sect. E, p. 7.

         Thanks LH for "what might be interpreted as her
         Bicentennial present to the nation ... a chilling re-
         minder of a way we must never forget so that we may
         never see it again."

VIIC50.  *New Yorker*, LII (Apr. 26, 1976), 147.

         Claims that LH has written "without self-pity or self-
         righteousness, and even at times with humor."

VIIC51.  "Notes on Current Books; *Scoundrel Time*," *Virginia
         Quarterly Review*, LIII (Winter 1977), 28.

Briefly recalls that "the complexities of her involvement with this Committee [HUAC] and Dashiell Hammett augment the individuality shown in previous memoirs."

VIIC52. Paul, Barbara. "Lillian Hellman Memoirs a 'Time' to Remember," Pittsburgh *Press*, May 2, 1976, Sect. F, p. 7.

Emphasizes that the "value of the book as a whole lies in seeing this shocking, shameful period of our history through the eyes of a sane civilized woman."

VIIC53. Phillips, William. "What Happened in the Fifties," *Partisan Review*, XLIII (Fall 1976), 337-340.

Declares inaccuracies in *ST* by noting that *Partisan Review* did, in fact, publish anti-McCarthy articles. Notes that the magazine did not come to the defense of McCarthy victims; however, LH did not come to the defense of those murdered in Stalin's death camps.

VIIC54. *Publishers Weekly*, CCIX (Mar. 1, 1976), 90.

Notes that *ST* is "an important document about a disturbing time."

VIIC55. Raymond, John. "Writer Refuses to Cut Conscience; Witch Hunt," Atlanta *Journal and Constitution*, May 2, 1976, Sect. C, p. 2.

Suggests that LH "is too complex and self-searching to claim any heroine's role, but she remains satisfied that she acted honorably."

VIIC56. "Recommended," Nashville *Tennessean*, May 9, 1976, p. 10.

Summarizes *ST* and recommends that others read it.

VIIC57. Roche, John. "Lillian Hellman Relies on Amnesia," San Francisco *Examiner*, Oct. 7, 1976, *Books*, p. 1.

Harshly criticizes *ST*. LH "relies on collective amnesia to make her impact...."

VIIC58. Rumley, Marjorie. "Joseph McCarthy Era; A Time to Test Courage," Seattle *Times*, May 16, 1976, Magazine, p. 14.

Concludes that "reviewing the events of the McCarthy period should be required reading periodically. No better way is there to do it than through [*ST*]...."

VIIC59.  Schroetter, Hilda N.  "Lillian Hellman; A Trying Time," Richmond *Times Dispatch*, May 9, 1976, Sect. K, p. 5.

Proclaims that *ST*, "for its small size, is a major piece of writing, a very real contribution to American letters."

VIIC60.  Sherrill, Robert.  "Wisdom and Its Price," *The Nation*, CCXXII (June 19, 1976), 757-758.

Maintains that LH divulges her story with detachment, not bitterness.  The detachment makes some events humorous which would not be ordinarily.  Her moral is that "few people act honorably."

VIIC61.  Sigal, Clancy.  "True Grit," *Guardian*, CXV (Nov. 14, 1976), 22.

Notes that the iron will of Regina in *LF* is found in LH in *ST*.  Her book is "elegantly written."

VIIC62.  Sperry, Ralph A.  "'Scoundrel Time,'" *Best Sellers*, XXXVI (July 1976), 116.

Reveals that *ST* is filled with a "gentle" style which one might not expect from LH.  There is genuine humor in some incidents.

VIIC63.  Steele, Mike.  "Memories of an 'Unfashionable Conscience,'" Minneapolis *Tribune*, May 16, 1976, Sect. B, p. 12.

Evaluates *ST* as "the most painful and most remarkable of her memoirs...."  It is filled with "hardwon insights of increasing understanding which, far from bringing cynicism or compromise, have stiffened her sense of moral direction."

VIIC64.  Thomas, Phil.  "The Bad 50's--Distilled," *Deseret News* (Salt Lake City), June 26, 1976, Sect. W, p. 4.

Summarizes *ST*, noting that "very few pages in Miss Hellman's book are devoted to her actual appearance before the [HUAC].  Her time before the committee was brief, although it seems much, much longer to her.  Rather, the bulk of her book is devoted to an examina-

tion of the years preceding the 1950's and how what
came about did so." LH "has survived, endured, and
her memories of what was [are] extremely interesting."

VIIC65.  Tyrrell, R. Emmett, Jr.  "The Worst Book of the Year,"
*The Alternative: An American Spectator*, X (Jan. 1977),
435-436.

Severely condemns *ST* for ignoring the evil of
"Stalinists" and their actions.  LH shows "almost
willful naiveté and impudence."

VIIC66.  Walker, Frank B.  "Liberal Silence," Montreal *Star*,
May 29, 1976, Sect. D, p. 3.

Claims that LH "is not an historian, but she is an
articulate and sensitive human being." *ST* "asks us
only to hear what happened to her because eventually
it can happen to anyone."

VIIC67.  Walker, Ruth.  "Exorcising an American Nightmare,"
Norfolk *Virginian-Pilot*, Apr. 25, 1976, Sect. C, p.
6.

Reports that *ST* is a "slender but impressive book."
It is LH's "recollection of those times with emphasis
on the day in May 1952 when she took her turn in the
witness chair and refused to cooperate."

VIIC68.  Warga, Wayne.  "West View; From Hollywood to HUAC
with Hellman," Los Angeles *Times*, May 23, 1976, *Book
Review*, p. 3.

Claims that *ST* is "the best piece of writing yet
about a very bad time."

VIII. GRADUATE STUDIES


VIIIA. Doctoral Dissertations


VIIIA1. Ackley, Meredith E. *The Plays of Lillian Hellman*. Ph.D. Dissertation, University of Pennsylvania, 1970.

Contains individual chapters on *CH*, *DC*, *LF*, *WR*, *AG*, and *TIA*.

VIIIA2. Angermeier, Brother Carrol. *Moral and Social Protest in the Plays of Lillian Hellman*. Ph.D. Dissertation, University of Texas, 1972.

Includes a biographical chapter on LH. Chapters on *CH*, *DC*, *LF/APF*, *WR/SW*, *AG/TIA* are also found.

VIIIA3. Brockington, John. *A Critical Analysis of the Plays of Lillian Hellman*. Ph.D. Dissertation, Yale University, 1962.

VIIIA4. Hasbany, Richard. *Rituals of Reassurance: Studies in World War II American Drama*. Ph.D. Dissertation, Michigan State University, 1973.

Considers Maxwell Anderson, Sherwood, LH, Wilder, and others.

VIIIA5. Haller, C. David. *Social and Moral Themes in the Plays of Lillian Hellman*. Ph.D. Dissertation, Tulane University, 1967.

Examines the concept of moral failure in the eight original plays of LH.

VIIIA6. Johnson, Annette Bergman. *A Study of Recurrent Character Types in the Plays of Lillian Hellman*. Ph.D. Dissertation, University of Massachusetts, 1971.

Maintains that LH is not of the school of playwrights made up of Odets, Rice, Irwin Shaw, and others, and thus will be enduring.

VIIIA7.    Keller, Alvin Joseph. *Form and Content in the Plays of Lillian Hellman*. Ph.D. Dissertation, Stanford University, 1966.

Includes chapters on "Action," "Character," and "Thought" in the eight original plays by LH.

VIIIA8.    Larimer, Cynthia C.M. *A Study of Female Characters in the Eight Plays of Lillian Hellman*. Ph.D. Dissertation, Purdue University, 1971.

VIIIA9.    Ledere, Katherine G. *A Critical Reaction to the Dramatic Works of Lillian Hellman*. Ph.D. Dissertation, University of Arkansas, 1967.

VIIIA10.   Whitesides, Glenn E. *Lillian Hellman, A Biographical Critical Study*. Ph.D. Dissertation, Florida State University, 1978.


## VIIIB.  MA Theses


VIIIB1.    Crane, Joshua. *A Comparison of G.B. Shaw's "Saint Joan" and Lillian Hellman's Adaptation of "The Lark" by Jean Anouilh*. M.A. Thesis, University of Florida, 1961.

VIIIB2.    Thompson, Robert Wayne. *A Production and Production Book of Lillian Hellman's "The Children's Hour."* M.F.A. Thesis, University of Texas, 1964.

INDEX